Business Planning for Turbulent Times

Business Planning for Turbulent Times
New Methods for Applying Scenarios
Edited by Rafael Ramírez, John W. Selsky and Kees van der Heijden

Vaccine Anxieties
Global Science, Child Health and Society
Melissa Leach and James Fairhead

A Web of Prevention
Biological Weapons, Life Sciences and the Governance of Research
Edited by Brian Rappert and Caitrìona McLeish

Democratizing Technology
Risk, Responsibility and the Regulation of Chemicals
Anne Chapman

Genomics and Society
Legal, Ethical and Social Dimensions
Edited by George Gaskell and Martin W. Bauer

Nanotechnology
Risk, Ethics and Law
Edited by Geoffrey Hunt and Michael Mehta

Business Planning for Turbulent Times

New Methods for Applying Scenarios

Edited by
Rafael Ramírez, John W. Selsky and
Kees van der Heijden

publishing for a sustainable future

London • Sterling, VA

First published by Earthscan in the UK and USA in 2008

ISBN: 978-1-84407-567-6
Typeset by JS Typesetting Ltd, Porthcawl, Mid Glamorgan
Printed and bound in the UK by Cromwell Press, Trowbridge
Cover design by Susanne Harris

For a full list of publications please contact:

Earthscan
Dunstan House
14a St Cross St
London, EC1N 8XA, UK
Tel: +44 (0)20 7841 1930
Fax: +44 (0)20 7242 1474
Email: earthinfo@earthscan.co.uk
Web: **www.earthscan.co.uk**

22883 Quicksilver Drive, Sterling, VA 20166-2012, USA

Earthscan publishes in association with the International Institute for Environment and
Development

A catalogue record for this book is available from the British Library

Library of Congress Cataloging-in-Publication Data
Business planning for turbulent times : new methods for applying scenarios / edited by
Rafael Ramirez, John W. Selsky, and Kees van der Heijden.
      p. cm.
   ISBN 978-1-84407-567-6 (hardback)
   1. Business planning. 2. Strategic planning. I. Ramírez, Rafael, 1956– II. Selsky,
John W. III. Van der Heijden, Kees.
   HD30.28.B848 2008
   658.4'01–dc22

                                                       2008015771

The paper used for this book is FSC-certified.
FSC (the Forest Stewardship Council) is an
international network to promote responsible
management of the world's forests.

Mixed Sources
Product group from well-managed
forests and other controlled sources
www.fsc.org Cert no. TT-COC-2082
© 1996 Forest Stewardship Council

Contents

List of Figures and Tables

Figures

Tables

List of Contributors

Lynn Allen is a professorial fellow at the Curtin Business School, Curtin University of Technology, Perth, Western Australia. She has co-developed a methodology that combines systems thinking, futures methods and narrative to create holistic approaches to planning and problem solving. Lynn was chief executive officer of the Library and Information Service of Western Australia (LISWA) from 1989 to 2001, when she contributed widely to policy and strategy development across government. She has worked at a senior level in academic libraries, as well as in the software industry. Her senior management experience extends over the university, private and public sectors. Her research interests are systems thinking, narrative and creativity.
Lynn.Allen@cbs.curtin.edu.au

Niklas Arvidsson works with strategy development, innovation environments and business scenarios. His prime focus is on organizing for creativity, managing creative processes and understanding innovative environments – often with the help of scenarios. He is employed at the Centre for Banking and Finance at the Royal Institute of Technology in Stockholm and is an associated partner of NormannPartners AB. He is published in *Management Science* and has – in collaboration with Richard Normann – edited a book called *People as Care Catalysts: From Being Patient to Becoming Healthy* (John Wiley and Sons, 2006) that proposes new ways of designing healthcare systems.
nikarv@infra.kth.se

Andromache Athanasopoulou completed her MBA, MSc in Management Research and DPhil in Management at the Saïd Business School, University of Oxford, UK. In her doctoral thesis, Andromache explored how managers make sense of the corporate social responsibility implementation process adopted by large multinational enterprises (MNEs). During her DPhil, Andromache also worked as a teaching and research assistant for Saïd Business School's executive education programme, the Oxford Scenarios Programme. Andromache has presented her research at international conferences and has served as a reviewer

of papers submitted to the British Academy of Management and the Academy of Management. Before her Oxford studies, Andromache worked in banking.
andromache.athanasopoulou@oba.co.uk

Mary Bernard is the first associate vice president of research at the Royal Roads University, British Columbia, a new and innovative Canadian university for those wishing to advance in the workplace. Formerly, Mary Bernard was with the Faculty of Environmental Studies at York University, Ontario, as well as the York Centre for Applied Sustainability, the Native/Canadian Relations Theme Area, and Action Learning Resources, a research, learning and consulting group founded by Eric Trist. Mary Bernard holds a PhD in Sociology from York University, a Master in Environmental Studies (MES) also from York University, and a BA in English from the University of New Brunswick, Canada.
Mary.Bernard@RoyalRoads.ca

George Burt is a senior lecturer in strategic management at the Department of Management, University of Strathclyde Business School (SBS), Glasgow, Scotland. George is co-founder and track chair of the Strategic Foresight Special Interest Group at the British Academy of Management, and co-founder of the Centre for Scenario Planning and Future Studies at SBS. His research interests focus on the organization–environment relationship and the processes of strategic change. He has extensive scenario-planning consultancy and training expertise. George Burt is co-author of the book *The Sixth Sense: Accelerating Organisational Learning with Scenarios* (Wiley and Sons, 2002).
burt@gsb.strath.ac.uk

Ged Davis is co-president of the Global Energy Assessment at IIASA and was previously managing director of the World Economic Forum, responsible for global research, scenario projects and the design of the annual Forum meeting at Davos. Before joining the Forum, Ged spent 30 years with Royal Dutch Shell. He was the vice president of global business environment for Shell International in London, and head of Shell's scenario planning team. In this capacity he participated in a wide variety of scenario projects many with a special focus on energy and environment. He has worked on many global projects for international institutions, including IPCC, IUCN, WBCSD, WEF and UN agencies.

Shirin Elahi is a scenario architect, specializing in scenario projects on complex global risk issues across multiple dimensions: political, economic, societal, technological, ethical, environmental and historical. She has examined knowledge risks for the European Patent Office (EPO), health risks for the Joint United Nations Programme on HIV/AIDS (UNAIDS), societal risks for the UK Health and Safety Executive, Shell UK and Electricité de France, and environmental risks

for the insurance industry. Her interests lie in using scenarios to examine the risk trade-offs that societies make and how this takes place at a global level within the context of trust, equity and scientific uncertainty. She has interviewed and lectured widely and contributes regularly to academic publications.
shirin.arch@btinternet.com

Jaime Jiménez has a PhD in Social Systems Sciences from the University of Pennsylvania, US. He is a full-time researcher for the Institute of Applied Mathematics and Systems (IIMAS), Universidad Nacional Autónoma de México (UNAM). Currently, he is involved in research in science and technology, education and health systems. He is a specialist in scenario planning, development processes, participative strategic planning, quality of working life, total quality, and group dynamics associated with organizational change. He has conducted research projects for United Nations Educational, Cultural and Scientific Organization (UNESCO), OIT, and Mexican public and private agencies. He has published several books and research papers in specialized journals.
jjimen@servidor.unam.mx

Trudi Lang is currently undertaking her doctoral studies at the Saïd Business School, University of Oxford, UK, where she also works as a graduate assistant on the Oxford Scenarios Masters Class and the Oxford Scenarios Programme. Prior to coming to Oxford, Trudi consulted and taught in the area of scenario planning mostly within Australia, although she has also delivered executive education courses in Singapore and Malaysia, and taught on the International Management Programme in Reims, France. From 2001 to 2004, she was the manager of the Scenario Planning and Research Unit at the Graduate School of Business, Curtin University of Technology, Australia.
trudi.lang@sbs.ox.ac.uk

Joseph E. McCann is dean of and professor of management in the Davis College of Business, Jacksonville University, Jacksonville, Florida, US. He is an internationally acknowledged consultant, researcher and author of many books and articles on organization change, change management, rapidly growing technology companies and new business venturing. He serves on the editorial board for a leading technology management journal and for *People & Strategy*, for which he was an associate editor. He earned his MA and PhD in Business and Applied Economics at the Wharton School of the University of Pennsylvania, US.
jmccann1@ju.edu

Rafael Ramírez is professor of management at Hautes Etudes Commerciales (HEC)-Paris and at the University of Oxford, UK, and occupies the posts of senior research fellow in the James Martin Institute for Science and Civilization

and fellow in strategy at both Templeton College and the Saïd Business School, University of Oxford. Rafael has studied causal texture theory since 1979, having been a student of both Fred Emery and Eric Trist in the Wharton School of the University of Pennsylvania, where he received his PhD, and at York University, Ontario, Canada, where he received his MES. At York University, he was Eric Trist's graduate assistant and worked with him in various action-learning projects. Rafael has worked with scenarios and search conferences for 28 years and was visiting professor of scenarios and corporate strategy at Shell for three years until 2003. This is his sixth book.
rafael.ramirez@sbs.ox.ac.uk

Rob E. Roggema is a landscape architect. His expertise lies in designing sustainable energy, climate adaptation and sustainable development measures. Currently, he works as a manager in strategy and regional planning for the province of Groningen, The Netherlands, and started his PhD at Technical University Delft and Wageningen University on the subject of climate change, energy supply, water supply and spatial design. He developed the swarm-planning paradigm: to reach long-term goals by implementing measures in daily practice. He publishes articles in both scientific and popular journals and acts as an expert and speaker at conferences and workshops. Recently, he published his first book on adaptation to climate change: *Tegenhouden of meebewegen* [*Withstand or Adapt*] (http://duurzaambouwen.senternovem.nl/publicaties/tegenhouden_of_meebewegen-2857/).
r.roggema@provinciegroningen.nl

John W. Selsky is an associate professor of management at the University of South Florida, US, where he teaches strategic and international management. His interest in turbulent organizational environments was sparked by his association with Eric Trist while pursuing his doctorate at the Wharton School of the University of Pennsylvania, US. It was there that his long-standing collaboration with co-author Joe McCann and more recent collaboration with Rafael Ramírez began. John has worked at universities in Australia, New Zealand and Turkey, and has published in such journals as *Academy of Management Review, Journal of Management, Organization Studies, Journal of Management Studies* and *Journal of Applied Behavioral Science*.
jselsky@lakeland.usf.edu

Martin Thomas holds Masters degrees in financial control and change management. He has lived and worked in France, The Netherlands, Colombia, Kenya, Israel and England. He was head of business planning in Unilever and managing director of an international division of Tate & Lyle. He studied for the Oxford/HEC change management MSc in 2004, the dissertation for which was

on scenarios and turbulence in Venezuela. He works in English, French, Spanish and Dutch. His particular interest is in enabling emergent visionary change to become a reality. He is a founding member and former chair of the Change Leaders community of practice. He coaches business leaders.
martin@call4change.com

Kees van der Heijden is an associate fellow at Saïd Business School, University of Oxford, UK. He is an emeritus professor at the University of Strathclyde, Glasgow, Scotland, where he taught general and strategic management from 1991 until 2003. Prior to 1991, he headed the business environment division of Royal Dutch Shell, London, where he oversaw scenario planning, including monitoring and analysing the business environment and communicating with top management on strategic implications. Previously, he headed Shell's internal strategic consultancy group. He is a Global Business Network co-founder. He is the author of *Scenarios: The Art of Strategic Conversation* (John Wiley and Sons, 2005, 2nd edition) and many other publications.
keesvdh@aol.com

Angela Wilkinson is the director of scenario planning and futures research at the James Martin Institute, University of Oxford. She is an experienced business executive, a reflexive scholar, an effective coach and teacher and a seasoned scenario-to-strategy practitioner. Prior to Oxford, Angela spent a decade as a leading member of Shell International's Global Scenario team. She has directed several ambitious public–private initiatives including: *AIDS in Africa: Three Scenarios for the Future*, for UNAIDS, *Aspire Australia: 2025* for the Business Council of Australia, and, *The Future of Water: Navigating a Sustainable Course* for the World Business Council on Sustainable Development. She holds a PhD in Physics.

Preface

That the world is turbulent is not a new insight. Heraclites[1] around 500 BC observed that the world is in flux – in continual change. His view, that nothing in the world ever stays the same, was summarized as, 'one cannot step in the same river twice'.

One might argue that turbulence was increased with the advent of scientific thinking, and the commencement of the Industrial Revolution in the 18th century, for humankind has been continually disrupted by new technologies and profound social change. This was observed by many, but in particular Jules Verne and H. G. Wells, who used their understanding of change and the medium of fiction, to address future possibilities and to comment on the present.

Understanding change requires a view of what persists. And what persists and what changes is very much a function of how we represent the world, and those representations can vary widely. Epicetus around 100 AD commented that 'all is opinion'.[2] Thus it is no surprise that just as opinions vary widely about present phenomena they vary more widely when we consider future possibilities. This already hints at the import of reflection on alternative futures in considering current and strategic actions, especially in large organizations containing many people with differing views.

The first half of the 20th century was a turbulent time, by any measure, with two world wars and an economic depression. We also saw the massive rise in the power of the state, large private institutions and international organizations. This accelerated the need for new administrative disciplines to improve the effective management of large public and private enterprises, including consideration of the environment they were operating in.

This was also a period of great intellectual ferment with important changes in our scientific worldview (for example, the theory of relativity and quantum mechanics) and in philosophy (for example, Karl Popper's theory of scientific enquiry). It was in this context that the paper by Tolman[3] and Brunswik in 1935, addressing the relation of the individual to the 'causal texture of the environment', was written. This paper provided a conceptual basis for Emery and Trist's seminal work on the causal texture of organizational environments in 1965.

Following the Second World War we saw a maturing of ideas in cybernetics, open systems theory, systems dynamics, dynamic modelling, and paradigm shifts in science. All have provided a set of ideas and tools for considering, interpreting and engaging with the enterprise's environment. The book[4] on systems thinking, edited by Emery, provides a good introduction to leading edge ideas of the 1960s.

The advent of scenario planning

Enterprises seek their own sort of persistence, that is organizational resilience and persistence of identity. They do so in a world in which the environment is subject to sudden change. This increasingly requires a capacity to understand the environment in which the organization is embedded, consider and simulate possible futures, and examine and select relevant strategies of adaptation. This is at the core of the practice of scenario planning.

Thus the need to address the challenge of how to act in the face of unknown and uncertain futures was an issue emerging in public and private enterprises in the 1960s. This was recognized in a number of institutions, as different as the RAND corporation, Délégation à l'Action Régionale et à l'Aménagement du Territoire (DATAR) and Royal Dutch Shell. Each took from a common intellectual heritage, but developed different approaches, reflecting a difference in style and organizational needs. The development of scenario planning in Shell is particularly interesting, showing how diverse ideas shaped one of the most successful scenario-planning teams.

In the mid 1960s Shell's Unified Planning Machinery was a model of its kind. A comprehensive forecasting mechanism focused on the coming few years and supporting traditional financial activities. Project evaluation was predominantly a matter of calculating returns and comparing them with targeted hurdle rates. But the 1960s was no normal decade for the oil industry, the formation of the Organization of the Petroleum Exporting Countries (OPEC) in 1960 and the rise of the independent oil companies was challenging the established regime of the Majors. In addition, the long-standing, stable pricing regime was potentially at risk. There was no adequate way to include these new political and business risks in investment considerations. Some proposed simply raising hurdle rates for 'riskier' projects. But this seemed inadequate and provided no new information as to how to handle the risks identified. The search for an alternative approach led to the experimentation with and eventual commitment to a process of scenario planning in Shell.

The two leaders of the new unit, Pierre Wack and Ted Newland, were well aware of Herman Kahn's work in RAND. Indeed Shell had a close relationship with the Hudson Institute in the late 1960s, where Kahn was working on the civilian application of scenarios. But they brought a unique approach and insight into how to think about scenarios and use them.

Wack who had already initiated scenarios in Shell's French company was an avid 'seeker of truth'. He became a disciple of Swami Prajnapad of Channa, Northern India, an intellectual who was a master in Vedanta. He suggested to Wack that he practice his yoga in his job. In Wack's words,[5] 'When I came back to my job in a large International Company, where I was occupied with economic studies, I was asked to make market forecasts. I talked to Svamiji about it when I went to see him the following winter. After he'd asked me precisely what my work consisted of, he said "That is your yoga. It will be the test that will allow you to testify whether you see things as they are".'

Wack's relentless approach to understanding and deconstructing his business environment, identifying new connections and insights, and to constructing scenarios relevant to the leadership team in Shell, became the hallmark of his work. As he said:

> *At the time, forecasting was essentially an econometric activity, that consisted of looking for 'development laws' in the past course of a phenomenon and applying them to the future. This way, it was possible to make forecasts from behind one's desk about elements with which one didn't have any contact whatsoever. This way of doing it was almost the rule. Svamiji's obligation for me to 'see things' was revolutionary. Instead of econometric calculations from global statistics, 'seeing' demands, firstly, the identification of the forces at work and the chain(s) of cause and effect behind the development of a market, and secondly, information about a chain that is much finer than global statistics, a ladder where significant differences appear. 'Seeing' certainly was a much more demanding and strenuous discipline than regular forecasting, but the managing directors who had to make use of forecasts quickly saw the difference and my field of activity expanded first to all of France and then to all the group on an International level. For me this was a great privilege, because the essence of my work was to try to 'see clear' in a situation where there were more and more parameters.*

He harnessed the benefits of systems thinking and dynamic modelling to a set of powerful narratives of change, highlighting new risks and opportunities. Like most new initiatives, views as to the value of scenarios were many, with passions strong both with supporters and detractors. But without question he catalysed an internal process to improve and finesse scenario applications, which over time has inspired many outside of Shell.

An art searching for its scientific basis

It may seem self-evident today that the world is turbulent or, more exactly, requires continual and explicit reframing to be made sense of. This is where scenario planning and its associated processes have become invaluable – most importantly as a basis for the development of new strategy.

The last half century has seen remarkable economic and political successes, as population doubled, world income quadrupled, and both colonialism and the Cold War ended. However, the large increase in productive capacity poses significant potential environmental and resource constraints in the coming century. For the first time we need to take into account the impact of our actions several generations ahead, and scenarios have a very significant role to play in clarifying the risks we face and communicating them widely. In addition, developments in computing power and tools for simulation of large systems in a post-modernist ethos that recognizes a diverse set of ideas, underpin the practice of scenario planning. With new opportunities have come new responsibilities for scenario practitioners, in particular to ensure that scenarios are ethically implemented.

The question of why scenarios work well in some situations and not others is of profound interest to practitioners. It is here that this book plays a special role in bolstering the art of scenario planning, with some glimpses as to what a science of scenario planning might be. Also of special interest are the case studies highlighting the wide range of current applications.

The prime aim of any planning system is to transform the enterprise's relationship to a turbulent environment into one which can be managed. Scenario planning has a unique role in this regard, through the institutionalization of risk management and risk monitoring, and provision of the tools to enterprise leaders for relating to the wider society. This book helps us better understand how to undertake this challenge and build resilient enterprises that can contribute to improving the world.

Ged Davis
Sevenoaks
May 2008

Notes

1   Heraclites (~535–475 BC) was a pre-Socratic Ionian philosopher, a native of Ephesus on the coast of Asis Minor. Heraclitus is known for his doctrine of change being central to the universe.
2   Epictetus (~50–130 AD), one of the most influential teachers of Stoicism. He stated 'Men are disturbed not by things that happen, but by their opinion of the things that happen.'
3   Tolman, E. C. and Brunswik, E. (1935) 'The organism and the causal texture of the environment', *Psychological Review*, vol 42, pp43–77.
4   Emery, F. E. (1969) *Systems Thinking*, Penguin Books, London.
5   Roumanoff, D. (1993) *Svâmi Prajñânpad – Biographie*, La Table Ronde, Paris 6, pp262–266.

Acknowledgements

The editors thank Templeton College, University of Oxford, UK, for supporting the 2005 Oxford Futures Forum (www.oxfordfuturesforum.org.uk) that became the foundation for this book. Our special thanks are also to two Oxford DPhil students: Andromache Athanasopoulou, who was crucial to running the 2005 forum successfully, and Trudi Lang, whose editorial help made a huge difference to the quality of this volume.

List of Acronyms and Abbreviations

AD	Accion Democratica party (Venezuela)
AIC	appreciate, influence, control
AIDS	acquired immune deficiency syndrome
AMA	American Management Association
ANC	African National Congress
ANC	Assemblea Nacional Constituyente (Venezuela)
CATWOE	customers, actors, transformation process, *Weltanschauung*, owner, environmental constraints
CEO	chief executive officer
CIAM	International Congress of Modern Architecture
cm	centimetre
CO_2	carbon dioxide
COPEI	Christian Democrats (Venezuela)
CSR	corporate social responsibility
DATAR	Délégation à l'Action Régionale et à l'Aménagement du Territoire (French Delegation for Regional Action and Space Planning)
DLPFC	dorsolateral prefrontal cortex
DP1	first organizational design principle
DP2	second organizational design principle
EPO	European Patent Office
ERU	emission reduction unit
ETSP	Emery–Trist systems paradigm
EU	European Union
GAVI	Global A Vaccine Initiative
GBN	Global Business Network
ha	hectare
HEC	Hautes Etudes Commerciales
HRI	Human Resource Institute
IIASA	International Institute of Applied Systems Analysis
IIMAS	Institute of Applied Mathematics and Systems
IPCC	Intergovernmental Panel on Climate Change

IPY	International Polar Year
ISA	International Seabed Authority
IT	information technology
JI	Joint Implementation
KNMI	Royal Dutch Meteorological Institute
LISWA	Library and Information Service of Western Australia
LULU	locally unwanted land use
m	metre
MNE	multinational enterprise
MNP	Dutch Environment Assessment Agency
NAIP	National Agricultural Innovation Project
NATO	North Atlantic Treaty Organization
NGO	non-governmental organization
NGT	Nominal Group Technique
OECD	Organisation for Economic Co-operation and Development
OED	*Oxford English Dictionary*
OEM	original equipment manufacturer
OFF2005	Oxford Futures Forum 2005
OPEC	Organization of Petroleum Exporting Countries
R&D	research and development
RAINS	Regional Acidification Information System
SC	search conference
SBS	University of Strathclyde Business School
SO$_2$	sulphur dioxide
SSM	soft systems methodology
SSM(c)	SSM content sub-system
SSM(p)	SSM process sub-system
SUV	sports utility vehicle
TOB	tobacco company
TRIPS	Trade Related Aspects of Intellectual Property Rights Agreement
UK	United Kingdom
UNAIDS	Joint United Nations Programme on HIV/AIDS
UNAM	Universidad Nacional Autónoma de México
UNESCO	United Nations Educational, Scientific and Cultural Organization
UNFCCC	United Nations Framework Convention on Climate Change
US	United States
UTIL	public-service utility

Part I

1

Introduction: Why Write This Book and for Whom?

Rafael Ramírez, Kees van der Heijden and John W. Selsky

What surrounds us as we finish this book

As we finish writing this book in early 2008, oil prices have reached US$100/barrel, NATO is neither winning nor losing a war with the Taliban in Afghanistan, Iraq continues to be in a bloody quagmire and is receiving incursions from Turkey, the Darfur genocide is well under way, banks are wary to lend to each other following the 'sub-prime' mortgage meltdown in the US, the gap between poor and rich continues to be exacerbated, and Colombia has written off huge parts of its territory that are controlled by 'rogue' guerrilla groups. Moreover, the Kyoto Protocol and carbon trading initiatives are failing to avert the growth of carbon dioxide (CO_2) in the atmosphere, making climate change an ever higher priority policy-making issue, perhaps even more than military security in this era of nuclear proliferation.

Possible futures over the next five to ten years, as seen by a corporate executive, a government planner or a non-governmental organization (NGO) head in 2008 hold both great promise as well as great risks. Most decision-makers would acknowledge that complexity in the context of their organizations appears to be increasing. Most would also recognize that failure to effectively address this contextual complexity is expensive. The destructive, even catastrophic, consequences of these failures have been well examined in the literatures on public policy and corporate strategy. Two recent examples point this out sharply. First, the Stern report commissioned by the UK government and issued in October 2006 examined the real cost of climate change to 2050, concluding that it would lead to the biggest ever recorded economic meltdown if it was not averted (Stern, 2006). Second, Nobel Prize winner Joseph Stiglitz together with a colleague have calculated that the failures of the Bush administration to comprehend the complexities of Iraq have led to a cost overrun of the war from the administration's original estimate of $US60 billion to well over $US3 trillion (Stiglitz and Bilmes, 2008).

While we express all these situations as threats, each and every change constitutes opportunities for growth and development. For example, the increasing use of technology in society stimulates interconnections and, thus, greater complexity (e.g. households spend more on telecommunications, and more people travel and travel more – between 1972 and 2000, the average annual distance travelled by Britons grew 53 per cent).[1] As assets in the world are becoming more liquid with rapidly developing technology (Normann, 2001), they can be linked to each other in more ways, and the increasingly rich connections pattern can produce unforeseeable surprises. For example, economic growth and globalization increase our awareness of overall constraints, affecting activities which we considered unrelated until now, many of which have destructive unintended consequences.

This book is about how threats convert into opportunities – and how increasing threats turn into increasing opportunities. In order to think in these terms we need to look to the future. For reasons that will become clear, we consider the future through the spectacles of the scenario approach. While we do that, we reflect on our practice in the light of the perspective offered by a school of thought in the social and organizational sciences called social ecology, in particular its description of the 'turbulent environment'. We will show how scenarios and social ecology inform each other, allowing us – as managers, consultants and scholars – to become more effective and successful navigators in an increasingly turbulent world.

Scenario work: Success without understanding

Scenarios are descriptions of plausible future contexts in which we might find ourselves. Scenarios are typically presented as a small set of stories about how our surrounding environment might have evolved into the future. They are produced by carefully analysing and structuring relevant and challenging possibilities (for a good methodological overview, see van der Heijden, 2005).

Available data suggests that the use of scenarios to address complex conditions has been increasing. Scenario thinking and practice have occurred in military circles and policy think tanks, as well as in companies, for many decades. There are indications that its practice is spreading (see Figure 1.2). The thinking and practice of scenarios are characterized by a broad and confusing mix of methods and procedures with little explanation as to why and how they 'work' and variable criteria for success. In spite of its widespread adoption, scenario work remains theoretically underdeveloped.

Recognizing the need to clarify the theoretical underpinnings of scenario work, the three editors of this volume organized the first Oxford Futures Forum (OFF2005) at Templeton College, Oxford University, in October 2005. This forum attracted 70 'futures' practitioners and academic researchers for two days of dialogue about the relevance of complex environments – as conceptualized by the field of social ecology – to the practice of scenarios. Participants included many of the scenario planners who have shaped the practice over the last 50 years, as well as a cross-section of researchers and consultants from the social ecology school. We designed the OFF2005 as a 'strategic conversation' (see van der Heijden, 2005) and the event demonstrated that reflective dialogue between the two communities can be lively, mutually enriching and relevant. The chapters in this volume are drawn from contributions to the OFF which have been edited and updated. Hence, in an important sense, this book continues the conversations started in the Oxford Futures Forum 2005 and has no illusions of ending them.

This book seeks to provide academic rigour and scholarship to scenario work. So far, the field has been supported by practitioner books of varying quality. We aim to anchor scenario thinking more robustly in social science knowledge, based on better research that improves practice. For example, the 'Dialogue' section in the journal *Organization Studies* (vol 27, issue 12, 2006) had an interesting debate between Richard Whittington, and Gerard Hodgkinson and George Wright as to why a scenarios-based intervention by the two latter authors failed. They agree that the intervention was 'premature' (*Organization Studies*, 2006, vol 27, issue 12, pp1898, 1905) in relation to the emerging turbulence in the client organization's environment (*Organization Studies*, 2006, vol 27, issue 12, p1898). However, what is still missing is guidance as to when in the rising turbulence it would have been advisable for scenarios to be deployed. This book aims to clarify such issues.

Scenario work: Towards a practical theory

During the 1960s, a group of social scientists, focused on organizational research, theorized environmental complexity and uncertainty in terms of levels of what they called 'causal texture'. As part of this work they coined the term 'turbulence' to represent the most uncertain environments. The development of causal texture theory, particularly the concept of turbulence, was provoked by a growing need for social scientists to better understand increasing environmental complexity, environmental uncertainty and the indeterminate nature of such environments that was being experienced by managers. This need has not abated.

This book suggests that causal textures theory provides a robust conceptual underpinning for how scenario practices help to address environmental complexity. Grounded in state-of-the-art examples from across the world, the book examines how causal texture theory explains the effectiveness and limitations of scenario practices.

In broad outline we see two ways where scenarios help in coping with turbulence. First, they help stakeholders to develop a better systemic understanding of their surrounding environment and provide new insights into the turbulent environments they inhabit. A clearer (see Chapter 11 in this volume) awareness of predetermined elements in the environment (see Chapter 12) helps actors to make better sense of their subjective experience of turbulence.

Second, scenarios help in building common ground among disparate stakeholders in a turbulent environment. It enables them to focus their collective attention on a set of alternative futures. Multiple futures provide space for surfacing tacit assumptions, which can then be discussed and understood (see Chapters 6, 8, 9 and 12 in this volume). Understanding each other's perspectives on how the field they hold in common may play out in the future (see Chapters 6 and 10) allows stakeholders to come together to align and jointly strengthen their coping strategy.

Who this book is for

This is a book about how theory can be systematically and concretely applied to scenarios work. The key contribution is to connect a theoretical strand and a practical strand in the line of argument, bringing together theoretical insights to illuminate a practice: scenario work.

This is, therefore, not another 'scenarios book'. Nor is it an academic treatise on a particular management theory or trend in the social sciences. Instead, it links theory and practice to render theory more rigorous and practice more effective.

This key link is for those people who wish to reflect on and address uncertainty and complexity in their environment in a creative manner, with a focus on the future, in order to serve their present concerns. This theme of the 2005 Oxford Futures Forum is also the theme of this book.

We think this work will be of interest to *reflective practitioners* (Schön, 1983) in scenario work: those who use scenarios in their managerial or consulting work, and who want to know more about why, when and how they can be made more effective. We think the book will also appeal to scholars who want to understand better how managerial practice relates to tracking how uncertainty and volatility impacts upon businesses, governmental institutions and NGOs.

We expect this book to be of particular relevance to professionals directly or indirectly involved with strategic planning and management in private, public and NGO sectors, and who consider themselves reflective learners. This will include senior general management executives in small and large organizations, but also professionals involved in strategic planning, foresight, scouting, corporate affairs, intergovernmental relations, external communications, change management, corporate social responsibility and internal consultancy. We hope to provide these readers with new insights about practical issues such as forging common ground, responding to disruption, the role and scope of fairness in planning, different uses of scenarios, 'swarm planning', clarity in scenario work, and working with predetermined elements.

In the academic world, the book may be relevant to faculty and students in strategy, management studies and policy studies, as well as in social geography, sociology, economics, educational leadership, public administration, epidemiology, community psychology and engineering. The book will be specifically useful for faculty and students with an interest in strategy, leadership, sense-making, environmental studies, scanning, future studies, sustainability, corporate social responsibility, long-range planning, scenarios and entrepreneurship.

A special appeal of the material in this book is its global nature that is so often missing in policy studies and strategic planning books. The chapter authors are from Australia, Canada, England, Holland, Greece, Mexico, Scotland, South Africa, Sweden and the US. Moreover, the chapters use material from diverse cultural contexts ranging from Venezuela and India to the UK and Holland.

Environmental complexity and scenarios: Growing together

Key contributors to the creation of social ecology were Fred Emery and Eric Trist. Trained as a psychoanalyst, Trist co-founded after World War II the Tavistock Institute in London, where links between technical innovations and psycho-social possibilities were explored in the service of workers and managers in large organizations such as the British Coal Board.

Fred Emery, an Australian social scientist, was initially a student of Trist, but quickly became a colleague and, in Trist's view (personal information), a leader in much of their joint intellectual work. While over their working lives they collaborated with many other important social scientists and action researchers (such as Einar Thorsurd in developing industrial democracy in Norway and Russell Ackoff in developing interactive planning in the US), they continued collaborating together for many years despite their residing on different continents for several years at a time.

Emery and Trist's original statement (in 1965) concerning the causal textures of the environment may be seen as a high-level descriptive theory of environmental evolution (à la Toynbee, Darwin or Marx). However, they recognized from the beginning that it offered important direct implications for practice in the world. Others, including the authors in this volume, have taken up and developed these practical implications. An example of this is a planning and intervention method called the search conference, which Fred and Merrelyn Emery designed during the 1960s and then developed over the next 30 years. In this volume, Chapter 3 compares the features of the search conference and the scenario method.

We believe that reading causal textures as a macro-evolutionary theory alone would be incomplete and inaccurate for several reasons. First, causal textures theory ascribes to 'strategic choice' rather than determinism in social (including business) affairs – that is, actors are able to choose among possible responses to their environmental conditions and such choices are consequential. Second, as a part of open systems theory and social ecology, causal textures theory is underpinned by the notion that systems and their environments co-evolve – that is, actions by systems and their members can have the effect of changing the basic contours of environments; systems must then adapt to those changed contours. Third, causal textures theory is grounded deeply in human practice and ascribes to a deliberately normative stance towards an 'improved future' for humankind. Finally, the 'variant' on the original causal textures theory advocated by McCann and Selsky (1984) explicitly introduces the perceptions by actors of their environment as a key contingency in adaptation. That introduces the subtle link between the objective and the perceived environment that scenario work helps to explore as part of developing and strengthening adaptive behaviour.

In the decades since the publication of Emery and Trist's original article in 1965, research on complex environments and turbulence have increased in the field of organization and management studies, as shown in Figure 1.1.

Coincidentally, from 1965 onwards, while Emery and Trist were developing causal textures theory, people such as Hermann Kahn and Pierre Wack took a leading role in developing the method of scenarios as an aid to strategic planning. The links between their work are what we explored at OFF2005 and which this book makes available for a wider audience. We propose that causal textures theory (which we explain in Chapter 2) provides a uniquely well-informed understanding of:

- why scenario practices are growing; and
- how they work to address turbulence.

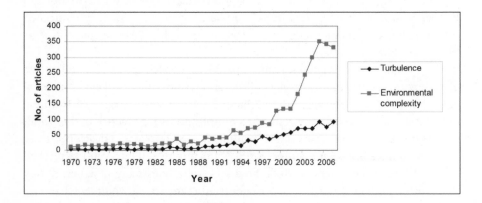

Source: Business Source Complete (EBSCO, 2008)[2]

Figure 1.1 Growth in the English language literature on 'turbulence' and 'environmental complexity' (1970–2007)

This understanding of scenario work has not been available before. As the chapters in this book show, attending to causal texture theory and its implications by scenario practitioners improve the effectiveness and quality of scenario work.

Scenarios

Several sources of data indicate that scenario use has increased significantly, particularly since the events of 11 September 2001. Figure 1.2 shows how the number of scholarly articles on scenarios published (in English only) in the social sciences has shot up. We believe this indicates the increasing interest in, and the importance of, scenario practice.

Figure 1.3 was produced by two professionals working in the US-based consultancy Bain and published in 2007 by the *Harvard Business Review* in its July–August issue. It suggests that scenario use among the parties surveyed by the consultants has gone up, as has satisfaction with the approach – presumably a good proxy for relevance. Similar statistics are available from the Conference Board, a US-based association of big companies. However, both surveys are less than rigorous in defining what 'scenario use' actually entails. As these definitions vary between users and have changed over time, the figures must be taken only as rough indicators of what is going on.

In a survey of the literature on scenarios covering 186 articles, books and chapters published between 1977 and mid 2007, Lang (2007) used a classification based on Morgan's (1986) eight-metaphor framework to identify social science

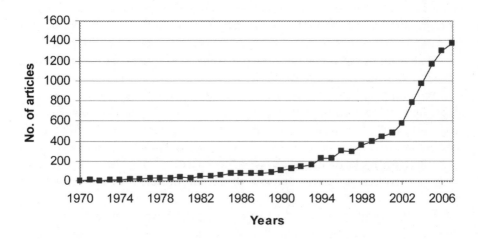

Source: Business Source Complete (EBSCO, 2008)[3]

Figure 1.2 Growth in the English language scholarly literature on scenarios (1970–2007)

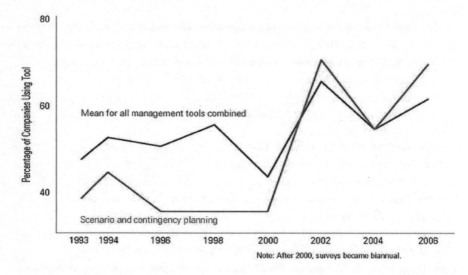

Figure axis label: Percentage of Companies Using Tool

Labels: Mean for all management tools combined

Scenario and contingency planning

X-axis: 1993 1994 1996 1998 2000 2002 2004 2006

Note: After 2000, surveys became biannual.

Notes: After 2000, surveys became biannual.
Planning catches on: for years, company use of scenario-and-planning contingency tools lagged behind the average for management tool use overall. This changed abruptly after the terrorist attacks of 11 September 2001.
Source: Rigby and Bilodeau (2007)

Figure 1.3 Increase in scenario usage

research on organizations. She found that the pattern of scenario research follows roughly that of research on organizations as a whole – that is, a majority of the publications fall within the mechanistic and organism metaphors reflecting concern with how to efficiently conduct scenario work and how to use the method to assist organizations in addressing environmental uncertainty. None of this, however, helps in explaining the growth in scenario use, particularly the explosive growth following 11 September 2001.

We propose that scenario use and relevance has increased because 9/11 brought home to decision-makers how turbulent causal texture has now become part and parcel of the field in which they live. We propose that since that time, it has become *legitimate* for senior people to express their inability to control some key uncertainties in their contexts. It is now accepted that these uncertainties need to be addressed through methods that accept the reality and inevitability of such uncertainties.

We also consider where, in the same light, scenarios would not be an appropriate or a helpful method. We will come to the conclusion (see Chapter 15) that scenarios are not helpful in environments which have a texture that is either more stable than a turbulent environment or even more uncertain and complex (see Chapter 9).

Outline of the book

Part I sets the scene for the rest of the book. It reviews the intellectual histories of *causal textures theory*, focusing on the turbulent field ('turbulence') and *scenario practices* to address complex strategic issues in corporate and public-sector contexts. These histories provide the foundation for an original and rigorous exploration of how scenario work succeeds and fails in addressing turbulence, leading to a new understanding of the effectiveness of the approach. This exploration is embodied in the chapters in Part I, which compare the causal textures framework with other conceptual frameworks and methods, the search conference method, soft systems methodology and the complexity theory of Ilya Prigogine.

In Chapter 2 the three editors of this volume review the intellectual history of the two key strands of the book:

1   the framework of environmental causal textures and turbulence, drawn from the original work by Emery and Trist during the mid 1960s and subsequent developments in social ecology up to the present day; and
2   the practice of scenarios, in terms of a comparison of a number of schools of thought and a mix of institutional homes (and how this has led to a lack of a coherent theoretical framework).

We then outline the two main ways in which scenarios help to cope with turbulence:

1   First, they help stakeholders to develop a better systemic understanding of the origins of turbulence in their contextual environment, leading to insights on the balance between predetermined elements and irreducible uncertainties.
2   Second, scenarios help to build common ground among disparate stakeholders by creating space for multiple interpretations and focusing collective attention on a constrained set of alternative futures.

In the next two chapters we aim to deepen this understanding by contrasting turbulence and the use of scenarios with other approaches designed to assist decision-makers in situations of considerable uncertainty. Chapter 3 elaborates upon the history of causal textures by comparing an intervention method normally associated with it – the search conference – with the scenario approach. This highlights the specific attributes of scenario practice. Chapter 4 demonstrates how the soft systems methodology developed by Peter Checkland can help us to understand how scenarios forge common ground among stakeholders in a turbulent environment.

Finally, Chapter 5 shows how the field of social ecology has moved on since Emery and Trist under the influence of complexity theory. Mary Bernard does this by comparing it with the work of Nobel Prize winner Ilya Prigogine on complexity and self-organization. This comparative analysis provides a more contemporary theoretical understanding of how change occurs in turbulent environments.

Coming out of Part I, the reader should have a clearer image of causal textures theory, of scenarios work, and of the interfaces between causal textures and scenarios that drive the rest of the book.

In Part II we find four cases, or stories, of specific turbulent environments and how scenarios were deployed to address these. These cases illustrate, in practice, the principles set out in Part I and prepare the reader for new conceptual and methodological insights presented in Part III.

The cases in Part II help the reader to appreciate the diversity of conditions and contexts in which turbulent causal textures arise, as well as the adaptability and versatility of scenario practices to address them. Originally, causal texture theorists proposed that turbulent environments could be addressed effectively by identifying and building common ground among stakeholders. The cases selected illustrate how this is facilitated by situating these common ground possibilities in possible futures with the help of scenario practices.

First, Chapter 6 discusses the shift from a 'placid-clustered' environmental texture to a 'turbulent' environmental texture, as Indian agriculture is gradually opened up to the logics and the pressures of world markets as part of the country's economic take-off. New dynamic, independent and autonomous processes take on an uncertain life of their own. Causal texture theory suggests that control of turbulence resulting from economic take-off requires collaboration among stakeholders based on their shared understanding of common ground among them. A scenario project was aimed at creating a 'strategic conversation' among the relevant actors, with the purpose of developing insights into what shape this common ground might take. This pointed to elements of possible future shared ideals being identified that might limit the potentially destructive consequences of turbulent conditions as a powerful step towards increasing the country's adaptive capacity.

Chapter 7 then examines how increasing environmental turbulence has led Dutch urban and regional planners towards methods that incorporate scenario practices. Rob Roggema emphasizes the role of the individual idea, next to the role of common ground collaborations, in the struggle to adapt to turbulence (as explained by complexity theory; see Chapter 5). These distinct roles in addressing the challenges of major climate change are discussed. On the basis of this, the author proposes 'swarm planning' as a possible future extension of scenario processes when deployed to address turbulent settings.

Chapter 8 examines how regulation and governance relate to addressing turbulence. It does so by exploring how scenarios were deployed in dealing with Swedish regional healthcare and its future. This case suggests that governance originally developed for more predictable environments than turbulent ones must, like Chapter 7's regional planning, be rethought and redesigned – and that failing to do so will lead to unacceptable conditions.

Finally, Chapter 9 highlights the limitations of scenario work in extreme environment causal textures, even beyond what is normally considered as turbulence, based on the original 1965 theory. Examples are McCann and Selsky's (1984) 'hyper-turbulent' and Babüroğlu's (1988) 'vortical' environmental textures. Thomas uses the case of Venezuela in 2004 to demonstrate the challenges of forging common ground in such highly turbulent conditions. He reflects upon his original analysis from the vantage point of hindsight (2008) and considers the possibilities of using scenarios in causal textures other than the turbulent.

Part III discusses key issues arising from exploring the links between causal textures and scenarios and reviews implications for scenario practice methods. We suggest that these issues affect all scenario work and all scenario practitioners. Real-world cases are also included here; but we as editors concluded that the power of these chapters lay in the conceptual and methodological issues that they raise.

Chapter 10 starts this section by focusing on the disruptive aspect of change in contextual turbulence. It examines several key features of disruptiveness in three forms: operational, competitive and contextual. Focusing on contextual disruption as key to coping with turbulent conditions, Selsky and McCann propose a shift in thinking about change, from viewing disruption as a deviation from normalcy or equilibrium, to viewing it as a normal condition of organizational life. Instead of an 'episodic' mental model of change, a search for equilibrium and adaptation, and strategy based on an inside–outside model of the organization, they call for a 'continuous' change model, a search for emergence and improvisation, and collaboration based on a networked field model of the organization. Selsky and McCann see an important role for scenarios in developing the improvisation skills of the organization. They suggest that envisioning the possibility of future disruptive change can galvanize stakeholders to come together to create, and foster or strengthen common ground as the basis for a more prosperous future.

Chapter 11 examines clarity and aesthetics in scenario practices. Rafael Ramírez focuses on how attending to 'clarity' in the process of scenario building helps to foster the creation of common ground. Clarity is an aesthetic quality or aspect of scenario practices. Ramírez argues that aesthetic judgements in scenario work come prior to forging common ground and, indeed, are a necessary precondition to it. He reports the results of an exploratory workshop to assess the role of aesthetics in scenario work. He concludes by suggesting that attending explicitly to 'clarity' as an organizing principle in scenario work helps to engage with the uncertainty of turbulent conditions.

Chapter 12 uses the case of a scenario project for an engineering original equipment manufacturer, serving the UK power industry, to explore how scenario practices can help the management team of such a company to understand possible future contexts of UK power generation. George Burt shows how the existing context of deregulation carries the seeds of increasing power shortages and blackouts. He focuses on how scenario work helps to assess the predetermined elements in an environment that will play out in all plausible conditions, and how attending to this aspect of scenario methods enables turbulence to be addressed.

Chapter 13 highlights how important it is to attend to the issues of fairness and equity among the stakeholders, especially in highly complex, inter-organizationally sponsored scenario initiatives. Collaborations under conditions of high uncertainty require understanding of generally accepted principles of fairness to generate confidence that even if things turn out differently from what is foreseeable, equity among stakeholders will be maintained. Shirin Elahi suggests that failure to attend to power and fairness will compromise the coherence of the collaboration and, therefore, the effectiveness of scenario practices.

The final chapter in Part III, Chapter 14, takes this a step further by comparing two case studies, in the tobacco and utility industries, where top management teams espoused explicit strategies on corporate social responsibility (CSR) and stakeholder responsiveness. Andromache Athanasopoulou situates CSR as a stabilizing mechanism to produce 'common ground' among a firm and its various stakeholders, helping to address and mitigate environmental turbulence. While neither company studied actually used scenarios, the author argues that the effectiveness of both companies' CSR strategies would have been strengthened if scenarios *had* been deployed by these companies. In turn, this points to how CSR may be strengthened in the future and how scenario practices may be informed by a CSR agenda.

Part IV consists of one chapter in which the three editors summarize the themes of the book, surface several hidden topics, and offer suggestions for future prospects and trajectories for research on turbulence and scenario practice. This includes reflection on issues such as the perceived versus objective nature of turbulence; how scenario work contributes to the better definition and development of causal textures theory; and dilemmas and challenges in forging common ground and deploying it to cope with turbulence. We conclude that causal texture theory offers a sound theoretical grounding of scenario practice, explaining why scenario work is more relevant in turbulent times than any other available alternative.

We end by highlighting some outstanding issues that either arose or were clarified from the material in the chapters. For example, there is the question of how we can write a book about addressing turbulence while it resides in the contextual environment where actors, by definition, have no direct influence. This is the social ecology equivalent of the design versus evolution dilemma that is being debated hotly in both biology and religion as we finish this book. It is a question of levels: how does the individual actor relate to emergent outcomes at the field level? More generally, how are we to link the macro- and the micro-level descriptions of a particular field? A way out may be offered by complexity theory, which relates very small fluctuations to very large structural change when the system is at the 'edge of chaos', or a 'tipping point', or, in Prigogine's terms surveyed by Bernard in Chapter 5, a bifurcation point. The patient reader at the end of this book will see that this issue is not merely an abstract conceptual one, but instead one that has important methodological implications for scenario practitioners. Let the conversation continue.

Notes

1   Centre for Transport and Society and Centre for Mobilities Research: see www. transport.uwe.ac.uk/research/projects/travel-time-use/background.htm.
2   Two searches were carried out in January 2008 for the full years indicated, one using 'turbulence' and one using 'environmental complexity' in the search fields of 'Abstract and Author-supplied Abstract' and limited to scholarly (peer-reviewed) journals. The figures are raw (i.e. the context within which the terms are used has not been checked).
3   This search was carried out in January 2008 for the full years indicated, using 'scenarios' in the search fields of 'Abstract and Author-supplied Abstract' and limited to scholarly (peer-reviewed) journals. The figures are raw (i.e. the context within which the terms are used has not been checked).

References

Babüroğlu, O. (1988) 'The vortical environment: The fifth in the Emery–Trist levels of organizational environments', *Human Relations*, vol 41, pp181–210

Emery, F. and Trist, E. (1965) 'The causal texture of organizational environments', *Human Relations,* vol 18, pp21–32

Lang, T. (2007) *An Initial Classification of the Organisational Scenario Literature Based on Morgan's Organisational Metaphors*, MSc (Management Research) thesis, University of Oxford, UK

McCann, J. and Selsky, J. (1984) 'Hyperturbulence and the emergence of type 5 environments', *Academy of Management Review*, vol 9, no 3, pp460–470

Morgan, G. (1986) *Images of Organization*, Sage, Beverly Hills, CA

Normann, R. (2001) *Reframing Business: When the Map Changes the Landscape*, John Wiley and Sons, Chichester, UK

Oxford Futures Forum (2005) www.oxfordfuturesforum.org.uk

Rigby, D. and Bilodeau, B. (2007) 'A growing focus on preparedness', *Harvard Business Review*, vol 85, July/August, pp21–22

Schön, D. (1983) *The Reflective Practitioner*, Basic Books, New York, NY

Stern, N. (2006) *Stern Review on the Economics of Climate Change*, www.hm-treasury. gov.uk/independent_reviews/stern_review_economics_climate_change/sternreview_ index.cfm

Stiglitz, J. and Bilmes, L. (2008) *The Three Trillion Dollar War: The True Cost of the Iraq Conflict*, W. W. Norton & Company, New York, NY

van der Heijden, K. (2005) *Scenarios: The Art of Strategic Conversation*, John Wiley and Sons, Chichester, UK

2

Conceptual and Historical Overview

Rafael Ramírez, John W. Selsky and Kees van der Heijden

Introduction

As mentioned in Chapter 1, our purpose in this book is to connect the conceptual body of work on the causal textures of organizational environments with the practice of scenario work. We intend that the former illuminates the latter.

Before exploring the links between the theory and the practice, it is important to deeply understand each of the components: the theory of causal textures and the practice of scenario work. To that effect we have organized this chapter as follows.

In the first section we review the causal texture theory and, in particular, examine what is called the 'turbulent' causal texture. This theory was produced by Fred Emery and Eric Trist and their colleagues in the Tavistock Institute in London during the 1960s. We focus on the original formulation as well as subsequent developments up to the present. In the second section we review the nature and history of scenario practices. This offers a comparative rendition of how scenario practices developed on both sides of the Atlantic, again from the 1960s to the present. In the final section of this chapter we outline how scenario work and causal texture theory inform and enrich each other.

This book rests on our belief that Emery and Trist's ideas about how to engage with open systems and their environments provides rich *conceptual* insights on why scenarios have become a major part of strategic and policy-making practices. In addition, their work offers important *methodological* insights that improve practice.

Emery and Trist's contribution: Causal textures theory

In the 20 years spanning the end of World War II and the publication of Emery and Trist's seminal paper 'The causal texture of organizational environments' in *Human Relations* in 1965, the field of social psychology had been most attentive to developments in biology. From that discipline, and particularly from the work of von Bertalanffy (1968) and Ashby (1960) on how organisms relate to their contexts, social psychology scholars had imported and then adapted the idea that systems should be treated as 'open' – that is, as fitting in, deriving form and sustenance from, and contributing to an environment around them. This perspective, which became known as 'open systems thinking', then influenced thinking in organizations, where strategic planners became increasingly interested in the business environment, setting parameters for strategic decision-making. Open systems thinking would be an essential part of Emery and Trist's work, and a central component of how their work would come to enlighten future scholars and practitioners.

A second important input into Emery and Trist's thinking came from their colleague Kurt Lewin (1952). In his work, Lewin found that to understand something in the social world, a social scientist engages with it, and that the inevitable changes caused by the engagement help the scientist to explain the system better. This idea was the foundation of the method of action research. Emery and Trist adopted this approach of 'engaging with', which they studied in their various field researches (Trist later highlighted this principle in the title of his three-volume trilogy of Tavistock work published by the University of Pennsylvania Press between 1990 and 1997, naming it *The Social Engagement of Social Science*). Open systems and engagement were decisive elements in how their work evolved, not only affecting what they researched, but also defining the role they developed as researchers relating to clients or subjects.

All this work then led to the development of causal texture theory, which Emery and Trist launched for the first time in their seminal 1965 paper, which we discuss below. In it they developed a taxonomy of causal textures of environments within which organizations aim to survive and thrive. The one they drew particular attention to was called 'turbulence'. Turbulence in colloquial English describes conditions that are uncertain, complex, and changing unpredictably and often quickly. In their paper, Emery and Trist (1965) defined 'turbulence' in a much more precise way that could refer to organizational environments. In this volume the word 'turbulence' is used in its more restricted and technical meaning, as described in detail below. Readers need to hang on to this point in order to understand the line of argument on why scenarios work and why they have grown as increasingly turbulent conditions have emerged. In the next section we return to the precise understanding of turbulence offered by causal texture theory.

Causal texture and organizational environments

Causal texture theory deals with systems trying to survive and thrive in their environments in a sustainable way. The inside (a system) and the outside (the environment of that system) 'co-evolve' in the sense that systems and their environments mutually and systematically influence each other, and they proceed into the future together (Selsky et al, 2007). System and environment both have links between variables that exist within them and links with each other. Several interacting systems, their shared environments and the links that connect them together are defined as a 'field'.

Causal texture is an emergent property of the whole field and concerns the behaviour of all systems within it. The causal texture of a field sets conditions on how these systems and their shared environments transact (Selsky et al, 2007, p74).

In their 1965 paper, Emery and Trist identified four distinct types of causal texture. The types were 'ideal' types in German sociologist Max Weber's (1962) sense – that is, a logically derived, hypothetical 'pure' category of existence unsullied by the clutter of the 'real' world. Ideal types can help practitioners to identify how close a given situation is to the 'textbook case' that the ideal type describes. For example, Weber used 'bureaucracy' (which he distinguished from charismatic and from traditional organizational ideal types) as the perfect form for his 'rational' ideal type of organization – yet everyone knows how irrational 'bureaucracies' can actually be in real life.

The differences among the four ideal types that Emery and Trist (1965) developed depended upon how systems in the field (systems they termed '1') and their surrounding environment (which they termed '2') are linked. They were particularly interested in links they called 'law-like' (i.e. links driven by a logic that pertains over a period of time). Four possible links between system and environment exist:

1   L11 (read as 'El one, one', not as 'El eleven') denotes links that remain internal to a system.
2   L12 links the system to its environment – system outputs, related to the planning function.
3   L21 links the environment to the system – system inputs, related to the learning function.
4   L22 denotes links between elements in the environment itself, and which occur independently of the system.

Distinctions among the causal textures are most helpfully characterized by which of the L11, L12, L21 and L22 links are most salient in the situation studied, as we show in Table 2.1 – that is, Emery and Trist worked out the causal textures logically in terms of field structure, and the type of coping or response strategy that would enable a system to do well in that causal situation (a more elaborate version of Table 2.1 is found in Chapter 9 as Table 9.1).

Table 2.1 *The four causal textures*

Type of causal texture	Structure of field	Most salient connections	Characteristics of successful coping/response strategy in the type
I: Placid Random	Resources, goals and noxiants are randomly distributed in the field. 'Perfect market' conditions.	L11	- Experience-based tactics. - Local optimization in the 'here and now'.
II: Placid Clustered	Resources, goals and/or noxiants are located in advantageous ('high ground') positions. Conditions of imperfect competition with market failure.	L11+L21	- Strategizing for securing or accessing 'high-ground' locations and identifying right placing of outputs. - Attending to distinctive competence and resources. - Centralizing operations.
III: Disturbed Reactive	Oligopoly. Similar organizations in head-to-head competition. More L21, L12 exchanges than in types I & II.	L11+L12+L21	- Game-based strategies, communicating with others to influence inputs. - Mounting operational 'campaigns'. - Rapid decision-making. - 'Coming to terms' with the other sharing the same field.
IV: Turbulent	The whole common shared ground is in motion. L22 becomes uncertain and changing, taking on a life of its own; distinctions between L12-L21 and L22 begin to break down.	L11+ L21+ L12+ L22; Distinctions between 1 and 2 begin to break down.	- No survival for systems acting alone. - Collaborative strategies among dissimilar organizations in field.

In developing the four causal textures, Emery and Trist's (1965) reasoning was logical and deductive. The distinctive contribution was to articulate for the first time the nature and properties of the environmental relationships L22.

The names they gave each causal texture were rather incidental, intended to make the types more accessible (Eric Trist told Ramírez and Selsky that the label 'turbulent' occurred to them while on a very unstable airplane flight). The depiction 'turbulent' has subsequently captured the imagination of many scholars and managers. In picking up on the label 'turbulence', they have made that 1965 article one of the most widely cited in the literature on management and organizations.

As one progresses from type I to type IV causal texture, increasing complexity of transactions *in* a field leads to an aggregate behaviour *of* that field that becomes less and less stable. The causal texture is a manifestation of this relative instability. From the point of view of any system in the environment (such as an organization), this means that its environment becomes less stable as the textures proceed – that is, the increasing instability of the field as a whole manifests itself as a 'relevant instability' of the environment of individual systems or organizations.

In Emery and Trist terms, as expressed in the 1965 paper, the L22 links are relevant to all systems in a field. For any system in this field, these links are perceived as the wider context in which it finds itself. This initially created a degree of confusion as it was less than clear how to distinguish L22 from L21 links. This dilemma was subsequently (post-1965) resolved by the definition of the transactional and contextual environments. Each system (organization) in the field has its own competitive and collaborative operations and relations with others, which are defined as the L21 and L12 links. This is the transactional environment, defined by the actions of the actors in it. Together these transactions in aggregate become part of the contextual environment. The latter is defined by the relevant L22 links, expressed not as agent actions but in terms of macro-factors. If an individual actor can influence the situation, she is in the transactional environment defined by L21 and L12 links. If an individual actor is looking at macro-phenomena that she cannot influence, she is looking at the contextual environment, defined by L22 links.

In the first two types of causal texture, the environment is recognized to be stable by the majority of the actors in it. In type III, with more interconnections, the field becomes more dynamic, or 'disturbed'. But even if competition can be severe, and some organizations will perish, these events happen in a mutually acknowledged and legitimate way. For this reason the actors in it recognize that the 'playing field' (i.e. the transactional environment) is still relatively stable. Systems in this environmental texture operate according to, and support, a set of institutional rules of the game (van de Ven and Hargrave, 2004) that characterize the field they constitute and inhabit.

Up to type IV causal texture, change occurs between and among systems encompassed in a stable and relatively predictable shared environment, even if life is not always totally agreeable and has its ups and downs. However, in the turbulent causal texture, the institutional arrangements governing the field as a whole start to break down, and the whole of the field, including the contextual environment of L22 links, becomes a source of instability. The (sudden) instability in the L22 relationships, signalling to actors that they can't rely on it anymore, makes the relevant uncertainty salient in a new way for decision-makers in organizations trying to survive and thrive.

How might this happen? Charles Perrow (1984) in his book *Normal Accidents* studied the set of conditions that led to the Three Mile Island nuclear power incident. He found that the nuclear reactor operators tacitly (and mistakenly) thought that what was going on had been predicted in advance and that ways to deal with it had been specified in their operating manuals. Yet, the situation that actually arose had not been predicted and anticipated in the manuals. So, in doing what the manuals said should be done, operators actually contributed to the accident coming about and made it worse. So, too, with turbulence – it may be caused by an aggregate of actors who are unaware that they are, in fact, co-producing the turbulent causal texture. For example, if actors or systems in a disturbed–reactive causal texture do not in aggregate attend to the externalities they produce in their normal competitive actions (including failure to attend to appropriate regulatory frameworks), they may unwittingly co-produce a turbulent causal texture (Selsky et al, 2007, p74; see also Chapters 8 and 14 in this volume).

The type IV causal texture reflects for a given observer conditions in the field that have been called 'wicked' problems (Rittel and Webber, 1973); 'messes', or systems of problems (Ackoff, 1979); and 'meta-problems' (Trist, 1979; Selsky and Parker, 2005).

Trist clarified later (1983) that the L22 contextual links supply the boundary conditions for any one system's transactional environment (its L12 and L21 relations with which it transacts with others). How the nature of the L22 relationships shape these transactions was the key contribution in the original analysis (Trist, 1983, p172). This is an important insight for the purposes of this book as it clarifies how and why scenarios help decision-makers – *specifically* in turbulent causal textures. In the first three types of causal texture, actors in aggregate maintain a degree of control over the field. But in the turbulent causal texture, the L21 and L12 transactions among systems become affected by highly uncertain L22 macro-relationships due to uncertain causality. It is because, in turbulent causal textures, the source of uncertainty stops being predictable that scenarios become highly relevant methods – it is in this respect crucial that the methods upon which scenario work rests neither depend upon nor deploy probability and predictability to be of help in assessing how the turbulence may play out.

We subscribe to the 'socio-ecological' position, proposed by Emery and Trist (1973) and further developed in causal texture theory. Here turbulence is understood as a distinctive field-based environmental texture, not only as an aspect of an individual organization's environment. Selsky et al (2007, p77) assert that 'To construe turbulence as a property of a particular firm's environment ... is to conflate it with the commercial challenges routinely faced by every firm.' Conflating turbulence with intense competitive challenges reflects the way in which the word 'turbulence' is used in everyday language, and has a rather different meaning from its usage in causal texture theory. The 'everyday view' of turbulence implies that strategizing in the final analysis *is* competing – a position more appropriate to the disturbed–reactive (type III texture) conditions than to turbulence in the strict causal texture sense. The technical view of turbulence used in causal texture theory suggests that competitive actions may not always be appropriate if they co-produce a turbulent field that leads to the collapse of systems (institutions and firms) in it. In effect, direct effects of competitive actions and unintended higher-order consequences may not be confined to other industry actors with whom one is competing. The logical conclusion of conflating turbulence with competitive challenges is that 'the more turbulent the environment, the more aggressive must be the firm's response' (Ansoff, 1988, p173). Causal texture theory, on the other hand, suggests that 'such "proactive" responses may produce highly problematic unintended consequences in extended social fields' (Selsky et al, 2007, p77).

Perceiving turbulence in practice

While the ideal types that Emery and Trist (1965) identified were clear, in practice it is not so easy to establish that one is in a situation that approximates a given ideal type of causal texture and not another. This is what happens when ideal types are used in real-world instances, which by definition only approximate this or that ideal type. In Chapter 9, Thomas wrestles with this upon analysing the case of Venezuela as it was in 2004.

Research by McCann and Selsky (1984) and Babüroğlu (1988) suggests that people's experience of turbulence is moderated by the adaptive capacities they perceive they can mobilize, both individually (say, inside a single system) and collectively. This contrasts with Emery and Trist's stance in the 1965 paper that considered turbulence as an objective condition of a field – through which it became a distinctive texture. Instead, McCann and Selsky (1984) and Selsky et al (2007) put the subjective perceiver of turbulence explicitly into the picture, suggesting that a given field condition will be experienced differently by different actors and therefore perceived differently. In other words, some may consider that they are operating in a turbulent causal texture, while others see themselves in a disturbed reactive one. The reason why they experience and perceive their environments differently is that they perceive their adaptive capacities differently. Some may believe they have the adaptive capacity to mobilize greater or more valuable stocks of resources and others may not have that perception. We revisit this distinction between the 'objective' (Emery and Trist, 1965) and the 'subjective' (McCann and Selsky, 1984; Selsky et al, 2007) nature of causal texture, and their mutual relationship and effects in the final chapter. This also is elaborated upon in Chapters 4 to 6 of this volume.

Coping with turbulence

So, how can anyone respond to a turbulent environment and escape from its negative or damaging effects? Emery and Trist (1965) – and their followers – suggested one could not do it alone. Systems in a field that is characterized by the turbulent causal texture conditions would have to come together and jointly determine, identify, uncover or even create grounds that they could share ('common ground') to act together. In other words, in a field with a turbulent causal texture, systems are advised to collaborate in order to identify a set of values that they can institutionalize to create common ground.[1] At a large-scale level, one can argue that this is what the process of civilization has successfully done throughout history. At a lower level, it entails creating inter-organizational collaborative 'island' arrangements that can keep turbulence outside (e.g. Normann and Ramírez, 1993, and their 'value constellations'). In Chapter 8, Arvidsson shows how Swedish healthcare is exploring how it might be done there, while in Chapter 6, van der Heijden presents four scenarios for Indian agriculture that suggest it might be the preferred future in that field.

In turbulent causal textures, attention must shift from understanding the competitive, often one-to-one, games in the existing transactional environment to understanding how the forces from the contextual environment (L22) may shape the transactional environment in the future. This is precisely what scenarios do – they attend to and work through plausible possibilities in the contextual environment, and the consequences for the transactional environment.

But prior to constituting these inter-organizational constellations, one must appreciate the nature of the turbulent causal texture and the new kinds of behaviours that it requires. To do so in the multiple (in a set of scenarios) rather than the singular (a forecast or reference projection) helps managers to acknowledge/recognize that the contextual environment is beyond their control or direct influence (Smith, 1983) in preparation for coming together and co-creating an island of collaboration that can shut out turbulence for all of them.

This strategy is not entirely unproblematic. Creating newly institutionalized rules and regulations means returning to head-to-head competition in the type III 'disturbed reactive' causal texture. Domain creation through successful inter-organizational constellations requires a mode of conversation in which such multiple perspectives are acknowledged as legitimate and helpful. Scenarios do that in a strategic conversation (van der Heijden, 2005). When, in this process, collaboration surmounts competition, then scenarios are effective; when competition wins in the conversation, scenarios fail (see Chapter 13 in this volume for a deeper analysis of this aspect of scenario work).

Whether collaboration is all that is needed to solve the 'problem of turbulence' is a moot point. Prigogine (see Chapter 5 in this volume) suggests that there are critical points in time, called bifurcations, when the entire future of a system depends upon minor fluctuations within or without. In Chapter 7, Roggema argues convincingly from examples in spatial planning that at these sensitive bifurcations, the creativity and innovative drive of one individual actor may be enough to determine the survival or demise of the field as a whole.

In summary, Emery and Trist (1965) considered that to stop the snowballing effect that gives rise to, feeds and is fed by turbulence, the salience of L22 relationships in the contextual environment would need to be reduced by institutionalizing new values. The idea is that shared values in these institutions would create an environment of lesser uncertainty than the type IV causal texture, pushing turbulence back and recreating a more stable ground for decision-making and investing in the future. However, at critical bifurcation points, a key role continues to be played by creative and innovative individuals who show new ways out of the messy and wicked problems caused by turbulence. Scenarios are a key method to assist in this imaginative and creative process.

Scenario practices

Scenarios have been used in companies for over four decades (Lesourne and Stoffaes, 2001; van der Heijden, 2005) and even longer by military planners and policy-makers. Because of their origins in military applications going back a long way, there are now multiple methodological versions in the public domain depending upon how they developed both conceptually and in practice. The early work in RAND that Herman Kahn (1962) made famous, along with the work at SRI, are considered pioneers in the Anglo-Saxon world. In the Francophone world, the school of *La Prospective* developed by Berger (1964) and furthered in the national planning work of the French Delegation for Regional Action and Space Planning (DATAR), the '*futuribles*' movement and journal (from '*futurs possibles*'), the '*comités de la prospective*' that were formed in public companies such as EDF and France Télecom (Lessourne and Stoffaes, 2001), and the work of Michel Godet and his colleagues shaped a whole community of practice.

An important milestone was the introduction of scenarios at Royal Dutch Shell by Pierre Wack[2] 40 years ago. Although a Frenchman, Pierre Wack was influenced more by Gurdjieff's (1963) philosophy, highlighting the essence of 'seeing' anew rather than by the highly technical and quantified methods of the French scenario school. He was followed in Shell by Peter Schwartz, who came from the SRI practice, having written early scenario books such as *Seven Tomorrows: Toward a Voluntary History* (1982) with Paul Hawken and James Ogilvy. The 'Shell school' became a private-sector benchmark, not only because of the role that scenarios had in helping the company to address the first oil shock (Schwartz, 1991; van der Heijden, 2005), but also because it became an interwoven practice across the company that has not been replicated elsewhere to the same degree. The Global Business Network (GBN) organization founded by Schwartz, together with van der Heijden, Ogilvy, Collyns and others, when he left Shell, continued more in the SRI tradition than the Shell one, just as the work of Godet and his colleagues carried on in the French tradition in a way that paid less attention to the US contribution than Shell did.

Because of the legacy of Pierre Wack and the Shell school, the core of non-military scenario work has moved from Herman Kahn's famous dictum 'to think the unthinkable' (in the context of a possible nuclear war), to focusing on seeing a new reality by identifying the driving forces in the contextual environment that determine plausible future transactional environments (see Chapter 12 in this volume).

The best-selling book by van der Heijden (2005, p115) explains scenario work in ways that build on Emery and Trist's (1965) understanding of transactional and contextual environments. Scenarios are considered to be methods to assess the causal texture by considering how L22 forces in the contextual environment interact systemically to affect a set of transactional environment (L12 and L21) possibilities. This is the methodological form of scenario work to which the chapters in this book refer.

As we noted in Chapter 1, the use of scenarios in corporate planning has increased substantially since the events of 11 September 2001. We believe that this book is the first publication to propose a clearly articulated, explicit and defensible reason for this. This is that decision-makers are increasingly seeing turbulence as part and parcel of the world in which they live, meaning that they cannot any longer count on a stable foundation for their activities. A long and growing list of large and unanticipated events, crises, wars, etc. drives home the message that this is not so much a problem of insufficient analysis and/or research or lack of data or information, but of the field itself having become turbulent and uncertain, requiring a fundamentally different response.

Causal texture theory, turbulence and scenario work

We have put together this book to explain in a scholarly *and* practical manner how causal texture theory helps decision-makers to understand, first, how scenario analyses help address turbulent environments; and, second, why scenario analysis is increasing as a consequence. Understanding how scenarios address turbulence has methodological implications in that it clarifies the purpose of deploying scenarios and the results one may expect from doing so.

During the 1930s, it was customary to say that scientists knew that bumblebees flew but that they did not know how. Magnan (1934) observed that the then-known laws of aerodynamics could not explain their ability to fly despite the obvious fact that they did. He postulated that new and unconventional aerodynamic laws must be involved. Some 70 years later scientists can now explain these laws in detail:

> Insects use a combination of newly discovered aerodynamic mechanisms, including clap-and-fling kinematics, leading edge vortices, rotational mechanisms, and wake-capture mechanisms to produce far more lift than conventional understanding, based on attached-flow aerodynamics, could account for.[3]

Thus, while bumblebees obviously flew, it took some time for scientists to understand why. In some way, scenario work at the beginning of the 21st century is in the same situation – it flies, but we have less than robust theories as to why.

In short, the core argument of this book is that as fields take on the characteristics of a turbulent environment causal texture, the use of methods such as scenarios to address turbulence is bound to rise. We argue that scenario methods would not be relevant in other than type IV causal texture conditions because the contextual complexity described by the L22 relationships is not salient, and so scenarios are not needed to address it. We have identified two main ways whereby scenario methods help in coping with turbulence. First, they help stakeholders to develop a better systemic understanding of the causal texture of the contextual environment and the salient L22 relationships. With scenarios, people responsible for their organizations' survival gain new insights and clearer understanding of these relationships in the environment, leading to a growing awareness of predetermined elements, reduced uncertainty and better insights on how the remaining uncertainties may play out. Second, scenario methods help in building common ground among disparate stakeholders because they provide space for multiple interpretations of the situation, leading to parties understanding each other's perspective on how the field they hold in common may play out under different plausible conditions. This helps create the common ground that shuts turbulence out.

In the 12 chapters that follow, the authors flesh out these two key linkages in a variety of ways and contexts.

Notes

1   After the 1965 paper, Fred Emery (1977) suggested that in addition to institutionalizing new values, systems in fields exhibiting turbulent causal textures should engage together in 'ideal-seeking'. He suggested that in the turbulent causal texture – and not in the other three – beauty would be an important ideal to pursue (see Chapter 11 in this volume).

2   From the French Ministry of Energy, prior to his joining Shell France (Wack, 1985; Kleiner, 1996).

3   We thank Dr Adrian Thomas from the Department of Zoology at the University of Oxford, UK (personal communication), for this example.

References

Ackoff, R. (1979) *The Art of Problem-Solving*, John Wiley, New York, NY

Ansoff, I. (1988) *The New Corporate Strategy*, John Wiley, New York, NY

Ashby, W. (1960) *Design for a Brain: The Origin of Adaptive Behaviour*, 2nd edition, Chapman and Hall, London, UK

Babüroğlu, O. (1988) 'The vortical environment: The fifth in the Emery–Trist levels of organizational environments', *Human Relations*, vol 41, pp181–210

Berger, G. (1964) *Phénoménologie du Temps et Prospective*, Presses Universitaires de France, Paris, France

Emery, F. (1977) 'Active adaptation: The emergence of ideal-seeking systems', excerpt from F. Emery (ed) *Futures We Are In*, Martinus Nijhoff, Leiden, The Netherlands, reprinted in E. Trist, F. Emery and H. Murray (eds) and B. Trist (assistant ed) (1997) *The Social Engagement of Social Science, Volume III, The Socio-Ecological Perspective*, University of Pennsylvania Press, Philadelphia, PA, pp147–169

Emery, F. and Trist, E. (1965) 'The causal texture of organizational environments', *Human Relations*, vol 18, pp21–32

Emery, F. and Trist, E. (1973) *Towards a Social Ecology*, Plenum, London, UK

Gurdjieff, G. (1963) *Meetings with Remarkable Men*, E. P. Dutton and Company Inc, New York, NY

Hawken, P., Ogilvy, J. and Schwartz, P. (1982) *Seven Tomorrows: Toward a Voluntary History*, Bantam Books, Toronto, Canada

Kahn, H. (1962) *Thinking About the Unthinkable*, Horizon Press, New York, NY

Kleiner, A. (1996) *The Age of Heretics: Heroes, Outlaws, and the Forerunners of Corporate Change*, Nicholas Brealey Publishing, London, UK

Lesourne, J. and Stoffaes, C. (2001) *La Prospective Stratégique d'Entreprise*, InterEditions, Paris, France

Lewin, K. (1952) *Field Theory in Social Science: Selected Theoretical Papers*, Tavistock, London, UK

Magnan, A. (1934) *La Locomotion Chez les Animaux, vol 1*, Hermann, Paris, France

McCann, J. and Selsky, J. (1984) 'Hyperturbulence and the emergence of type 5 environments', *Academy of Management Review*, vol 9, no 4, pp460–470

Normann, R. and Ramírez, R. (1993) 'From value chain to value constellation: Designing interactive strategy', *Harvard Business Review*, vol 71, no 4, pp65–77

Perrow, C. (1984) *Normal Accidents*, Basic Books, New York, NY

Rittel, H. and Webber, M. (1973) 'Dilemmas in a general theory of planning', *Policy Sciences*, vol 4, pp155–169

Selsky, J. and Parker, B. (2005) 'Cross-sector partnerships to address social issues: Challenges to theory and practice', *Journal of Management*, vol 31, no 6, pp849–873

Selsky, J., Goes, J. and Babüroğlu, O. (2007) 'Contrasting perspectives of strategy making: Applications in "hyper" environments', *Organization Studies*, vol 28, no 1, pp71–94

Schwartz, P. (1991) *The Art of the Long View: Scenario Planning – Protecting Your Company against an Uncertain Future*, Doubleday, New York, NY

Smith, W. (1983) *Organizing as a Power Process: The Creation and Testing of a Conceptual Framework and Its Application to the Design of Development Projects*, PhD thesis, University Microfilms International, Ann Arbor, MI

Trist, E. (1979) 'The environment and system response capability: A futures perspective', *Futures*, vol 12, pp113–127, reprinted in E. Trist, F. Emery and H. Murray (eds) and B. Trist (assistant ed) (1997) *The Social Engagement of Social Science, Volume III: The Socio-Ecological Perspective*, University of Pennsylvania Press, Philadelphia, PA, pp517–535

Trist, E. (1983) 'Referent organizations and the development of inter-organizational domains', *Human Relations*, vol 36, pp269–284, reprinted in E. Trist, F. Emery and H. Murray (eds) and B. Trist (assistant ed) (1997) *The Social Engagement of Social Science, Volume III: The Socio-Ecological Perspective*, University of Pennsylvania Press, Philadelphia, PA, pp170–184

Trist, E. (1997) 'Aphorism', in E. Trist, F. Emery and H. Murray (eds) and B. Trist (assistant ed) *The Social Engagement of Social Science, Volume III: The Socio-Ecological Perspective*, University of Pennsylvania Press, Philadelphia, PA

Trist, E., Emery, F. and Murray, H. (eds) and Trist, B. (assistant ed) (1997) *The Social Engagement of Social Science: A Tavistock Anthology, Volume III: The Socio-Ecological Perspective*, University of Pennsylvania Press, Philadelphia, PA, pv

van der Heijden, K. (2005) *Scenarios: The Art of Strategic Conversation,* 2nd edition, John Wiley and Sons, Chichester, UK

van de Ven, A. and Hargrave, T. (2004) 'Social, technical and institutional change: A literature review and synthesis', in M. Scott Poole and A. van de Ven (eds) *Handbook of Organizational Change and Innovation,* Oxford University Press, Oxford, UK

von Bertalanffy, L. (1968) *General Systems Theory: Foundations, Development, Applications,* George Braziller, New York, NY

Wack, P. (1985) 'Scenarios: Uncharted waters ahead', *Harvard Business Review*, vol 63, no 5, pp73–89

Weber, M. (1962) *Basic Concepts in Sociology*, translated and introduced by H. P. Secher, Peter Owen, London, UK

3

How Do Scenario Practices and Search Conferences Complement Each Other?

Jaime Jiménez

The increasing turbulence present in the current world environment has drawn attention to the incapacity of existing social institutions to produce the response capability necessary for human survival. A new response capability leading to both personal and social transformation seems to be required. This will need to be based on the primacy of symbiotic and collaborative, as compared with individualistic and competitive, relations. (Eric Trist, 1997, pv)

Introduction

The purpose of this chapter is to contrast scenarios with another method: search conferences, which will add clarity to how causal texture theory illuminates the way in which scenarios work and why.

The chapter is structured as follows: an overview is presented of key aspects of scenarios that differ from search conferences. Search conference methodology is then described. Finally, both are compared and the conclusion centres on how they can complement each other in practice.

Scenarios

It has long been recognized that organizations are immersed in turbulent environments, characterized by increasing uncertainty (Schön, 1971; Ackoff, 1974; Emery and Trist, 1997). In my view, this uncertainty is mainly due to the profound changes of people's values and ideals since the end of World War II (F. Emery, 1978), which have made for increasingly complex and sophisticated societies. From the second half of the 20th century onwards, society witnessed accelerated change in technology and the global economy, as well as in social and political relations. In addition, the generation and dissemination of information grew faster than the ability of individuals and organizations to analyse and assimilate it. My research shows that this additional source of uncertainty on the future of organizations greatly reduces their ability to actively participate in the planning and construction of their own future. Planning based on the gathering and analysis of past information is no longer enough under changing conditions:

> *... conventional methods are not appropriate to confront new challenges. Critical problems trespass across the boundaries set by organizations and social groups. Stakeholders are physically and organizationally dispersed, limiting their interactions to ritual acts, without realizing how their interests are interlinked – hence, they do not develop effective strategies aimed at a common shared future.*
> (Carvajal, 1994, p1, author's translation)

Scenario planning

Since scenarios are explained in Chapter 2, this section will provide only a brief description of various aspects that give a comparative basis with search conferences.

The construction of alternative scenarios is used by many organizations to assess or help develop long-term plans. It is understandable that this type of planning was first used by military intelligence to the extent that, although this fact is not properly documented, Sun Tzu (*The Art of War*, VI A C, 1997) may be considered a forerunner of scenario building. The concept was first introduced as *La Prospective* by Berger in 1964. These ideas were further developed by Herman Kahn, who first used the word 'scenario' in 1967, as well as by Godet (1987) in Paris. The 1970s oil shocks contributed to give this tradition prominence: just before 1973, planners at Royal Dutch Shell had begun using it (Wack, 1985).

Scenarios are helped by 'simulation games' prepared by a group of analysts to be manipulated by policy-makers. The 'games' include known possibilities about the future, such as demographics, geography, and social, technical, economic and political *trends* that are considered as *driving forces* which may shape one's contextual future. Scenarios seek to identify plausible and unexpected contexts that may have already begun appearing in the present. However uncomfortable, analysts select scenario features in order to challenge assumptions and perceptions of the present. Scenario planning helps decision- and policy-makers to anticipate hidden weaknesses and to address inflexibilities in organizations and social systems. A major challenge of scenario planning is to ensure that these decision- or policy-makers use the scenarios in settings where they may not know what their actual information needs are.

After going through the different stages of scenario building, the participants end up with two to four robust scenarios. Uses include:

- *Identification of driver sets, systems or strings.* Scenarios are a framework for presenting single or collective *factors* (*drivers*) so that they become easily available for decision-makers' use as practical concepts about possible future developments in their own right.
- *Positive perspectives.* One of the major benefits derived from scenarios comes from the alternative 'types' of futures that their different perspectives offer. It is a common experience that participants get startled by the insight scenarios offer when they finally emerge.

A key value of scenario planning is that it allows one to make and learn from mistakes without risking the organization in real life. Policy-makers can make mistakes in a pleasant, unthreatening, game-like setting, while responding to a set of possible contextual situations.

The search conference

The search conference (SC) is a method ordinarily embedded in an intervention process, requiring a careful pre-SC design and a post-SC implementation. Neglect of either of these two stages may lead to disappointment and frustration. The SC is a method that is designed to help social systems become adaptive. Adaptation is the ability of a system to modify itself or its environment when either has changed to the system's disadvantage in order to increase its efficiency with respect to its functions (Ackoff and Emery, 1972, pp123–124). The SC has been deployed in many hundreds of situations and in these contexts has proven to be a viable and adaptive way of planning for turbulent times (M. Emery, 1976; F. Emery, 1997a). In terms of M. Emery (1997, p389):

> *Planning within the type IV environment with its discontinuities and relevant uncertainties requires active adaptation (Emery and Trist, 1997) continuous manoeuvring as in the strategy of indirect approach (Sun Tzu, 1943; Hart, 1943, 1946). It also requires an adaptive organizational form. As a temporary organization, the Search Conference is structured on the second organizational design principle – redundancy of function ... (F. Emery, 1993). It is therefore a purposeful organization, a structure for learning and the emergence of ideal-seeking (F. Emery, 1997b, pp147–169).*

The SC method recognizes the fact that the system to be planned for is an open system (i.e. a system that continuously interacts with its immediate environment). The immediate environment constitutes the context of the system. Both the system and its context are continuously changing. The SC method provides a social 'space' where reflection and design can be accomplished in an environment free of self-imposed constraints (Jiménez, 1987, p1).

A planning community monitors the environment, sifting information to adapt and change as needed. This is why Merrelyn Emery asserts that 'the product of planning through a SC is therefore not "the plan", but the *continuing learning planning community*' (M. Emery, 1994, p9). The community does not necessarily follow a fixed path towards the desired future, but is prepared to adaptively change as the external conditions affecting it evolve.

Search conferences have many aspects: method, methodology, an event, an exercise in participation, a process. The SC method developed gradually from its incipient beginnings at the Tavistock Institute during the 1940s. The first search conference to be held, containing most of its current characteristics, was designed and managed by Fred Emery and Eric Trist in 1958 to 1959 (M. Emery, 1993, 1994). While the SC is a participative open-system event, not all participative open-system events are SCs (see, for example, Ackoff's idealized design, 1994; or Checkland's soft systems methodology, 1999).

The SC has been deployed for purposes other than strategic planning: to raise community awareness of transport issues (Anson and Willis, 1993); to redesign organizations (Axelrod, 1992); to enhance interpersonal cooperation in economic revival (Tandy, 1991); to explore the future of dietetics as a profession (Parks et al, 1994); to search into the nourishment of the future (Vergara et al, 1982, 1983); and to design a Masters programme in environmental sciences (Jiménez et al, 1986). This serves as evidence that SC democratic principles are the appropriate framework for different participative searches into the future. A major feature of the SC is that during the conference all participants are at the same hierarchical level: there are no bosses or employees.

In order to meet its objectives (invent a desirable future agreeable to all and produce a learning planning community), the SC must observe the following characteristics (Carvajal, 1994, p2). It has to:

- Ensure participation of representatives of all stakeholders of the system in question in the appreciation and conceptualization of a complex problem or system of problems.
- Generate a shared vision of a desirable future for the system in question and an awareness of the main obstacles and opportunities to reach it.
- Facilitate a learning and maturation process that enhances the group's capacity to face external change and crisis.
- Create a new understanding among stakeholders to facilitate the generation of novel alternatives based on an effective cohesion and cooperation.

The SC has a 10- to 15-year orientation towards the future irrespective of context. This allows the participants to mentally get rid of the current obstacles and propose bold, original designs, never envisioned heretofore. It is necessary to observe the following conditions in order to conduct an SC to that its objectives can be met (Morley and Trist, 1993, pp674–78; Carvajal, 1994, p3):

- Participants of an SC must come from all the parts that compose the system. Stakeholders who are affected by the actions of the system have to take part in planning the shared future.
- The event has to take place in an environment of mutual trust. The 10- to 15-year future horizon, in addition to allowing the participants to mentally get rid of current obstacles, helps to reduce mistrust among stakeholders because issues that separate stakeholders at present may not be visualized as such in the distant future.
- The individuals selected to participate must reflect the composition of the organization, minimizing the possibility of over-representation of a system's part.
- The people selected come as individuals and should not represent the interests of the part to which they belong. Individuals should leave behind their parochial interests and integrate themselves into the wider community. This will help them to enhance the creativity called for by the exercise.
- There are no hierarchies; all participants are at the same level. What matters is their ability to reflect and design in an environment free of self-imposed constraints.
- The event has to take place under 'social isolation' conditions, without common distracters such as daily work duties or family affairs. Depending upon the number of participants, it ordinarily lasts from three to five days.
- Participants must attend the conference from the beginning to the end. Individuals who enter after the conference has started are not able to share the experience of gradual integration within the collaborative environment that the rest enjoy.

When the membership is less than 20, the SC can proceed through all its phases in one single group. When it is larger – say, 40 or 60 members – most of the work is done in small working groups of 10 or less, who report back their detailed work for general discussion in plenary sessions (Morley and Trist, 1993, p675).

In order to permit thorough exploration of multifaceted issues, search conferences require a considerable commitment of time. It is difficult for an SC to complete the task in less than two and a half days. A longer time is preferred: three to four or even five days (Morley and Trist, 1993, p675).

The search conference aims to open new paths of thought and to encourage innovation without usurping the role institutions play. The process gradually carries participants to reach a consensus about important system's issues. Step by step, it leads them to converge in creating a system's vision that inspires and provokes them to achieve a better future. As they do, they share a responsibility for that vision (M. Emery, 1994, p3).

The SC is in itself a learning environment (M. Emery, 1994, p3). By the very nature of its methodology, the SC mobilizes the knowledge stakeholders have acquired through a lifetime's perception of their system, and leads them through the stages of putting that knowledge to use, so they can exercise all their capacities toward designing and implementing a most desirable future. Participants take a new impulse that has to be demonstrated once they are back in their ordinary duties.

Assumptions and theoretical framework

According to M. Emery (1994, p4), four basic assumptions support the SC. It assumes that people:

1   are purposeful and can, in the appropriate conditions, be ideal-seeking;
2   want to learn, and want to create and exercise control over their futures;
3   have consciousness and can be cognisant of their awareness (Chein, 1972);
4   can make judgements and learn to act wisely through exploring possible future worlds.

They are conscious of their past, their present and changes in their environment. Actually, people may not have all these attributes at a given time; but with some training through the SC, they come to exercise their potential.

The conceptual underpinning of the SC method

The major concepts underlying the search conference are as follows:

- open systems and directive correlation;
- environmental change and causal texture;
- the second organizational design principle;
- ecological learning, from direct experience (M. Emery, 1994, p4).

As demonstrated in Chapter 2, the open systems concept acknowledges the fact that interrelations between the system and the environment are governed by links that are lawful (L) and known. A comprehensive understanding of systems behaviour requires some knowledge of each of the Ls, where L indicates a potentially lawful connection, and the suffix 1 refers to the system, while 2 refers to the environment, as follows:

- L11, L12;
- L21, L22.

Here L11 refers to links *within* the system: the area of internal interdependencies; L12 and L21, the exchanges *between* the system and its environment: the area of transactional interdependencies from the system to the environment and from the environment to the system, respectively; and L22 to links through which parts of the environment become related to each other – called by Emery and Trist (1997, pp53–65) the causal texture of the environment: the area of interdependencies that belong within the environment itself. The L12 relationship is the planning process; the L21 relationship is the learning from the environment process.

Directive correlation implies that any new state of affairs will be jointly determined by *system* and environment (see also Chapter 10). When system and environment are in correspondence, the relationship between them is adaptive. Open systems articulate and provide a picture of a point in time with change expressed through learning and planning, while directive correlation offers a film. Open systems include adaptive and maladaptive relations, whereas the directive correlation expresses over time when adaptation is or is not occurring. Environmental change refers to the changes that are constantly taking place in the environment, independent from the system in question. As was shown in Chapter 2, the causal texture of the environment in which a system is embedded influences the behaviour of the system and has to be taken into account for the strategic planning of the system – that is, in the realization of an SC (for a detailed explanation of the causal textures, see Emery and Trist, 1997, pp53–65).

The second organizational design principle (DP2) that Emery (F. Emery, 1997c, p537) defined – redundancy of functions – yields a system where responsibility is located with those doing the work, learning and planning. An SC, although temporary, is a social system in which its members play different roles, as prescribed by DP2. The first organizational design principle (DP1), redundancy of parts, is variety decreasing and error amplifying, whereas DP2 is variety increasing and error reducing. DP2 'translates directly across to a "fully working learning conference" which takes responsibility for its own control, coordination and outcome. The SC is designed as a pure DP2 event' (M. Emery, 1994, p10).

Ecological learning from direct experience refers to the ability of the individual to learn from the environment *directly*, in general, and during the SC, in particular.

> As the environment contains limitless information, then any person with an intact perceptual system can, in principle, access what they need. Access is restricted by habit, lack of confidence and physical or psychological isolation from the informational field. (M. Emery, 1994, p10).

The environment consists of affordances, properties that define what it means to be a perceiver and what they can do with it. The perceiver has effective, potential purposeful behaviours that both act upon and define the environment. Taken together, affordances and effectiveness express the process of living in a meaningful world (M. Emery, 1994, pp10–11).

The facilitators' role

The search conference is managed by a team of facilitators whose role is essentially to encourage an environment of collaboration and creativity. This team is headed by a conference manager who explains each of the conference's stages, keeps the meeting on schedule, and uses rationalization of conflict procedures during the process. Facilitators do not intervene in the 'substance'; they only ensure that the method's rules are observed, which encourages people to participate.

They also must avoid sterile confrontations. People may hold different views of the same issue. The facilitators' role is to make sure divergent viewpoints are properly explained by the proponent and understood by the rest. A 'common ground' may gradually be reached after participants properly assess the opposite views. A facilitator may set apart those participants with opposite views and, making use of the appropriate techniques, facilitate the communication among them to reach a deep understanding of either position. Consensus may gradually be reached after participants assess the opposite view. However, if differences remain, the facilitator must register discrepancies and include them in the final report.

The five stages of the search conference

What follows is a brief description of the process involved in managing a search conference. The event starts by explaining the conference objectives, the rules and procedures that have to be observed, the stages to be covered, and the expectations to be satisfied, as expressed by the participants. Reflection goes from the general to the specifics. Participants are organized in small working groups of 10 to 12 people each. Groups have to be small to allow all participants to take part in the deliberations. The conference stages are:

1   exploration of the contextual environment – this is the environment surrounding the system;
2   analysis of the current system's situation;
3   design of the ideal desired state of the system;
4   identification of obstacles and opportunities to reach the desired state of the system;
5   selection and design of courses of action.

During the first four stages each small group works separately, holding a plenary session at the end of each stage. In the fifth stage, new small groups are formed according to the individual's interest in specific courses of action. At the end of the fifth stage a plenary session is held to report and share with everyone the designs developed by the new small groups, and to make collective decisions of strategic importance.

Questions regarding the objective of each stage are included when explaining the stages. They are a helpful tool in conducting the sessions without distracting the attention from other issues. A brief explanation of each stage follows.

Exploration of the contextual environment

The first question participants must explore is *what are the relevant external factors affecting the future of the organization or system?*

In this stage, the external factors surrounding and affecting the system in question are to be explored. These may be factors that are currently present or that are believed to continue being present in the next 10 to 15 years. They must have a major impact on the future of the organization. They may be of an economic, technological, social, political or cultural nature.

The second question posed to the participants is *what is the future image of the external environment if nothing is done?*

Participants are asked to reflect upon and form an image of the world's future if nothing different is done to change current directions. This image is the reference projection of the system's external social environment, assuming things go on as usual and the external factors materialize. Participants are also asked to describe the most desirable world possible in the timeframe, given that many people are trying to improve the current world situation.

Analysis of the current system's situation

An analysis of the current system's situation is then made, including the factors responsible for the situation. Likewise, an analysis is made of the system's capacity to confront the crisis and opportunities that the external factors will generate in the future.

The first question to be explored is *how are we now?* The next question is *how did we get to be in this situation?* The third question is *what is the system's capacity to confront the foreseeable external factors identified in the first stage?*

Design of the ideal desired state of the system

The audience is encouraged to design, free of self-imposed constraints and of current problems, the ideal situation of the system in a future located 10 to 15 years at a distance. The idealization process involved leads those engaged in it to become conscious of these constraints, making it easier to remove them (Ackoff, 1974, p30). The time span helps to reduce discrepancies among people sustaining opposite views of the current system's situation. It is easier for people confronted with each other to converge in a common design since the current reasons for opposition (e.g. budgetary issues) become meaningless when the ideal system is located far in the future. The only restrictions to the system's design are that they have to be technically feasible and operationally viable – that is, there is no room for utopia. The question to be explored is *what is the ideal state of the system we wish to have in a future located 10 to 15 years from now?*

Identification of obstacles and opportunities

Once the idealized future is described, the audience returns to the present, and the identification of obstacles and opportunities for reaching such an ideal is carried out. Opportunities are often visualized when examining possible restrictions. Having recognized these factors, the small groups work on the courses of action which could lead to a result that approximates the future ideal state.

Participants will reflect first upon the following question: *what obstacles and opportunities are foreseen to reach the future ideal state?* At times, the same obstacle could also be visualized as an opportunity.

The second question is *starting at the present stage, what are the courses of action that the SC participants could carry out in order to approach the ideal state?*

Selection and design of courses of action

At this stage, a number of action proposals to approximate the desired future are available for further elaboration. Since the number of proposals is usually more than the ones the audience can work on, a democratic ranking procedure is used to select those with the highest priority. Now the participants organize in small groups of three to six in order to work on the design of the course of action they most prefer. Enough time is allowed for the elaboration of courses of action since it is one of the most sensitive parts of the exercise.

Finally, the designs are presented in a plenary session to the rest of the participants. Depending upon the nature of the particular SC, personal commitments may be assumed in this last stage in terms of assuming full responsibility for the realization of their designs, including timetables and allocation of tasks to each of the new small group members. As asserted by Williams (1979), the SC is a task-oriented event.

Participants are gradually guided from a reflection of the state of affairs in the external environment (first stage), to the focal problem (second to fourth stages), until arriving at the design stage (fifth stage). Figure 3.1 is an illustration of the way in which the SC goes from the general to the specific.

Similarities and differences

Conceptual differences

Based on my experience of working with both methods, scenario planning and search conferences (although similar in a variety of aspects) are in my view conceptually different in some key aspects. Table 3.1 briefly describes the major differences.

Although both scenario planning and SC are planning methods aimed at addressing, containing and, ultimately, reducing environmental turbulence, a fundamental difference is that scenario planning *focuses on one actor* (e.g. an

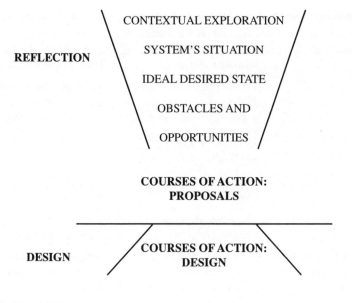

CONTEXTUAL EXPLORATION

SYSTEM'S SITUATION

REFLECTION

IDEAL DESIRED STATE

OBSTACLES AND

OPPORTUNITIES

COURSES OF ACTION:
PROPOSALS

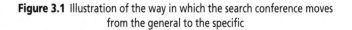

DESIGN   **COURSES OF ACTION:**
DESIGN

Source: Jiménez, 2005

Figure 3.1 Illustration of the way in which the search conference moves
from the general to the specific

executive, a policy-maker or a company) with the aim of helping this actor best address the turbulence it faces, whereas the SC *focuses on one issue*, upon which different stakeholders try to find a common ground from which to build a desired future – hence, mitigating turbulence.

However, the major difference between scenario planning and search conference refers to the fact that the construction of scenarios is *the visualization of possible futures* according to what we have *now* and the *drivers* detected in the environment, whereas the search conference produces *one desired future* to be approached gradually in the next 10 to 15 years. Scenario planning can be thought of as a set of *reference projections* of what can happen in the future. The product of a search conference is, on the one hand, the image of *a future desired by all* the stakeholders present in the conference and, on the other, a set of *courses of action* that stakeholders will carry out *to approach the desired future*.

Procedural similarities

Scenario planning and the search conference share some similarities that are not necessarily explicit in the definition of methods; however, they are present in practice. The most important similarities and differences that I have found in my work are listed in Table 3.2.

Table 3.1 *Conceptual similarities and differences between scenario planning and search conference*

Category	Scenario planning	Search conference
Definition	A strategic planning method to consider how contextual environmental driving forces may shape the transactional environment in which the focal actor is embedded.	A strategic planning method involving *stakeholders* of all levels to visualize a future desired by all and ways of approaching it.
Adaptation to the environment	Pre-active adaptation to the environment.	Active adaptation to the environment.
Time span	Time span depends upon context particulars and purpose.	10 to 15 years' time span, independent of context.
Who solves the problems?	Problems are proposed and analysed by a team of 'experts' consulting a wide field of remarkable people.	Problems are proposed and 'solved' by an ample spectrum of stakeholders.
Discipline	Interdisciplinary/transdisciplinary.	Actors are not selected by discipline, but by their commitment to contribute with their knowledge to the common cause. Widely participative.
Direction of planning	Actor-centred strategic planning.	Issue-centred strategic planning.
Mode of planning	Pre-active planning. Can be interactive (Sharpe and van der Heijden (2007).	Interactive planning.
Approach to the future	Futurology combined with 'presentology': how do we expect the future might be? What can we do about it? What does the future say about the present? Context considered as independent from organization.	'Presentology': what can we do *now* to approach the future desired by all? Context and organization considered as interdependent.
Possible futures	There are two to four *possible* future contexts (scenarios) based on current tendencies *and* expected changes in the environment.	There is no such a thing as *the* future. The future may be 'modified' by our actions *now*.
Social accountability	Less socially responsible. Responds to the needs of a limited set of stakeholders.	More socially responsible and reflective. Responds to a large set of stakeholders.

Source: Author's elaboration

Table 3.2 *Procedural similarities and differences between scenario planning and search conference*

Characteristics	Scenario planning	Search conference
Participants must come from all parts of the system.	No (see Chapter 13 in this volume)	Yes
The event has to take place in an environment of mutual trust.	Yes	Yes
The individuals selected to participate must reflect the composition of the organization or system, minimizing the possibility of over-representing a system's part.	No	Yes
The people selected come as individuals and do not represent the interests of their association.	Yes	Yes
There are no hierarchies: all participants are at the same level.	Yes	Yes
The event has to take place under 'social isolation' conditions, without common distracters such as daily work duties or family affairs.	Yes	Yes
Ordinarily the number of participants is as follows:	Variable: as little as three and as many as hundreds	10 to 60
The length of the process (scenarios can be multi-workshop processes) is:	Two to three days to 18 months or less than two years	Two to five days
Participants must attend the conference from the beginning to the end.	Yes (although in multi-workshop designs they may differ from workshop to workshop)	Yes
Number of 'scenarios' ('futures') assembled:	Two to four	One

Source: Author's elaboration

How can scenario planning and the search conference complement each other?

How to make the most of both methods? I think one combination would be to deploy scenarios first. A search for a desired future could then produce the expected results. The SC should start from the 'design of the ideal desired state' stage since the previous stages should have been covered by the scenarios method. The great advantage of combining them in this order is that the following questions will be answered thoroughly through the scenario construction:

- What are the relevant external factors affecting the future of the organization or system?
- What is the future image of the external environment if nothing is done?

The visualization of the desired future will benefit from a richer environmental scan made by scenario building.

Another possible combination of both methods would be the independent realization of both exercises made by two different teams addressing the same organization or social system, and then the comparison of results. The question would be: how do the courses of action compare between both methods? Are they similar or do they differ significantly? Actual decision-making would benefit from this comparison and be made with more certainty since the search for possible futures could have covered all thinkable alternatives and nothing would be left to the *drivers* in the external environment.

When to use scenario planning and when search conferences?

My work has so far not found a reason to think that one method is more suitable than the other for specific environmental situations, type of organizations or social systems. Combining both, as described above, may be the best way of extracting all possibilities.

However, scenario building – having been used primarily in the context of large corporations, government departments and the military, where hierarchies are dominant – may have evolved to suit this type of organization best. The search conference has been used in a wide variety of contexts, including urban and rural planning, education and community development, but also in the strategic planning of middle and large corporations. Therefore, the use of either method may be attached more to particular aesthetic reasons than to the formal conditions of the system addressed.

Planning enhances the ability of members of an organization to better adapt to changing environments. However, since the level of uncertainty in turbulent environments is not predictable, planned courses of action must be oriented towards values and ideals giving sense and coherence in a commonly agreed upon direction. Search conferences do this more explicitly than scenarios have – and scenarios can learn from this feature and profit from the contribution that search conferences make in this regard.

References

Ackoff, R. (1974) *Redesigning the Future*, John Wiley and Sons, New York, NY

Ackoff, R. (1994) *The Democratic Corporation: A Radical Prescription for Recreating Corporate America and Rediscovering Success*, Oxford University Press, New York, NY

Ackoff, R. and Emery, F. (1972) *On Purposeful Systems*, Aldine-Atherton, Inc, Chicago, IL

Anson, G. and Willis, K. (1993) 'Planning with vision: The development of traffic strategies for Melbourne', *Transportation*, vol 20, no 3, pp59–75

Axelrod, D. (1992) 'Getting everyone involved: How one organization involved its employees, supervisors, and managers in redesigning the organization', *Special Issue: Large Groups Interventions, Journal of Applied Behavioral Science*, vol 28, no 4, pp499–509

Berger, G. (1964) *Phénoménologie du Temps et Prospective*, Presses Universitaires de France, Paris

Carvajal, R. (1994) *El Movimiento de Calidad en México: Conferencia de Búsqueda* [*The Quality Movement in Mexico: Search Conference*], Red T de Competitividad, Mexico City, Mexico

Checkland, P. (1999) 'Soft systems methodology: A 30-year retrospective', in P. Checkland and J. Scholes (eds) *Soft Systems Methodology in Action*, John Wiley and Sons, Chichester, UK

Chein, I. (1972) The *Science of Behaviour and the Image of Man*, Basic books, New York

Emery, F. (1978) 'Youth – vanguard, victims or the new vandals …?' in F. Emery (ed) *Limits to Choice*, Australian National University Press, Centre for Continuing Education, Australian National University, Canberra, Australia

Emery, F. (1993) 'The second design principle: Participation and the democratization of work', in E. Trist and H. Murray (eds) *The Social Engagement of Social Science, Volume II: The Socio-Technical Perspective*, University of Pennsylvania Press, Philadelphia, PA

Emery, F. (1997a) 'Passive maladaptive strategies', in E. Trist, F. Emery and H. Murray (eds) *The Social Engagement of Social Science, Volume III: The Socio-Ecological Perspective*, University of Pennsylvania Press, Philadelphia, PA

Emery, F. (1997b) 'Active adaptation – The emergence of ideal-seeking systems', in E. Trist, F. Emery and H. Murray (eds) *The Social Engagement of Social Science, Volume III: The Socio-Ecological Perspective*, University of Pennsylvania Press, Philadelphia, PA, pp147–169

Emery, F. (1997c) 'Industrial democracy and regional decentralization', in E. Trist, F. Emery and H. Murray (eds) *The Social Engagement of Social Science, Volume III: The Socio-Ecological Perspective*, University of Pennsylvania Press, Philadelphia, PA

Emery, F. and Trist, E. (1997) 'The causal texture of organizational environments', in E. Trist, F. Emery and H. Murray (eds) *The Social Engagement of Social Science, Volume III: The Socio-Ecological Perspective*, University of Pennsylvania Press, Philadelphia, PA

Emery, M. (1976) *Searching*, Occasional paper in continuing education no 12, Australian National University Press, Centre for Continuing Education, Australian National University, Canberra, Australia

Emery, M. (1993) 'Introduction to the 1993 edition', in M. Emery (ed) *Participative Design for Participative Democracy*, Australian National University Press, Centre for Continuing Education, Australian National University, Canberra, Australia

Emery, M. (1994) *The Search Conference: State of the Art*, Australian National University Press, Centre for Continuing Education, Australian National University, Canberra, Australia

Emery, M. (1997) 'The search conference: Design and management of learning with a solution to the "pairing" puzzle', in E. Trist, F. Emery and H. Murray (eds) *The Social*

Engagement of Social Science, Volume III: The Socio-Ecological Perspective, University of Pennsylvania Press, Philadelphia, PA

Godet, M. (1987) *Scenarios and Strategic Management*, Butterworths, London, UK

Hart, L. (1943) *Thoughts About War*, Faber and Faber, London, UK

Hart, L. (1946) *The Strategy of the Indirect Approach*, Faber and Faber, London, UK

Jiménez, J. (1987) *El Papel de la Reunión de Reflexión y Diseño en Procesos de Evaluación* [*The Role of the Reflection and Design Conference in Evaluation Processes*], *Comunicaciones Técnicas*, Serie Amarilla: Desarrollo, No 70, Institute of Applied Mathematics and Systems, National Autonomous University of Mexico, Mexico City, Mexico

Jiménez, J., Mazari, M., Fa, J. E., Bayona, M. and Sarukhán, J. (1986) *Reunión de Reflexión y Diseño sobre la Maestría en Ciencias Ambientales* [*Reflection and Design Conference on the Environmental Sciences Masters Program*], *Comunicaciones Técnicas*. Serie Amarilla: Desarrollo, No 55, Institute of Applied Mathematics and Systems, National Autonomous University of Mexico, Mexico City, Mexico

Jiménez, J. (2005) *Participation and Development in Mexico*, PhD Thesis, University of Pennsylvania, Pennsylvania

Morley, D. and Trist, E. (1993) 'A brief introduction to the Emerys' "search conference"', in E. Trist and H. Murray (eds) *The Social Engagement of Social Science, Volume II: The Socio-Technical Perspective*, University of Pennsylvania Press, Philadelphia, PA

Parks, S., Babjak, P., Fitz, P., Maillet, J. and Mitchell, B. (1994) 'Future search conference helps define new directions in practice, education, and credentialing', *Journal of American Dietetics Association*, vol 94, no 9, pp1046–1047

Schön, D. (1971) *Beyond the Stable State*, W. W. Norton, New York, NY

Sharpe, B. and van der Heijden, K. (2007) *Scenarios for Success: Turning Insights into Action*, Wiley and Sons, Chichester

Sun Tzu (VI A C) *The Art of War*, El Arte de la Guerra (1997), Translation from *The Art of War*, Enrique Toomey, Ediciones Coyoacán S.A. de C-.V., Mexico City, Mexico

Sun Tzu (1943) *The Art of War*, in T. R. Philips (ed) *Roots of Strategy*, Bodley Head, London

Tandy, K. (1991) 'Participative planning from a Jungian viewpoint', *Journal of Mental Health Counseling*, vol 13, no 1, pp69–78

Trist, E. (1997) 'Aphorism', in E. Trist, F. Emery, and H. Murray (eds) *The Social Engagement of Social Science, Volume III: The Socio-Ecological Perspective*, University of Pennsylvania Press, Philadelphia, PA

Vergara, J., Díaz, P. and Carvajal, R. (1982) *Primera Conferencia de Búsqueda. Proyecto: 'La Alimentación del Futuro'* [*First Search Conference. Project: 'Nourishment of the Future'*], *Comunicaciones Técnicas*, Serie Amarilla: Desarrollo, No 34, Institute of Applied Mathematics and Systems, National Autonomous University of Mexico, Mexico City, Mexico

Vergara, J., Díaz, P. and Carvajal, R. (1983) *Segunda Conferencia de Búsqueda. Proyecto: 'La Alimentación del Futuro'* [*Second Search Conference. Project: 'Nourishment of the Future'*], *Comunicaciones Técnicas*, Serie Amarilla: Desarrollo, No 34, Institute of Applied Mathematics and Systems, National Autonomous University of Mexico, Mexico City, Mexico

Wack, P. (1985) 'Scenarios: Uncharted waters ahead', *Harvard Business Review*, vol 63, no 5, pp 73–89

Williams, T. (1979) 'The search conference in active adaptive planning', *Journal of Applied Behavioral Science*, vol 15, no 4, pp470–483

4

Reflecting on Scenario Practice: The Contribution of a Soft Systems Perspective

Trudi Lang and Lynn Allen

Introduction

This chapter analyses how soft systems thinking and, in particular, Peter Checkland's soft systems methodology (SSM), can contribute to the further development of scenario practice in addressing turbulence. In doing so we explore the philosophical links between the two methodologies and outline a number of soft systems thinking principles and SSM technologies that can be applied to scenario practice.

When organizational leadership groups engage in exploring their long-term future it can appear that everything under investigation is interconnected. In a complex world, this interconnectedness can generate a sense of uncertainty. Once this connectedness is perceived, it becomes difficult to apply simple cause-and-effect logic and to find easy 'solutions' or pathways. Systems thinking can provide processes and methods to cope with this complexity.

To be a 'systems thinker' is to recognize the need to give an account of the world as a perceived hierarchy of systems. It is also to 'set some constructed abstract wholes (often called "systems models") against the perceived real world in order to learn about it' (Checkland and Scholes, 1990, p25).

Systems thinking is familiar to many scenario practitioners, particularly in their quest to understand deep, systemic changes in the environment. However, to date, much of the usefulness of a systems approach to scenario practice has come from a 'hard' perspective that assumes systems exist in the real world and that they can be described objectively. Hard systems tools used by scenario practitioners include causal loop diagrams that are used to explore driving forces of change and scenario logics (see, for example, van der Heijden, 2005).

While 'hard' systems thinking tools have their value, a 'soft' systems perspective makes another contribution by proposing that human activity systems (a series of purposeful activities that exhibits emergence) may exist in the real world, but they exist only as 'notional systems' – that is, they only make sense through the perspectives, in the sense of worldviews (or *Weltanschauungen*) of the persons describing them. Therefore, by focusing on perspectives or worldviews, SSM offers an 'organized way of tackling perceived problematical (social) situations' through learning (Checkland and Poulter, 2006, pxv–xvii). Learning occurs when individuals bring their different worldviews to the table, come to appreciate those differences and develop a new shared meaning and agree on ways forward through what Checkland calls 'accommodation'. Checkland (1999) suggests that the enquiry process itself can be organized as a learning system.

There is evidence that scenario practice and the SSM developed in parallel over the last four decades. However, we argue that the opportunities presented by a 'soft' systems perspective for enhancing scenario practice have not been sufficiently explored.

As a result of working together on a scenario project, we realized the potential that lay in the intersection of these two fields, and invited Professor Kees van der Heijden, a global leader in scenarios, Professor Peter Checkland, the creator of the soft systems methodology, and Jaap Leemhuis, Global Business Network (GBN) Europe, an experienced practitioner with both methodologies, to participate in a Deep Conversation in Australia in 2003 (full details of the Deep Conversation can be found at www.cbs.curtin.edu.au/files/DeepConversation.pdf). The aim of the conversation was to explore the synergies, as well as the commonalities and differences, between the SSM and the scenario methodology. Many of the points discussed in this chapter draw inspiration from that meeting.

In exploring the bearing of SSM on scenarios in this chapter, our central argument is that a soft systems approach contributes to scenario practice not by trying to determine how human activity systems operate in the real world, but by applying systems principles to the way in which we study the future, while taking the multiple perspectives on that future as an opportunity to generate alternative perceptions and ways forward.

We commence this chapter by outlining the parallel emergence of scenario practice and soft systems thinking (in particular, the SSM). We then proceed to outline a key observation from the Deep Conversation that provided the impetus for the more detailed exploration of how a soft systems perspective can inform scenario practice. We then discuss these ideas under the headings of systems concepts and the application of SSM processes to scenarios. Finally, we summarize the insights generated in relation to each phase of a scenario project.

Co-emergence of scenarios and soft systems thinking

Two major developments in the field of management occurred during the 1960s and early 1970s that led to a shift in the way in which long-term planning and general problem-solving were approached.

Scenario practice and long-term business planning

The first development was related to the perception of increasing uncertainty and complexity in the environment. When high levels of uncertainty and complexity persist, Emery and Trist (1965) characterized such environments as turbulent fields, one of the four 'causal textures' of the environment as discussed in Chapter 2. The effect of turbulence for managers is a sense that the 'ground is in motion', which is caused by interactions of organizations as they compete with each other and from developments in the environment itself (driven by innovation, inter-dependencies between economic and other aspects of society, etc.). Managers therefore experience a gross increase in their area of 'relevant uncertainty' (Emery and Trist, 1965).

In such a situation, single-line forecasts, with unique end-point predictions prevalent in planning during the 1960s, became problematic because they presumed the environment was characterized by a high degree of certainty and stability. This realization, as well as empirical experience, led to the introduction of scenario practices (originally developed by Kahn and others at the RAND corporation in the US and by Gaston Berger for the French government) into all kinds of organizations by people such as Wack (1985a, 1985b). In this context, scenarios provided a way of dealing more comprehensively with uncertainty.

Over time, a number of scenario processes and schools evolved (Bradfield et al, 2005). The type of scenario practice referred to in this chapter is part of the so-called 'intuitive logics' school best known through the work of Royal Dutch Shell and the writings of Wack (1985a, 1985b), van der Heijden (1996, 2005) and Schwartz (1991). The intuitive logics approach emphasizes the participants (often managers) as the ones to develop the scenarios, tends not to use detailed computer modelling, and works with all scenarios that are regarded as equally probable (Bradfield et al, 2005).

One of the earliest findings of Pierre Wack in his pioneering work at Royal Dutch Shell was that scenarios had to connect with managers' assumptions, beliefs and concerns for the future in order to be of real use to them. In other words, scenario practice had to impact upon the mental models of decision-makers. As he (Wack, 1985a, p84) writes:

> *From the moment of this realization, we no longer saw our task as producing a documented view of the future business environment five or ten years ahead. Our*

real target was the microcosms of our decision makers: *unless we influenced the mental image, the picture of reality held by critical decision makers, our scenarios would be like water on a stone... We now wanted to design scenarios so that managers would question their own model of reality and change it when necessary, so as to come up with strategic insights beyond their minds' previous reach. This changing in perspective – from producing a 'good' document to changing the image of reality in the heads of critical decision makers – is as fundamental as that experienced when an organization switches from selling to marketing* [emphasis added].

The main point we want to make in this chapter is that this concept of the 'microcosm of decision-makers' in our view paralleled the emerging work of Peter Checkland in highlighting the concept of worldview (or *Weltanschauung*) in the SSM. Checkland drew attention to the fact that managers act from their mental image or view of the world. For example, there may be a prison in the real world; but to one set of correctional officials it is an instrument of retribution, while to another it is a place redolent with potential for rehabilitation. Each set of officials will manage the prison based on their particular worldview. Similarly, Wack argued that the mental image that managers hold of the future shapes the strategic decisions they make and that a corporate strategic viewpoint is essentially their shared mental models. It is thus clear that the intuitive logics approach to scenarios, with its focus on perceptions and the subjective and tacit knowledge of the participants, provides many philosophical links with soft systems thinking.

Soft systems thinking and problem structuring

Another major development that occurred in the field of management during the 1960s and 1970s was the realization that many organizational, industry and policy issues were 'wicked' (Rittel and Webber, 1973), 'ill structured' (Mitroff and Emshoff, 1979) or 'messes' (Ackoff, 1979). In these situations, solutions cannot be easily found because there is a lack of agreement about the nature of the problem, let alone the solutions. It is within this context that soft systems thinking emerged.

Soft systems thinking was part of a second wave of systems thinking that challenged the notion that models were 'representations of reality rather than as aids for the development of inter-subjective understanding' (Midgley, 2002, p191). Soft systems thinkers such as Checkland declared that such a reductionist scientific approach to dealing with human activity was less than adequate because each individual had their own view on what constitutes a problem situation, potential solutions and barriers to resolution. Therefore, systems and their objectives could not be taken as given. Over many years, through working with his Masters students in real-life situations in industry, he developed the SSM, publishing extensively from the 1970s up to the present day.

Checkland also challenged the assumption that human activity is goal-seeking. Influenced by Geoffrey Vickers's work, he adopted the premise that the maintenance and constant balancing of relationships in a system was a more fruitful basis for examining problem-solving behaviour in organizations. Checkland greatly admires Vickers's work, especially his ideas on the theory of appreciative systems. Vickers (cited in Checkland, 1985, p761) explains appreciation as 'a mental, evaluative act in which conflicting norms and values determine what "facts" are relevant, whilst "facts" perceived or envisaged demand attention because they are seen to be relevant to particular norms and values'. Thus, SSM provides what Checkland (1985, p761) calls 'a practical orchestration of the process of appreciation'.

The SSM assists with addressing 'wicked' or 'ill-structured' situations by placing different actors' perceptions or worldviews about the issue at the heart of its enquiry and working with these (through a process of appreciation) to generate learning about the situation. If anything, awareness of the 'wickedness' of many organizational and public policy challenges has increased over the decades. Both scenario practice and the SSM offer ways of addressing uncertainty, thereby assisting managers to deal with 'wicked' issues.

Exploring the potential benefit of soft systems thinking and SSM to scenarios

The outcome of the Deep Conversation mentioned in the introduction was the identification of commonalities and differences between the methodologies, as well as challenges that could be addressed by using them together. In particular, van der Heijden and Checkland (undated) suggested that scenarios are a particular type of human activity system, the purpose of which is to generate learning, what they called 'a "knowledge mobilizing" process'. Van der Heijden (undated) also posited that a scenario project can be designed as a purposeful human activity system using SSM. By doing so, he says, the question of purpose is placed on the table, enabling managers and practitioners to see that a scenario project never exists on its own (and therefore does not have an inherent purpose), but always as a part of a bigger project such as strategizing (which has a built-in purpose, such as survival and growth).

These insights had not been previously expressed. They represented a useful conceptual development that could link two important managerial interventions for coping with wicked issues. Based on these insights, and further research, we went on to examine the application of soft systems thinking and SSM processes to scenario practice.[1] Below we discuss these, focusing first on insights about systems.

Systems concepts

In this section we discuss two key soft systems concepts that we believe can inform scenario practice. These are the implications of seeing boundaries as judgements and viewing the contextual environment as a subject domain.

Boundaries as judgements

Scenario practitioners distinguish between two levels of the environment. The first is called the transactional and is that aspect of the environment that managers feel the organization has influence over and in which it can be a significant player. The second, the contextual environment, is that part of the environment that managers believe the organization has no influence over and which contains the 'referees' that set the rules for the way in which the organization can 'play' in the transactional environment (van der Heijden, 2005, p115). Or to use Trist's (1997, p172) phrase, the contextual environment provides 'the boundary conditions for transactional relations'. Scenarios then focus on appreciating and illuminating possible developments in the contextual environment by mapping the major driving forces of change that could influence the future transactional environment.

Thus, scenario practitioners must make decisions about where to draw the boundary between the contextual and transactional environments before they can develop scenarios. This boundary decision is often determined in consultation with the client and is dependent upon the topic and purpose of the enquiry. The value of a soft systems perspective in this regard is to remind scenario practitioners and managers that drawing these boundaries is a judgement. As such, they are freed up to 'shift' them to experiment conceptually with personal, group, community and other stakeholder perceptions of their organizational futures.

An example of this is provided by Ramírez and van der Heijden (2007, p96). The authors argue that extending the boundary of the transactional environment into the perceived contextual environment increases the area of the environment over which managers believe they have influence, thus revealing new options and opportunities for action that might not otherwise have been perceived. They offer the example of the VISA corporation who bought together banks, retailers, consumers and technology providers to convert the technological and others forces of the contextual environment 'into effective processes, standards and protocols', thereby opening up new business opportunities for the banks in particular.

Conceptualizing the contextual environment as a subject domain

The contextual environment in scenario practice is by definition a shared environment among a set of organizations that is delineated by an issue or subject (e.g. superannuation). We would like to suggest that there are times when it is useful for organizations to think of their contextual environment as a subject domain and to develop scenarios in reference to this domain rather than more directly to the organization. One time, in particular, would be developing scenarios for what Morgan (1997) refers to as 'egocentric' organizations.

Such organizations, says Morgan (1997, p259), have a 'fixed notion of who they are or what they can be and are determined to impose or sustain that identity at all costs. This leads them to overemphasize the importance of themselves while underplaying the significance of the wider system of relations in which they exist.' This means, as Morgan points out, that they potentially miss important environmental changes.

An example is provided by Claus (2007), who suggests that traditional music companies did not successfully anticipate the impact of digital providers such as Napster and iTunes because the identity of these companies was defined more as 'selling CDs' than 'providing home entertainment'. Thus, the traditional companies kept taking actions that were congruent with their identity (such as programming CDs so that they couldn't be played or copied on computers) even though 'the environment' indicated something different was needed. Another example is if libraries had always seen themselves as collectors of books, then they would not have thought of new information storage formats as part of their activities.

We believe, therefore, that encouraging managers in organizations with egocentric tendencies to think of their contextual environment as a subject domain and to develop scenarios in reference to this domain can help them better understand the interdependencies of the systems to which they belong and avoid becoming wedded to outdated identities.

Checkland's (1999) experience in developing task- and issue-based models or holons within SSM is helpful here. Task-based models, he says, 'map existing organisational structures', while the latter focus on the issue. He says the benefit of issue-based holons is that they 'lift the thinking in the situation out of its normal, unnoticed, comfortable grooves' (Checkland, 1999, pA21).

We believe that the same cognitive benefits can be achieved for organizations with egocentric tendencies. The organization would still be the client with their transactional environment, but instead of thinking of the contextual environment as 'our' environment (Burt et al, 2006), the managers of the organization would be encouraged to think of it as a subject domain and to reference the scenarios to this domain. By doing so they would be loosened up to perceive their contextual environment more 'accurately'. This proposal is consistent with some scenario scholars who have pointed to the need to develop alternative ways of deploying scenarios to deal with organizations with egocentric tendencies (Lang, 2007).

Application of SSM processes to scenarios

In this section we focus on what we see as five main contributions of the SSM to scenario practice.

Conceptual modelling

The link between the developed scenarios and action is not always clear within scenario practice. Sometimes groups can struggle in taking the outcomes of scenarios forward. This does not occur to the same degree with the SSM because a number of tools have been designed specifically within the framework to enable action. We believe these tools could provide a structured way for scenario groups to take the outcomes of their scenarios forward into action.

The particular tool we have in mind here is conceptual models or 'holons'. These are purposeful human activity systems defined as 'the abstract idea of a whole having emergent properties, a layered structure and processes of communication and control which in principle enable it to survive in a changing environment' (Checkland, 1981, p22). The holons are not representations of the real world, but are simplified devices or transitional objects (Winnicott, 1965) to encourage discussion and learning about pathways forward. For example, any production system can be modelled as a holon, consisting of a set of activities that transforms resources into a finished product and is controlled by processes that sustain ongoing production.

A basis for developing the conceptual models is the CATWOE mnemonic. Checkland (1993) explains that CATWOE stands for *customers* (the beneficiaries or victims of the system), *actors* (the person or persons who carry out the activities in the system), *transformation process* (the purposeful activity undertaken within the system), *Weltanschauung* (the worldview which makes this purposeful activity meaningful), *owner* (the person or persons who could prevent the activities from occurring), and *environmental constraints* (things which the system must take as given). Checkland (1999, pA22) suggests using these to form a 'root definition' in the form of a sentence that answers three questions: What to do? How to do it? Why do it? After these are defined, the elements of the holons are then developed by listing and mapping out the necessary activities to achieve the stated transformations.

The difference between holons and scenarios is that holons directly incorporate the actions that the client organization would take as implied by the scenarios. At the Deep Conversation, it was suggested that the strategies suggested by each scenario could be modelled. These models or holons would then help structure a discussion to assist managers progress the outcomes of the scenarios.

CATWOE and scenario narratives

Developing scenario narratives is not easy. While many texts offer guidelines to assist writers in developing scenario narratives, we feel that the CATWOE mnemonic (as discussed above) provides a specific 'technology' for this task. In structuring the scenario narrative, CATWOE helps users to provide/identify responses to the following questions (the CATWOE order has been rearranged to reflect the scenario context):

- What is the nature of the activity, especially the driving forces, being described in the scenario (the *transformation* in SSM language)? What is the plot of the tale, the conflict and resolution within the scenario? (T)
- What is the declared worldview or point of view from which the scenario is being told? Who should be the narrator and why are the plot and activities in the scenario important? (W)
- Who are the victims or beneficiaries of the main activity being pursued in the scenario and what are their perspectives? (C)
- Who are the main actors of this point of view who would undertake the activity within the scenario? What are the relationships between them? (A)
- Who are the people who could prevent the main activity or transformation in the scenario from occurring? Who is in charge of this world? (O)
- What are the predetermined factors and other information that the scenario narrative should take as given? (E)

Flowers (2003), who has ghostwritten many of Shell's scenarios, argues that a declared point of view is a neglected part of scenario writing. She also notes that having scenarios told from an 'outside' point of view (to the organization) is extremely valuable. The questions above show that the CATWOE technology can assist scenario writers to think through and declare the point of view from which the story is being told (see Chapter 11 in this volume). Such a declared point of view enables a consistent voice throughout the scenario, while explicitly including the voices of others, especially those external to the organization.

The other advantage of applying such a 'technology' is to achieve a degree of uniformity across the scenario set such that their elements (the actors, the activities, the taken as givens, etc.) are at the same system level. This contributes to consistency among the scenarios.

Separating process and content sub-systems

We also feel that scenario practitioners can benefit from adopting what is known in the SSM as the process (SSM(p)) and content sub-systems (SSM(c)). The *process* sub-system is owned by the enquirer or facilitator and is concerned with questions such as available resources, skills required, choice of methods, people to involve, etc. On the other hand, the *content* sub-system is owned by the client who is more focused on issues of success, content outcomes, the givens or not-negotiables related to the enquiry, etc. The 'owners' of these two sub-systems have different roles; and by making these as explicit as possible, scenario practitioners can gain more clarity for designing the enquiry and clarifying the contract with the client. In addition, this explicitness can help with clarifying the purpose of a scenario project ensuring that these two sub-systems are aligned so that the client's expectations are in line with the resources, skills and time available to the scenario project.

We have developed a series of questions (after Checkland, 1993, pp294–298) to develop an understanding of the important factors in each sub-system that will aid in designing and conducting the scenario project. These questions complement more generic ones in scenario practice (such as what timeframe will the scenarios focus on) to elicit and then cater for the different worldviews and perceptions related to why and how an enquiry should be conducted.

Questions to guide clarification of the *processes* related to the scenario project:

- Who is the facilitator?
- What are the roles and responsibilities of the facilitator?
- What skills need to be available to the facilitator in this enquiry?
- What resources are needed to conduct the scenario project?
- What cultural issues and power dynamics need to be considered in setting up and conducting the enquiry?
- How will the facilitator know when the process is complete?
- What governance structures are needed for the scenario project?
- What reporting lines will be followed in the enquiry?
- What communication processes will be used to report the progress of the scenario project?

Questions to guide clarification related to the *content* of the scenario project:

- Who is the client? Who is the action taker as a result of this enquiry?
- What is the focal topic or issue of the scenario project?
- Who are the essential 'owners' of the topic or issue – that is, who will gain the most from the exploration of this topic?
- Why do the client and the owners feel this topic is so important to be investigated?
- Who is the decision-taker(s) (the person(s) who controls the resources related to the enquiry and the implementation of its outcomes)? What are their views of the enquiry and its expected outcomes?
- How will the client and owners judge this enquiry to be successful?
- What are the limits of the enquiry – that is, what must be taken as given or not-negotiable?

It is important to note that asking questions related to the content sub-system of the project helps to surface the multiple perspectives about the topic of the enquiry and how it should be conducted. Scenario enquiries seek to involve many people from different functional and subject areas to build an understanding of potential developments related to the future. However, this diversity can risk creating 'representational gaps' (Cronin and Weingart, 2007, p761), which in scenario practice are differences in how individuals define the focus of the enquiry because of their backgrounds. By surfacing these different definitions they can be shared with the whole group, thus building understanding and facilitating communication.

Finally, it is useful to note that questions regarding the content sub-system will also help to clarify the roles of the client and the decision-taker for the project. The client is typically the person(s) commissioning the project and liaising with the facilitator, whereas the decision-taker is the individual(s) who can stop the project at any point and who will approve or veto its outcomes. It is important to understand the decision-taker role. Churchman (1971, p48) once noted that it is this person or persons who 'co-produces the future' for an organization along with the environment. Appreciating the client and the decision-taker as two distinct roles may reveal that they may be incorporated in the same person or persons – but they may not. For example, the client may be the chief executive officer; but the decision-takers might be situated at the board level. If the project does not take into account the perspectives of the board members, it could meet with limited success (see Chapter 13 in this volume).

Appreciating the social and political context

We believe scenario practice could be further strengthened by giving more explicit attention to the social and political context in which a scenario project is conducted and in which the outcomes of the scenarios must contend. Selin (2006, p6) makes a good case for this when she states that:

> *The future is very much staked out within existing strategies, agendas and hierarchies. Scenarios are not innocent or distanced from these regimes, but rather often support or oppose them. Despite the aim to create objective or equally plausible scenarios, specific future worlds are sketched out and in the end scenarios are always selective and political.*

Checkland (1999, pA19) added what he calls analyses two and three to SSM, 'comprising a framework for the social and political analyses'. These are processes for staying alert to information that signals the nature of roles, norms, values and power in the situation (Checkland, 1999). Of particular interest to our discussion is the focus on power in analysis three. Relevant questions for scenario work suggested in this analysis are 'Who are the powerful people in a scenario project?' and 'What modalities of power can be determined: positional; informational; access to resources; networks; knowledge of technology; previous practice; corporate memory, to name a few?' Because scenario projects are conducted within sociopolitical contexts, the power interactions will influence the design, conduct and outcomes of the project (see Chapter 8 in this volume).

In a review of the organizational scenario literature, Lang (2007) did not find any similar socio-political analysis tool discussed within scenario practice. We therefore propose that consideration be given to developing one. A socio-political contextual analysis in a scenario project would include being alert for information about the history of the focal topic, the values of the participants and stakeholders, and the power dynamics (positional, informational, decision-making, etc.) in the situation. Much of this information would emerge through the use of the questions above to design the process and to gather information about the content of the scenario project. However, this information would also emerge during the course of the enquiry, and it is important that practitioners be on the lookout for it so they can develop a progressively richer understanding of the context in which the enquiry is being conducted and in which the scenarios are to be used.

Reflective scenario practice

We encourage practitioners to reflect at every point of a scenario project to redesign it if necessary and to capture what has been learned. Such reflective practice (Schön, 1983) is important because, as Checkland (1999) points out, the facilitator is one of three interrelated elements in using a methodology. The other two are the situation and the methodology itself. It is the interaction of these three elements that results in a particular scenario approach being designed by the facilitator for a specific situation. We believe this emphasis on reflective design for a particular situation can serve to remind scenario practitioners, first, to pay attention to the continuous (re)design of their enquiry (not just in the early design phases), and, second, to develop over time a deep sense of what techniques work for them within what contexts (for a useful discussion related to reflective scenario practice, see Hodgkinson and Wright, 2002, 2006, and Whittington, 2006a, 2006b). Some chapters in this book also contribute to a reflective practice in scenario work: see especially Chapter 11).

First, attention to continuous redesign is important because the situation in which a scenario project is applied is dynamic. There can be staffing changes in key positions within the organization, resource and political developments affecting the enquiry, unexpected reactions by those participating in the project, stakeholder or competitor developments impacting upon the focus and relevance of the enquiry, etc. In these circumstances, a good facilitator reflects in action (Schön, 1983) by revisiting the design to see if, and how, it needs to be adapted.

Second, reflective practice encourages facilitators to develop a deep sense of what techniques work for them in particular situations and to capture this learning for subsequent use. Ison et al (2007, p220) also suggest that reflecting in action can assist practitioners to 'explicate their understanding of the theory/practice dialectic'. This enables them to articulate the theory behind each phase in the practice and to justify why a particular set of methods has been chosen. This reinforces the connection between theory and practice and encourages facilitators to reflect on what has been learned as a result of using the methodology.

Conclusion

In this chapter we have sought to highlight the parallel emergence of, and philosophical links between, scenario practice and the SSM. We then discussed what we see as the opportunities presented by applying soft systems concepts and selected SSM processes to scenario practice. These included the idea that boundaries in scenario work are judgements and, as such, practitioners and managers are free to shift them to experiment and thus explore new opportunities for action. We have also suggested that encouraging managers in organizations with egocentric tendencies to think of their contextual environment as a subject domain and to develop scenarios in reference to this domain can help them to better understand the interdependencies of the systems to which they belong and to avoid becoming wedded to outdated identities.

In particular, we have sought to argue that designing a scenario project as a purposeful human activity system using the proven methodology of SSM helps to clarify its purpose. It also helps to accommodate the various perspectives that exist within scenario participant groups regarding the nature and intensity of turbulence and what is to be done about it.

We then explored the value of specific SSM processes to scenario practice. These included the use of conceptual models to provide a structured way of taking the outcomes of scenarios forward; the use of the CATWOE mnemonic as a technology for writing scenario narratives; separating the process and content sub-systems to assist with designing and conducting an enquiry; analysing the social and political context of the enquiry and the scenarios; and, finally, reminding scenario practitioners to reflect on their design in all phases of the enquiry, as well as at the end to capture what has been learned.

In Table 4.1, each of these contributions has been placed alongside the relevant phase of a scenario project. (These phases are drawn from Shell International's, 2003, guide to their scenario process. We use it given the firm's extensive experience in the field.) One of the particular things to note is that 'appreciating the social and political context' is relevant to four of the five scenario phases. However, despite this high degree of relevance, the scenario practice literature does not include a well-developed tool for understanding the socio-political context of a scenario project.

Both SSM and scenario practice are attempts to avoid simplistic framing of ill-structured or wicked situations arising from environmental turbulence. By focusing on reframing, both methodologies have the capacity to 'shift mental furniture' (Deep Conversation) about the situation being faced. While scenario practice focuses on knowledge generation about an organization's contextual environment, SSM addresses the human complexity that is generated by turbulence and wicked problems. In this chapter, we have sought to demonstrate that the knowledge generation process of scenario practice can be enhanced by adopting

Table 4.1 *Summary of the contribution of soft systems concepts and soft systems methodology processes to each phase of a scenario project*

Phases within a scenario project (Global Business Environment, Shell International, 2003)	Contribution of soft systems concepts and SSM processes to these phases
Preparation: clarifying goals and resources to design the enquiry	Separating process and content sub-systems; appreciating the social and political context
Pioneering: undertaking research and outlining the scenarios	Boundaries as judgements; conceptualizing the contextual environment as a subject domain; reflective scenario practice
Map-making: developing the scenarios and gaining endorsement	Boundaries as judgements; CATWOE and scenario narratives; appreciating the social and political context; reflective scenario practice
Navigation: communicating and using the scenarios	Conceptual modelling and discussions; appreciating the social and political context; reflective scenario practice
Reconnaissance: using the scenarios to develop implications, interpret signals, share perspectives and recognize differences	Appreciating the social and political context

soft systems concepts and specific SSM techniques that place the human being and his or her perceptions at the centre of the enquiry – that is, by designing a scenario project as a purposeful human activity system using SSM, the purpose of the project as well as the multiple perspectives of the issue and how it is to be explored are more easily rendered. This facilitates the generation of alternative insights and increases the likelihood of success of the project.

This chapter has outlined a number of soft systems principles and SSM concepts that we believe can be applied to scenario practice, thereby enhancing its capability to address turbulence. While it can be argued that experienced and reflective practitioners may already apply some of the suggestions we have made in this chapter, our aims here have been to make these practices explicit and to link them systematically, thus filling an important gap in the literature.

Acknowledgement

We would like to particularly thank John Selsky for his extremely helpful comments on earlier drafts of this chapter. Rafael Ramírez also provided useful feedback and we would like to express our thanks to him as well.

Note

1   In other work we have integrated scenarios within a wider methodology for clarifying strategic intent. The methodology is called *ariadne*. Further details can be found in Allen and Lang (2006). In addition, that methodology forms the basis of an action learning programme for senior managers called Navigating the Maze.

References

Ackoff, R. (1979) *The Art of Problem-Solving*, John Wiley and Sons, New York, NY

Allen, L. and Lang, T. (2006) 'Here be dragons: Mapping future possibilities using an emergent framework', *12th ANZSYS Conference: Sustaining our Social and Natural Capital*, Katoomba, NSW, Australia

Bradfield, R., Wright, G., Burt, G., Cairns, G. and van der Heijden, K. (2005) 'The origins and evolution of scenario techniques in long range business planning', *Futures*, vol 37, pp795–812

Burt, G., Wright, G., Bradfield, R., Cairns, G. and van der Heijden, K. (2006) 'The role of scenario planning in exploring the environment in view of the limitations of PEST and its derivatives', *International Studies of Management and Organisation*, vol 36, no 3, pp50–76

Checkland, P. (1981) *Systems Theory, Systems Practice*, John Wiley and Sons, Chichester, UK

Checkland, P. (1985) 'From optimizing to learning: A development of systems thinking for the 1990s', *Journal of the Operational Research Society*, vol 36, no 9, pp757–767

Checkland, P. (1993) *Systems Thinking, Systems Practice*, John Wiley and Sons, Chichester, UK

Checkland, P. (1999) 'Soft systems methodology: A 30-year retrospective', in P. Checkland and J. Scholes (eds) *Soft Systems Methodology in Action*, John Wiley and Sons, Chichester, UK

Checkland, P. and Poulter, J. (2006) *Learning for Action: A Short Definitive Account of Soft Systems Methodology and Its Use for Practitioners, Teachers and Students*, John Wiley and Sons, Chichester, UK

Checkland, P. and Scholes, J. (1990) *Soft Systems Methodology in Action*, John Wiley and Sons, Chichester, UK

Churchman, C. (1971) *The Design of Inquiring Systems: Basic Concepts of Systems and Organization*, Basic Books, New York, NY

Claus, C. (2007) 'Creating identity dynamics: How the major music labels failed to make sense of future insights while new entrants set the pace', Presentation at the *25th Standing Conference for Organizational Symbolism: Signs of the Future: Management, Messianism, Catastrophe*, 1–4 July, Ljubljana, Slovenia

Cronin, M. and Weingart, L. (2007) 'Representational gaps, information processing, and conflict in functionally diverse teams', *Academy of Management Review*, vol 32, no 3, pp761–773

Emery, F. and Trist, E. (1965) 'The causal texture of organizational environments', *Human Relations*, vol 18, pp21–32

Flowers, B. (2003) 'The art and strategy of scenario writing', *Strategy & Leadership*, vol 31, no 2, pp29–33

Global Business Environment (2003) *Scenarios: An Explorer's Guide*, Shell International Ltd, London

Hodgkinson, G. and Wright, G. (2002) 'Confronting strategic inertia in a top management team: Learning from failure', *Organization Studies*, vol 23, no 6, pp949–977

Hodgkinson, G. and Wright, G. (2006) 'Neither completing the practice turn, nor enriching the process tradition: Secondary misinterpretations of a case analysis reconsidered', *Organization Studies*, vol 27, no 12, pp1895–1901

Ison, R., Blackmore, C. and Armson, R. (2007) 'Learning participation as systems practice', *Journal of Agricultural Education and Extension*, vol 13, no 3, pp209–225

Lang, T. (2007) *An Initial Classification of the Organisational Scenario Literature Based on Morgan's Organisational Metaphors*, MSc (Management Research) thesis, University of Oxford, UK

Midgley, G. (2002) *Systemic Intervention: Philosophy, Methodology and Practice*, Kluwer Academic, New York, NY

Mitroff, I. and Emshoff, J. (1979) 'On strategic assumption-making: A dialectical approach to policy and planning', *Academy of Management Review*, vol 4, pp1–12

Morgan, G. (1997) *Images of Organization: New Edition of the Best Seller*, Sage, Thousand Oaks, CA

Ramírez, R. and van der Heijden, K. (2007) 'Scenarios to develop strategic options: A new interactive role for scenarios in strategy', in B. Sharpe and K. van der Heijden (eds) *Scenarios for Success: Turning Insights into Action*, John Wiley and Sons, Chichester, UK

Rittel, H. and Webber, M. (1973) 'Dilemmas in a general theory of planning', *Policy Sciences*, vol 4, pp155–169

Schön, D. (1983) *The Reflective Practitioner*, Basic Books, New York, NY

Schwartz, P. (1991) *The Art of the Long View*, Doubleday, New York, NY

Selin, C. (2006) 'Trust and the illusive force of scenarios', *Futures*, vol 38, pp1–14

Trist, E. (1997) 'Referent organizations and the development of inter-organizational domains', in E. Trist, F. Emery and H. Murray (eds) and Trist, B. (assistant ed) *The Social Engagement of Social Science: A Tavistock Anthology, Volume III: The Socio-Ecological Perspective*, University of Pennsylvania Press, Philadelphia, PA

van der Heijden, K. (1996) *Scenarios: The Art of Strategic Conversation*, John Wiley and Sons, Chichester, UK

van der Heijden, K. (2005) *Scenarios: The Art of Strategic Conversation*, 2nd edition, John Wiley and Sons, Chichester, UK

van der Heijden, K. (undated) 'Scenario thinking as a purposeful activity system', pers comm

van der Heijden, K. and Checkland, P. (undated) 'Model to express the relationship between SSM and scenarios', pers comm

Wack, P. (1985a) 'Scenarios: Uncharted waters ahead', *Harvard Business Review*, vol 63, no 5, pp73–89

Wack, P. (1985b) 'Scenarios: Shooting the rapids', *Harvard Business Review*, vol 63, no 6, pp139–150

Whittington, R. (2006a) 'Completing the practice turn in strategy research', *Organization Studies*, vol 27, no 5, pp613–634

Whittington, R. (2006b) 'Learning more from failure: Practice and process' *Organization Studies*, vol 27, no 12, pp1903–1906

Winnicott, D. (1965) *The Maturational Process and the Facilitating Environment*, Hogarth Books, London, UK

5

New Forms of Coherence for the Social Engagement of the Social Scientist: The Theory and Facilitation of Organizational Change from the Perspective of the Emery–Trist Systems Paradigm and the Ilya Prigogine School of Thought

Mary Bernard

Let us look, therefore, into the black hole. We have to be alert to opportunities and create new spaces. (Trist, in Burgess and Trist, 1993)

We are observing the birth of a science that is no longer limited to idealized and simplified situations but reflects the complexity of the real world, a science that views us and our creativity as part of a fundamental trend present at all levels of nature. (Prigogine, 1996, p7)

In this chapter I explore the theories and approaches inherent in the Emery–Trist systems paradigm (ETSP), including related work of their close collaborators (Babüroğlu, 1992)[1] on change and uncertainty through the perspective of scientific theories on chaos, complexity and dissipative structures from the Ilya Prigogine school of thought. In 1977, Ilya Prigogine won a Nobel Prize for his work on the thermodynamics of non-equilibrium systems, focusing on dissipative structures arising out of non-linear processes. I suggest in this chapter that finding parallels between the paradigm and the school of thought provides both theoretical and practical insights for the social scientist involved in the study, appreciation, application and facilitation of organizational change theory and process. In this chapter I pay particular attention to insights gained from applying the Prigoginian lens to Emery and Trist's (1965) seminal article on contextual and turbulent environments and, more broadly, to the body of Trist's work as well as that of Trist and Emery and their colleagues who over decades involved themselves in research that relates theory and practice in a way that Trist refers to as *The Social Engagement of Social Science* (Trist and Murray, 1990, 'Preface').

Studying the behaviour of dissipative structures near bifurcation shows that systems seem to pause from time to time along their potential evolutionary courses. At such points, a small fluctuation may change the whole system – a feature that has parallels in the biochemical domain and in social systems. In such systems, both chance and necessity become descriptors of behaviour (see Chapter 7 in this volume). In this sense, irreversibility is the source of order. Prigogine and Stengers (1984) emphasize, then, that time can no longer be considered a concept developed by humankind and thrust upon a timeless universe. On the contrary, time becomes an autonomous contributor to behaviour.

The structure of this chapter is as follows. First, I present the philosophical assumptions of social science as synthesized by Burrell and Morgan (1979) in order to lay the ground for the subsequent demonstration of the impact that Prigogine's work has had on social science. Second, I summarize Ilya Prigogine's work on dissipative structures, including a comparative review of classical science, thermodynamics, the three stages of equilibrium, the principle of order through fluctuation, the relation between chance and necessity, the relation between permanence and change, rediscovering time, irreversibility, and the entropy barrier. Third, I apply the assumptions of the first section to chaos and self-organization theories in order to highlight where Prigogine's theories lie in Burrell and Morgan's (1979) schema. The fourth section discusses a new framework for the 'nature of society' debate in social sciences in the light of the application of the new scientific developments. Positioned within that framework, I examine, in the final section, the key concepts from the Emery–Trist systems paradigm and relevant works from their colleagues and appropriate methods for the engaged social scientist, and, by inference, for the scenario planner.

Philosophical assumptions underlying social science

Burrell and Morgan (1979) divide the philosophical assumptions underlying social science into four categories: ontology, epistemology, human nature and methodology. The paragraphs that follow draw from this categorization.

Ontology, defined as 'the branch of metaphysics dealing with the nature of being' (Morehead and Morehead, 1976), is concerned with *realism* and *nominalism*, which are at opposite ends of a continuum. The *realist* sees the nature of reality as 'out there', hard and concrete, while the *nominalist* sees the social world as the result of individual cognition and considers it made up of names, labels and concepts that the individual uses to structure reality.

Epistemology is 'the study of the nature, basis, limits and validity of human knowledge' (Morehead and Morehead, 1976). At one extreme of epistemology is *positivism*, which seeks to explain and predict what happens in the social world by searching for regularities and causal relationships between its constituent elements. *Anti-positivism*, at the other extreme, is characterized by understanding events and behaviour in subjective terms from the perspective of the individual involved.

The third category proposed by Burrell and Morgan, *human nature*, is concerned with relations between human beings and their environment. At one end of this continuum is *determinism*, where it is assumed that human beings are controlled by external environmental forces; at the other extreme is *voluntarism*, which assumes that human beings make an autonomous contribution to the creation of their own environment. In other words, determinism assumes the individual as the play ball of his or her situation, and voluntarism signifies that the individual is free willed.

The fourth category Burrell and Morgan (1979) considered, *methodology*, is to a large extent directed by one's position along the continua of each of the other three categories. Among the hundreds of methodological approaches to science studies, they identify a continuum with, at one extreme, the *nomothetic* approach and, at the other, the *ideographic* approach. The first one is concerned with methods that consider reality as external and knowledge as objective, while the latter refers to a more internalized view of reality and a subjective perception of knowledge.

Burrell and Morgan (1979) further describe *sociological positivism* and *German idealism* as the intellectual traditions that represent the most used combination of each of the four categories at each end of their respective continua. The *sociological positivist* assumes that the methods and theories of the hard sciences can be applied to the social sciences, while the *German idealist* sees the essence of the universe as 'spirit' or 'idea'. This is commonly referred to as the objective–subjective dimension. In the past half century, there has been a tendency to move along this continuum as opposed to being at either extreme.

To complete their framework, Burrell and Morgan (1979) categorize assumptions about the nature of society according to either *regulation* or *radical change*. This is based on two views of the nature of society; the first implies *order* and the second implies *conflict*. Most of the historical and contemporary study of societal (including organizational) change focuses on stability, social order and equilibrium, where the *order* perspective dominates. Burrell and Morgan refocus the debate by replacing the terms order and conflict with the *sociology of regulation* and the *sociology of radical change*. The sociology of regulation explains why society holds together rather than falls apart, while the sociology of radical change seeks to find out why there is radical change and structural conflict. The Prigogine exploration in the next section helps to place the debate in a new perspective.

Order out of chaos: Chaos and self-organization theories

In this section I shift to the natural sciences in order to consider how the Prigoginian perspective explains the emergence of order out of chaos. Following from that I consider how the theories can be applied to the human world and, subsequently, to the Trist–Emery Systems Paradigm.

All of Prigogine's work is based on the view that science is not independent from society. Rather, science participates with the society in which it is located in a rich network of idea feedback loops. In other words, its development is fostered by its cultural milieu, which, in turn, reacts to its major theories and findings.

Prigogine (Prigogine and Stengers, 1984; Prigogine, 1996) presents a comprehensive theory of change that recognizes that most of reality is in a process of change and disorder as opposed to being orderly and stable. Central to this theory is the idea that order arises spontaneously out of chaos through a process of self-organization – islands of order in a sea of change. He considers that we live in a multifaceted world where there are some processes that are deterministic and reversible, and others that are irreversible with various degrees of uncertainty, randomness and fluctuation. Rather than being viewed as an exception to order and reversibility, randomness and irreversibility are beginning to be perceived as closer to normality.

The body of Prigogine's work addresses two primary themes. The first theme is the apparent contradiction between two ways of seeing the world, both current in science, between what could be called the 'static paradigm of dynamics' and, on the other hand, the 'evolutionary paradigm of thermo-dynamics'. The first view considers reality expressible in terms of laws of nature, valid for all times, while the second view considers reality essentially related to and dependent upon time.

The second theme is the relationship between order and disorder. One view paints a picture of a world which evolves from order to disorder, with structures crumbling and everything eventually returning to dust. This is the sort of world described by the laws of thermodynamics and chemistry. Biology and social evolution, however, provide an opposing picture: the simple evolving into the complex.

In order to explain how Prigogine connects the apparent unconnectable paradoxes, it is helpful to examine past worldviews, beginning with classical mechanics. During the 17th century, Newton assumed that dynamic interaction between all objects could always be reversed. However, in chemistry, processes are known to go irreversibly to a state of greater disorder. Here one sees the origin of the first paradox mentioned above – that is, reversible dynamics cannot lead to the irreversible thermodynamics that is observed in nature as the second law of thermodynamics.

Philosophically, classical mechanics or Newtonianism coincided with the rise of industrialism – the universe and societies were viewed as machines. Laplace (1799–1825, vols 1 to 5) whose science represents the classical views of his time, claimed that given enough facts, one could always derive timeless state laws from time behaviour. In the 19th century, the discovery of the laws of thermodynamics challenged this timelessness of the machine metaphor. If the world was a big machine, it was running down and could not go on forever. On the other hand, Darwin introduced a contradictory thought – biological systems at least, under the influence of evolution, were becoming more organized. The machine metaphor that became further undermined by Einstein and quantum physics nevertheless remained a powerful reference point in both the natural sciences and the social sciences.

Over the past 200 years, a dichotomy has existed between science and common-sense knowledge. Prigogine states that this period is passing, and that the first step towards a reunification of knowledge has been the discovery of the laws of thermodynamics, which appeared as the first form of the science of complexity. The second law of thermodynamics led to the first scientific expression of irreversibility. This led to a dichotomy of images between 'dynamics' that referred to the world of reversible motion, and 'thermodynamics', a complex world with an irreversible evolutionary direction (Prigogine and Stengers, 1984). Thermodynamic change was expressed as the dissipation of 'entropy' and the evolution towards random disorder. At the turn of the 20th century, Boltzmann (German) and Poincaré (French) held a passionate debate on the nature of irreversibility. At the time, Poincaré appeared to prove mathematically that reversible dynamics and irreversible thermodynamics could not co-exist, which only served to intensify the paradox as both were irrefutably observed to occur in nature. The question, then, became how can we understand how irreversible thermodynamic behaviour emerges from reversible laws of dynamics?

It was Prigogine who finally solved this problem in 1973 by showing how irreversible thermodynamics can only occur in systems of 'sufficient complexity'. Prigogine showed experimentally that order sometimes emerges out of chaos. Where once there was nothing but disorder, in some systems there can be the spontaneous evolution of ordered states. All large systems contain sub-systems that are continually in a state of flux. At times, a single fluctuation or a combination of fluctuations may grow and become so powerful (as a result of positive feedback) that it shatters the pre-existing order, and a new higher level of order called a dissipative structure may appear (so called because the new structure requires energy to sustain it). These ordered states can appear as:

- Spontaneous bifurcation between diverse branches of development: if a single fluctuation becomes so powerful as a result of positive feedback that it shatters the existing order, this revolutionary moment is called a *bifurcation*.

For example, if an ant colony is provided with two routes in order to move from one point to another, they may initially follow each of the two routes with some of the total ant group in each route. However, at one point, all ants will together take one of the routes.

- Spontaneous evolution of macroscopic order: this occurs, for example, when water randomly going down a drain switches to highly ordered behaviour at the macro-structural level and forms a vortex.

In order for either of these phenomena to occur, Prigogine suggested that the two following conditions must be met:

1   The system must be sufficiently large.
2   The system must be sufficiently complex.

Prigogine provided precise mathematical definitions for 'sufficiently' for each of the above conditions – for which he received the Nobel Prize.

In view of the above, an alternative view of the world materializes. Having reached a spontaneous bifurcation point, the system behaves in a way that is:

- discontinuous and non-evolutionary (i.e. unlike Darwin, who theorized that biological systems are becoming more organized rather than less and that the universe gets better organized in a gradual and continuous fashion as it ages);
- non-deterministic and contrary to the uniform mechanistic worldview (that has had such tremendous influence on industrial society and underlies forecasting methods with statistical outcome predictions);
- richly interconnected with its wider environment.

Self-organizing structures manifest all of the above characteristics. Note parallels with the build-up of knowledge and order seen in biological systems, contradicting the loss of order dictated in chemical systems by the second law of thermodynamics. Yet, as we saw above, biology is built on chemistry. This suggests the non-linear (discontinuous) and non-local (richly interconnected) feedback mechanism as a necessary condition.

In summary, many systems in the world are sufficiently complex to show three characteristics:

1   Prediction is possible, but not all of the time.
2   Allowance must be made for the possibility of a spontaneous bifurcation (settling down in one of two possible stable states).
3   The possibility of the emergence of a spontaneous self-organizing structure must be acknowledged.

All three characteristics directly contradict the deterministic view of the world.

Following this line of argument allows evolution to be seen as something that occurs in stages with spontaneous alternative evolutions or discontinuous change (Goodman, 1983) interspersed with periods of stability. As we saw above, the thermodynamic perspective projects change in terms of dissipation of entropy and the evolution towards disorder. Prigogine shows how this process gives rise to the emergence of dissipative structures, manifesting as spontaneous evolution that makes entropy central to the characterization of the evolutionary process.

How can such bifurcation and self-organization occur? Understanding this requires thermodynamics to be divided into:

- equilibrium (entropy production and forces in balance), close-to-equilibrium or linear thermodynamics (where thermodynamic forces are weak); and
- non-linear or far-from-equilibrium thermodynamics, which manifest more complicated functions of the thermodynamic forces (Prigogine and Stengers, 1984).

Close-to-equilibrium or linear thermodynamics describes the predictable behaviour of systems, in which the system can move in all directions but will reach a predictable state of organization, determined by its boundaries.

But within far-from-equilibrium situations, spontaneous, often dramatic reorganizations of matter take place. Add to this the notion of a movement calling up a reaction that encourages further production of the movement. In systems science, this is called a positive feedback loop and in chemistry, autocatalysis. Biologists have found that life itself is underpinned by such processes (for example, lumps of DNA becoming living organisms). They cause very small fluctuations to become 'gigantic structure-breaking waves' (Prigogine and Stengers, 1984). The system may eventually evolve to a new steady state. But in far-from-equilibrium conditions, new phenomena may eventually appear prior to chemical instability. Beyond a critical threshold, the system spontaneously leaves the stationary state as the result of fluctuations.

The distinction between equilibrium and far-from-equilibrium systems is described in mathematical terms. Prigogine's colleague Isabelle Stengers suggested that to the extent that social systems can be described in the same terms, they will manifest similar behaviour. This means that also in the social world, we will observe limited predictability, spontaneous bifurcation and self-organizing structures.

Most systems (in both the physical and in the social world) operate like open systems, are richly interconnected and can potentially become subject to these far-from equilibrium forces. This suggests that reality is not stable and orderly and equal, but changing, disorderly and process oriented (Prigogine and Stengers, 1984). Any single fluctuation may become so powerful as a result of positive feedback that it may shatter the existing order. This revolutionary moment is called a *bifurcation*. Whether the system will disintegrate into chaos or leap to a new order cannot be predicted in advance. This new order is the *dissipative structure*, so called because the new structure requires energy to sustain it (dissipation of entropy).

Summarizing, at equilibrium or near equilibrium there is only one steady state. In far-from-equilibrium states, self-organization processes may occur in many different directions. Beyond this threshold into far-from-equilibrium states, bifurcations occur. The road to chaos is characterized by complex spatial and temporal activity beyond the bifurcation at the threshold. The temporal path along which the system evolves is characterized by a series of stable states and unstable ones with further bifurcation points in which the system 'decides' among possible futures. The choosing processes generated by random fluctuations are connected in terms of one 'choice' affecting the next one. The dissipative structures are related – the structure behaves as a whole.

Order through fluctuation

When deterministic description breaks down at a bifurcation point, the type of fluctuations present in the system will determine the direction that the system is to follow. Prigogine's theory of 'order through fluctuation' can assist in understanding the interplay between individual and collective aspects of behaviour with clear bifurcation points where an individual fluctuation (or, in the social world, an individual idea) can have a profound effect through positive feedback. Small causes can have large effects.

With the evolution of equilibrium thermodynamics, it seemed plausible that rather than irreversible processes being an exception, in far-from-equilibrium states, these new spontaneously generated dissipative structures could be the norm. Each of these dissipative structures is one unique association between a system and its environment emerging as chance events out of many possibilities. On the other hand, systems near equilibrium behave in a more predictable repetitive manner.

However, with dissipative structures near bifurcation, irreversibility becomes the source of order and time becomes the autonomous contributor to behaviour. Time is critical in understanding the evolutionary process.[2] Prigogine and Stengers (1984) question what it is about dynamic systems that permit them to distinguish past from future. Prigogine interpreted the second law of thermodynamics by showing that it does not merely suggest a downward slide into disorganization, but that under certain conditions entropy becomes the progenitor of order (i.e. dissipative structures). He, in effect, suggested that it is these irreversible processes that are the source of order; it is through processes involving randomness and openness that higher levels of organization are created. This led to the conclusion that 'Only when a system behaves in a sufficiently random way may the difference between past and future, and therefore irreversibility, enter its description' (Prigogine and Stengers, 1984).

As determinism became more problematic over the centuries in terms of what people saw happening around them, new efforts were made to 'recognize the co-presence of both chance and necessity … as partners in a universe that is simultaneously organizing and de-organizing itself' (Prigogine and Stengers, 1984). Prigogine's work underlies a new relationship between chance and necessity. He describes how a complex system is forced into a far-from-equilibrium state where it approaches the moment of bifurcation, at which point it is impossible to determine the next state of the system. It is chance that directs the system down a new path of development. At that point, determinism takes over until the next bifurcation point – with both chance and necessity playing a role. Coveney and Highfield (1995) uniquely describe the bifurcation point as, in effect, announcing: 'Expect novel behaviour here.'

Prigogine's re-perception of the world, and the way in which it works, shifts the focus from *being* to *becoming* – from *permanence* to *change*. It shatters confidence in the idea that there is only order in nature. Symmetry and all-embracing predictive schemes are no longer what is being found in biology, chemistry, physics and ecology. A new paradigm is emerging based on order appearing out of chaos.

Prigogine argued that the old universal laws are not universal at all, but describe special conditions applying only to local regions of reality, subject to change following new bifurcations. As the world moves away from an industrial-based society to one focusing on high technology, services and information, we may be moving into such a new world where new scientific models apply.

The Prigogine paradigm shifts attention to those aspects of reality that characterize today's accelerated change: 'disorder, instability, diversity, disequilibrium, non-linear relationships (in which small inputs can trigger massive consequences), and, temporality – a heightened sense of the flows of time' (Prigogine and Stengers, 1984).

The second law of thermodynamics altered our perception of classical science, introducing time into the laws of physics and distinguishing between reversible processes that are not dependent upon time and irreversible processes that are. The Newtonian model meant a success of procedure for the positivist. The recent evolution of physics has realized the reality of time (Prigogine and Stengers, 1984). I have already suggested the link with the social sciences, which I will now work out further in the next section.

Social science assumptions, intellectual traditions and societal nature in light of Prigogine's scientific chaos and self-organization theories

Can the social sciences learn from the natural sciences? In Prigogine's and, especially, Stengers's view, this age-old question takes on radical new dimensions and presents a strange paradox when their ideas on chaos and self-organization theory come into play. Those leaning towards the objective dimension of the basic social science assumptions would most likely say yes from the perspective of a realist ontology. In this section I employ the scientific developments of Prigogine, based on the behaviour of far-from-equilibrium states, to add insight to the social sciences, pointing to a direction that is fundamentally different from the realists. Prigogine's school of thought, as scientific theory, leads to a degree of subjectivity, anti-positivism, nominalism, voluntarism and ideographic methods. The premises of Prigogine's theories are far removed from those of classical science.

Although in this chapter I apply scientific theory to the social sciences, I emphasize that this is not the positivist epistemology of applying the traditional methods of the natural scientists to the social sciences. In my research (Bernard, 1999), I found that Prigogine's views on chaos and self-organization theory established a new paradigm within the natural sciences itself. Predictability and determinism are only appropriate for closed and contained situations. And most of the world is not in this state. Prigogine and Stengers (1984) state that the new insight which Prigogine's research afforded in thermodynamics opens new possibilities for the natural sciences that influence the way in which we view social reality. In this section, I explore the implications for social science, laying the groundwork for my exploration of the Trist school of thought.

Social scientists have often identified the environment as an external force – impacting upon the organization, but separate from it. Within this context they identify components (functions) within an organization that are related to environmental factors perceived to be external to the organization. These functions, such as parameters and structure, are then measured. Ordered pairs are formed (environmental factors paired with internal functions) so that a function and its matching variables become separate sets that are isolated from one another. Therefore, the understanding of a complex environment becomes fragmented and cause and effect are broken up. This implies what is known as 'locality': the ability to separate environment from effect. In contrast, a system with its own internal feedback mechanism cannot be broken down into cause and effect in this way, a condition called 'non-locality'.

Articulation of cause and effect leads to a Laplacian variant of the deterministic view attempting to identify all environmental variables (given enough facts, one can always derive time behaviour from timeless state laws). The assumption of knowing the social interactions and processes leads the social scientist to try to predict future interactions and, therefore, events. Indeed, the ability to predict based on known laws is sometimes taken to be the definition of 'science'. Given that many social science paradigms still adopt this deterministic view of the universe, movement from this Laplacian starting point generally occurs by gradual evolution as evidence points elsewhere. Social science 'laws' are in a sense Darwinian (survival of the fittest). There is a strong awareness within the social science community that all theories of organization are based on a philosophy of science and a theory of society (Burrell and Morgan, 1979). Reality, locality and causality are often underpinnings of conventional Western thought. Within the realm of much of conventional social science theory around organization, 'reality' subsumes the ontological notion of realism, 'causality' subsumes the epistemological notion of positivism, and 'locality' subsumes the human nature assumption of determinism. Methodologies selected tend to be germane to these perspectives. Each of these aspects is now confronted by recent scientific theories such as Prigogine's. For example, quantum theory has proven that the nature of reality as conventionally perceived is not correct, at least at the sub-atomic level. There is evidence in quantum mechanics that also shows that the assumptions of local reality or causality must be unfounded (d'Espagnat, 1979). Prigogine's work calls into question both locality and causality.

If we look at Prigogine's work from the perspective of the Burrell and Morgan (1979) framework, we conclude that a new position in the objective–subjective dimension is called for in the social sciences. This new position is as follows: an ontology characterized by both realism and nominalism; an epistemology leaning towards anti-positivism; human nature characterized by a degree of voluntarism (specific to state and position of the individual); and a methodology leaning towards the ideographic. The nature of society is characterized by both order and disorder, but not in terms of the extreme ends of the continuum. Instead, Prigogine reached the startling conclusion that the pull towards disorder is, in fact, the source of order.

Table 5.1 is based upon the Burrell and Morgan (1979) framework. It combines the social science assumptions into one table to demonstrate the continuum position of the categories from a Prigoginian chaos and self-organization perspective.

Prigogine proposed that most of reality is in a process of change and disorder as opposed to being orderly and stable, and that order arises spontaneously out of chaos through a process of self-organization. In the light of this, his theories, if projected onto the social sciences, point towards a recognition of both objective and subjective dimensions. The new paradigm, combining a number of older positions, supports a description of the nature of society as akin to the order out of chaos perspective. In such a reality, the role of the social scientist in the process of change should change to reflect this new perspective.

Table 5.1 *The Burrell–Morgan social science framework as applied to Prigogine's theories on chaos and self-organization*

The Burrell–Morgan social science framework	Prigogine's theories on chaos and self-organization	
Ontology assumptions	both	
	Realism ------------------	nominalism
Epistemology assumptions	towards →	
	Positivism ------------------	anti-positivism
Human nature	both	
	Determinism ------------------	voluntarism
Methodology assumptions	towards the ideographic →	
	Nomothetic ------------------	ideographic
Intellectual tradition	a new position	
	Objective ------------------	subjective
Societal nature	order out of chaos	
	Order ------------------	disorder

Source: based on Burrell and Morgan (1979)

The Emery–Trist systems paradigm and related approaches: Towards the social engagement of the social scientist

Using the conclusions I reached in projecting Prigogine's theories to the social sciences, in this section I focus specifically on the Emery–Trist systems paradigm, the Eric Trist body of work and related works of their colleagues. My research suggests that examining this work against the Ilya Prigogine school of thought leads to new insights on change theory, and on the active role of social scientists in facilitation of change and learning.

The conceptual dialogue between their ideas in my view brings back a measure of hope that has been lost over the years in an increasingly complex world where clarity has been progressively replaced by confusion. Specifically, clarity (see Chapter 11 in this volume) is gained in relation to:

- a theoretical position that allows for coherence and hope as guiding principles;
- availability of new and relevant methods, interventions and facilitation practices; and
- new inter-organizational activities and collaboration based on this.

While social science tends to reflect the contemporary scientific mode of thought, there is always a cultural lag compared to the leading edge. Over several decades, both Prigogine and Trist and Emery and their colleagues have drawn attention to outdated analytical frameworks based upon obsolete scientific theories that hold back progress.

In particular, from the beginning of his career, Trist was concerned with the role of social science. When the Tavistock Institute was founded in 1946, its purpose was described as actively relating the psychological and social sciences to the needs and concerns of society. At the end of his life, Trist was still engaged in the question of the relevance of the social sciences. He took the word 'engagement' to mean 'the process by which social scientists endeavour actively to relate themselves in relevant and meaningful ways to society' (Trist and Murray, 1990, 'Preface'). In these terms, he felt social science was under-delivering. But as Eric Trist's work progressed over time – through the social-psychological, the social-technical and the social-ecological perspectives – it was increasingly convergent with the latest available natural science scientific paradigms. In this section I will consider these three perspectives as they have been categorized in the Tavistock anthology (Trist and Murray, 1990; Trist and Murray, 1993; Trist, et al, 1997).

The first perspective, the socio-psychological, covers work that began during the mid 1940s and continued into the 1950s. It includes Trist's seminal work on the development of a single frame of reference for the socio-psychological perspective, as well as the significance of groups in experiential learning and the importance of group process. In terms of organizational theory, he pursued the theme of internal organizational choice, which grew to become a most important contribution to the organizational change literature in that it promoted an alternative to the Taylorist rationalist planning perspective. This theme runs parallel to Prigogine's primary theme of non-deterministic behaviour and self-organizing process. Through the creation of these themes, Trist simultaneously began to focus on the articulation of what at that time was a new role for the social scientist – a theme inherent in Prigogine and Stengers's (1984) positioning of their scientific theories in relation to social science.

The second perspective, the socio-technical, incorporated concepts from the socio-psychological perspective specific to organizations, building on new ideas at the time on open systems theory in biology. During the late 1950s and into the 1960s, the concept of socio-technical systems broke new ground in terms of debunking the technological imperative of how organizations are defined, therefore developing a non-deterministic theme. A great deal of the conceptual development on the socio-technical organization was articulated during this period, including concepts such as 'redundancy of functions', 'requisite variety', and 'minimum critical specifications' (Trist and Murray, 1990). In the early 1970s, innovative organizational ways of working were actively promoted and evaluated (for example, quality of working life). The changing role of the social scientist continued to be expanded upon by Trist and his colleagues, including Fred Emery, in the theoretical and conceptual development of the perspective and in the practical role in the field, including the importance of evaluation.

The third perspective, the socio-ecological, covers work from the mid 1960s until Trist's death in 1993. A number of major themes can be distinguished in Emery and Trist's work over this period.

The first major theme, turbulent environments, was articulated during the mid 1960s and is the most significant part of Emery and Trist's work when related with Prigogine's concept of chaos. A further development, 'permanent white water', again names another salient condition, this time describing a post-turbulent state or a state of hyper-turbulence (see Table 5.2) in which previous response capacities alone are insufficient. In addition, McCann and Selsky (1984) describe two types of domains that can emerge in an environment where the prospect of hyper-turbulence occurs: the social enclave and the social vortex.

Table 5.2 *Ontological constructs: Acknowledgement of realism and nominalism*

Emery–Trist systems paradigm and related work	Prigogine
Permanent white water characterizes the large-scale global state – this is the current contextual environment.	Prigogine's paradigm shifts attention to those aspects of reality that characterize today's accelerated change and a heightened sense of the flow of time.
There is fundamental uncertainty: only futures, not *the* future.	In non-equilibrium conditions, initial states are irrelevant for outcome; the state of the organization is determined by its boundaries.
There is the danger of a vortical state.[a]	An undesirable state is maintained by the patterns of self-similarity.[b]
The symbiotic paradigm[c] is a new, higher, logical type.	Dissipative structures.
Individuals and organizations communicate in order to reach new states.	Small fluctuations are capable of creating new dissipative structures. This occurs only in the far-from-equilibrium state. At equilibrium, molecules are 'asleep'.

Notes: [a] Trist described a limit, which he called a dark force or vortical state, in which adaptation becomes impossible (Trist and Murray, 1990).
[b] The far-from-equilibrium state in natural science is characterized by hyper-complexity and uncertainty. This is the 'strange attractor' type of chaos distinguished by disorder, leading to order arising from self-similarity. New order arises from symmetry-breaking activity.
[c] The symbiotic paradigm as developed by Perlmutter and Trist (1986) can be seen as a synthesis of two ends of a societal paradigm continuum, characterized at one end by advanced industrial society with growth and technological advancement, and at the other end by the 'small is beautiful' paradigm. Under turbulent conditions, neither paradigm is appropriate. The industrial society paradigm is eroded and the small is beautiful paradigm is not feasible, although it embodies many good aspects. The symbiotic paradigm is a synthesis of the two ends of the continuum. The resulting paradigm embodies, as a fundamental systemic principle, the nurturing of the formation of symbiotic partnerships.
Source: adapted from Burrell and Morgan (1979)

Table 5.3 *Epistemological constructs: Towards anti-positivism*

Emery–Trist systems paradigm and related work	Prigogine
The new organizational metaphor is more like a conscious organism than a machine.	Far-from-equilibrium self-organization leads to increased complexity.
The effectiveness of domain development[a] depends upon widespread experiential learning.	'Time and reality are irreducibly linked' (Prigogine, 1996). In terms of learning, to deny it is to deny reality.
The form of learning moves beyond outcome to the process of learning to learn itself. Action learning means the continuous creation of new mental models.	There is a recognition that 'irreversible processes play a fundamental constructive role in nature' (Prigogine, 1996).
The selection of issues, symmetry-breaking[a] and the reframing of issues are part of the action learning process.	Prigogine's theories support a non-linear, non-constant structural, non-static methodology.

Note: [a] New order arises from symmetry-breaking activity. Ontologically, each of the states is recognized as 'becoming' and may exist concurrently with states that are 'being' (stable); but each call for its own epistemologies and methodologies. Moreover, this far-from-equilibrium state is seen as a desirable state as it is from this condition that innovation and self-organization occur.
Source: adapted from Burrell and Morgan (1979)

The second theme, system transformation, describes organizational response capacities to turbulent environments – the core of this book. The category is characteristic of the vision and values reflecting Trist's work until the end of the 1970s. The symbiotic paradigm describes a vision and value base for a response capacity to the heightened sense of turbulence. The paradigm is comprehensive, describing social, political, ecological and organizational response capacities.

The third theme marks the development of the field of organizational ecology during the decade of the 1970s.

The fourth theme, action learning, builds upon the theory and practice of the role of the social scientist in affecting change, capturing the need for facilitation and playing down the role of the expert in the social change process (Morgan and Ramírez, 1984). The social engagement of social scientists builds on this evolving role as a facilitator of change and organizational learning.

From the vast amount of work referred to above, I now examine selected concepts of importance in the context of this book against Prigogine's theories.

Emery–Trist and Prigogine: Construct comparison summary

In my research I have found that looking at the juxtaposition of the social systems paradigm and the scientific school of thought in some detail informs understanding

Table 5.4 *Human nature constructs: Respect not control*

Emery–Trist systems	Prigogine
There are advantages as well as disadvantages in the current contextual environment (permanent white water).	Uncertainty fosters innovation.
Which of the possibilities will be realized depends upon the choices we make, which in turn depend upon our values.	Both chance and necessity become descriptors.
Communication and interaction are important.	The system must maintain a far-from-equilibrium state to be sensitive to be small changes.
Acting and making choices as opposed to non-action are crucial.	Bifurcation points exist: the critical points where the system must choose among developmental paths.
The action learning process is largely unpredictable and evolves as new needs and factors arise.	Probabilities are more than just a state of mind; they are states of the world.[a]
Action learning enhances the capacity of people to change situations with a minimum of external help.	Prigogine refers to a recent report to the European communities: 'The maintenance of organization in nature is not – and cannot be – achieved by central management; order can only be maintained by self-management' (Prigogine 1996).

Note: [a] Since the beginning of Western science, the exploration of causes, not chance, was dominant; and probabilities were not viewed as reality beyond states of mind. Prigogine shows that introducing probability and irreversibility to quantum mechanics the observer no longer became a necessity. He states: 'this does not mean a return to classical deterministic orthodoxy; on the contrary, we go beyond the certitudes associated with the traditional laws of quantum theory and emphasize the fundamental role of probabilities. We need not only laws, but also events that bring an element of radical novelty to the description of nature' (Prigogine, 1996). The basic laws of physics now become probabilities. The future is not a given: it is a construction.
Source: adapted from Burrell and Morgan (1979)

of both. This section provides a side-by-side projection of the two schools. I've put elements next to each other where I consider one informs the other.

The comparison takes the form of four tables covering the Burrell and Morgan categories (Tables 5.2 to 5.5).

Conclusion

In Table 5.6, I summarize both the Emery–Trist systems paradigm (and the related works of colleagues) and Prigogine's theories in relation to conventional organizational theory within the Burrell–Morgan framework. In breaking the moulds and challenging us to look at our world differently, Trist–Emery systems paradigm and related works and the Prigogine school of thought show remarkable affinity.

Table 5.5 *Methodology constructs: Towards the ideographic approach*

Emery–Trist systems paradigm and related work	Prigogine
The symbiotic paradigm, systemic transformation involving major paradigm shifts, and building new social institutions are key components.	Dissipative structures and emergent patterns are evident.
Action learning is a response to permanent white water.	The laws of nature change radically when instability is introduced.
Symmetry-breaking must occur for the next innovation to occur.	Instability breaks time symmetry.[a]
Challenge assumptions; participation encourages the detection and selection of issues.	Complex systems are sensitive to small fluctuations.
A context environment that allows innovation is created. Design principles include collaboration, negotiated order, democratization, participation and power-sharing, all of which are socio-ecological in nature.	The scientific recognition of complexity in the real world allows us to view our capacity for creativity.
The facilitator concentrates on process, leaving participants free to concentrate on content.	Constraints are required to create bounded instability.
There is strategy of process: an overall process of learning to learn.	Because of the ontological recognition of life as constantly evolving, certainty is an illusion.
Retrospection is part of the strategy of process.	There is recognition of the hidden order (relationships and patterns).

Note: [a] The singleness, the uniqueness, of time is certified by the entropy barrier. With the selection of possible initial states, this issue of practical probability was moved beyond the theoretical level. After the initial states are selected, the probability interpretation comes to bear. As Boltzman stated: 'the increase of entropy expresses the increase of probability, of disorder ... entropy is a selection principle breaking the time symmetry. It is only the unification of dynamics and thermodynamics through the introduction of a new selection principle that gives the second law its fundamental importance as the evolutionary paradigm of the sciences' (cited in Prigogine and Stengers, 1984).
Source: adapted from Burrell and Morgan (1979)

The Emery–Trist thinking, in my view, consists of both theoretical and practical insights to guide people in a safe journey through an increasingly complex world. Emery and Trist articulated concepts, methods and capacities appropriate to an unstable, indeterminate, creative, self-organizing universe. The development of the Emery–Trist systems paradigm and the majority of Trist's work was done prior to Prigogine's publications on the new dialogue with nature; and while Trist was encouraged by the presentation of the new scientific paradigm, it seems reasonable to assume that Trist's ontological and epistemological articulations would have continued independent of this further scientific knowledge. Support of this view is that Trist suggested, during the early 1980s, to his graduate students – such as Selsky, McCann, Jiménez, Ramírez and this author – that they read Prigogine's

Table 5.6 *A three-part comparison, following the Burrell–Morgan schema, conventional theory, the Prigogine school of thought and the Emery–Trist systems paradigm*

Burrell–Morgan social science framework	Majority of conventional organizational theory	Prigogine's theories on chaos and self-organization	Emery–Trist systems paradigm and related work
Ontology assumptions	← Towards Realism------Nominalism	Both Realism--------Nominalism	Both Realism------Nominalism
Epistemology assumptions	← Towards Positivism---Anti-positivism	Towards → Positivism-----Anti-positivism	Towards → Positivism---Anti-positivism
Human nature	← Towards Determinism----Voluntarism	Respect, not control Determinism---Voluntarism	Towards → Determinism---Voluntarism
Methodology assumptions	← Towards Nomothetic---Ideographic	Towards → Nomothetic-----Ideographic	Towards → Nomothetic---Ideographic
Intellectual tradition	← Towards Objective------Subjective	A new position Objective--------Subjective	A new position Objective------Subjective
Societal nature	← Towards Order-----------Disorder	Order out of chaos Order-------------Disorder	Order out of chaos Order----------Disorder

Source: Adapted from Bernard (1999), p440

work. Even so, while Trist and Prigogine were contemporaries, aware of each other's work, they followed their own path, enriching the thinking of the people who came after them.

By engaging with Prigogine's school of thought in this chapter explicitly, I think I further clarify the understanding of Emery and Trist's systems paradigm, and the related concepts, methodologies and inter-organizational capacity-building. A comprehensive picture emerges for a new role for the social scientist, encompassing both the micro- and macro-level of analysis and method, theoretical and practical approaches to deal with turbulence as explored in this book. The thoughtful scenario planner, as social scientist, deploys many of the characteristics and methods that Emery and Trist and many of their collaborators would have considered appropriate to address turbulence and chaos.

Many contemporary chaos theorists tend to present a view of chaos that is value free. Prigogine is not one of them; he, like Trist, adds values – and hope. Prigogine's fundamental insights bring forth a new culture that is relevant across disciplines. Prigogine describes himself as having always been concerned with the ethical problems of human freedom (Prigogine, 1996). Similarly, the work of Eric Trist and many of his colleagues is value laden. In particular, Trist's work reflects great concern for the betterment of humankind, its organization and its environment. The articulation of affinity between the Trist–Emery systems paradigm and the Prigogine school of thought entails an ideology as much as an understanding of turbulent conditions.

Notes

1   Oğuz Babüroğlu tracks the Emery–Trist systems paradigm to denote the value of the paradigm to critical system thinking, as well as to other system thinkers.
2   With the development of quantum mechanics by Schrödinger and others during the 1920s, reactions were still expressed as reversible in time in the equations that describe the dynamic interaction of atoms and molecules.

References

Babüroğlu, O. (1992) 'Tracking the development of the Emery–Trist systems paradigm (EMTP)', *Systems Practice*, vol 5, no 3, pp263–290

Bernard, M. (1999) *New Forms of Coherence: The Theory and Facilitation of Organizational Change from the Perspective of the Eric Trist and Ilya Prigogine Schools of Thought*, PhD thesis, York University, Toronto, Canada

Burgess, S. and Trist, B. (1993) *Eric Trist: Engaging Visionary, Memorial Video*, HPTV Communications Network, Hewlett-Packard Company, US

Burrell, G. and Morgan, G. (1979) *Sociological Paradigms and Organizational Analysis*, Heinemann Educational Books, London, UK

Coveney, P. and Highfield, R. (1995) *Frontiers of Complexity: The Search for Order in a Chaotic World*, Random House of Canada, Toronto, Canada

d'Espagnat, B. (1979) 'The quantum theory and reality', *Scientific American*, vol 241, no 5, pp158–181

Emery, F. and Trist, E. (1965) 'The causal texture of organizational environments', *Human Relations*, vol 18, no 1, pp21–32

Goodman, J. (1983) *The Genesis Mystery*, Times, New York, NY

Laplace, P. (1799–1825) *Traité de Méchanique Céleste*, reprinted as vols 1–5 of *Oeuvres 1878–1912*, Gauthier-Villars, Paris, France

McCann, J. and Selsky, J. (1984) 'Hyperturbulence and the emergence of type 5 environments', *Academy of Management Review*, vol 9, no 3, pp460–470

Morehead, D. and Morehead, A. (1976) *Normal and Deficient Child Language*, University Park Press, Baltimore, MD

Morgan, G. and Ramírez, R. (1984) 'Action learning: A holographic metaphor for guiding social change', *Human Relations*, vol 37, no 1, pp1–27

Perlmutter, H. and Trist, E. (1986) 'Paradigms for societal transition', *Human Relations*, vol 39, no 1, pp1–27

Prigogine, I. (1996) *The End of Certainty: Time, Chaos, and the New Laws of Nature*, The Free Press, Toronto, Canada

Prigogine, I. and Stengers, I. (1984) *Order Out of Chaos*, Bantam, New York, NY (original title, *La Nouvelle Alliance*)

Trist, E. and Murray, H. (eds), and Trist, B. (assistant editor) (1990) *The Social Engagement of Social Science, Volume I: The Socio-Psychological Perspective,* University of Pennsylvania Press, Philadelphia, PA

Trist, E. L. and Murray, H. (eds) and Trist, B. (assistant editor) (1993) *The Social Engagement of Social Science, Volume II: The Socio-Technical Perspective,* University of Pennsylvania Press, Philadelphia, PA

Trist, E., Emery, F. and Murray, H. (eds) and Trist, B. (assistant editor) (1997) *The Social Engagement of Social Science, Volume III: The Socio-Ecological Perspective,* University of Pennsylvania Press, Philadelphia, PA

Part II

6

Turbulence in the Indian Agricultural Sector: A Scenario Analysis

Kees van der Heijden

Introduction

The Indian agricultural sector is exposed to a complex economical, social and cultural environment characterized as 'turbulent' by Emery and Trist, resulting from the country's rapid economic development and the opening up of its markets to international competition.

A recent scenario project was aimed at exploring evolving aspects of this situation in a broadly based strategic conversation among stakeholders. This chapter describes how the process led to a deeper understanding of some the main driving forces in this situation, and how the causal textures framework helped in structuring this understanding.

Four scenarios were developed illustrating the consequences of different ways of dealing with the situation. Emery and Trist have argued that players exposed to a new turbulent environment cope with this by falling back on, or developing and institutionalizing, sets of shared values that reintroduce coherent behaviour in an otherwise unmanageable business environment. The four scenarios emerging from this project can be interpreted as being driven by four different values sets. The scenarios tell the stories of how these are mobilized to transform the turbulent environment into more placid causal textures in which rational decision processes can address the longer-term needs of the sector.

While some value sets seem to resonate more with Indian cultural assumptions than others, the project has shown that the country is some distance away from a condition of 'shared values' in the agricultural industry as a whole, as a basis for moving forward.

Even so, the project experience illustrates the value of using scenario planning in order to gain some control over new and problematic interrelationships in turbulent contextual environments.

Short summary of the causal textures framework and appropriate responses

As we overviewed in Chapter 2, in their seminal paper, Emery and Trist (1965) propose four types of environment that an open system, such as Indian agriculture, can be exposed to depending upon the causal texture of the variables defining it. For each environment, they indicate 'winning' responses that allow players to cope with its specific problems. The following is a brief summary, grouped from placid to turbulent:

1   Placid randomized environment:
    • perfect market model;
    • winning strategy → the simple tactic of doing your best on a purely local basis; local optimization in the 'here and now'.
2   Placid clustered environment:
    • imperfect competition model, with market failure;
    • winning strategy → knowing your environment and strategizing through the larger clusters of events to find the 'high ground'; keeping to the plan and avoiding local opportunism; large organizations and central control.
3   Disturbed reactive environment:
    • zero-sum game with head-to-head competition; battling it out with a limited number of comparable competitors;
    • winning strategy → the campaign (i.e. diverting others while aiming for the 'high ground'); success depends upon relative power and capabilities; some decentralization is advantageous to achieve speed of response.
4   Turbulent field:
    • dynamic unpredictable environment, driven by continuous societal and technological change emanating from the contextual environment; increasingly salient linkages between relevant contextual variables, and between these and events (labelled by Emery and Trist as 'L22') drive uncertainty; due to unpredictability optimization is no longer an option; organizational stability is in question – you cannot survive simply through your own actions;
    • the way in which players escape the paralysing influence of turbulence is by adopting a code of behaviour to which a significant number of players can subscribe; emergence of values (commandments, codes, coping mechanisms) that have overriding significance for all players;
    • winning strategy → creation of institutions whose role is to define and protect generally applicable behavioural codes, designed to divert turbulence; inter-organizational matrices, collaborative endeavours, sanctioning bodies.

The McCann and Selsky variant

In their seminal paper, Emery and Trist (1965) provide for the first time a precise definition of turbulence in terms of the causal texture creating it. They illustrate this by referring to a case example related to agricultural reform in the UK during the 1960s. The following is one of the possible interpretations of that case. In the case discussion, it becomes clear that Emery and Trist see turbulence as an objective reality of the given environment, and consideration of any strategic response starts from that point. This leads to 'active–adaptive' coping strategies (Emery, 1976) based on action levers within the immediate control of the actors, leading to sharing of values and behavioural institutionalization of mutual collaboration, as discussed above. These aim at reducing turbulence not in the given contextual environment, but on the playing field, by creating one or more actionable 'islands' of relative placidity where the players (or stakeholders) can anticipate and gain sufficient control to move forward on a longer-term basis. Policy then reverts to 'planning a campaign', the approach appropriate for 'disturbed–reactive' environments. In the battle for survival, these code-based organizations win out over others, which try (and fail) to find a viable strategy on their own in the turbulence they find themselves in.

McCann and Selsky (1984) have argued that turbulence can be experienced differently by different actors in the same field. The perception of the individual actor may or may not map with reality. Different observers will come to different conclusions as to the nature of the environment observed depending upon their 'perceived adaptive capacity' (Chapter 10 in this volume explores this in greater detail). An observer may experience the environment as turbulent, even if, objectively, the environment is disturbed/reactive (of course, the opposite is possible too). This may happen if people lack understanding of the entire field of L22 relationships and therefore perceive these as chaotic. Even experienced observers may suffer from this lack of understanding of the L22 if they analyse only a part of the total multifaceted causal texture.

If the experience of turbulence is subjective, then there is the possibility, in principle, of reducing turbulence by developing a more comprehensive understanding of the L22. McCann and Selsky's (1984) view provides space in the turbulent world for scenario planning, providing decision-makers with a sense-making tool in order to gain understanding of what seems chaotic at first sight. Scenario planners consider it productive to invest in analysing the environment in order to bring out its more stable L22 relationships (see Chapter 12 in this volume). Through enhanced systemic understanding, the complexity and unwieldiness of the perceived L22 relationships are minimized, uncertainty is reduced and, as a consequence, perceived turbulence diminishes and a more placid model, such as 'disturbed/reactive', is experienced. This requires that the whole L22 scene is considered involving all disciplinary perspectives on the situation. The role of scenario planning is to help decision-makers increase their perceived adaptive capacity. Arguably, the enhanced mental model of the situation provided by the scenario process helps the decision-makers to mobilize the appropriate kinds of resources (collectively?) in order to cope in the immediate situation. These resources can include new institutions that 'define and protect' new behavioural codes. With enhanced understanding, the experienced salience of L22 diminishes and the environment becomes less turbulent.

At first sight, the views of Emery and Trist and McCann and Selsky may seem contradictory, with Emery and Trist seeing codes emerge as an evolutionary process, while McCann and Selsky perceive room for collaborative proactivity by players in the turbulent environment. We don't think there is necessarily a conflict if we make the distinction between micro- and macro-perspectives. While at the micro-level, players may decide and act to the best of their ability, the question of which models will eventually survive at the macro-level may simultaneously be interpreted as being driven by autonomous evolutionary forces ('survival of the fittest').

In this chapter we have used a case study to illustrate dealing with a shared environment, experienced as turbulent by multiple actors, through scenario analysis. In the footsteps of Emery and Trist, we have selected a case study relating to agricultural reform in order to illustrate the causal texture perspective. During the project, the scenario team gradually came to recognize the overriding importance of a limited number of key variables in determining the overall L22 situation. Whether the situation was eventually understood well enough to characterize the situation as having reverted to a disturbed–reactive environment that could be tackled by the principle of 'planning a campaign' remains a moot point. Eventually, history will reveal whether turbulence was reduced enough for this to become an option for the policy-makers.

Background to the scenario project

The Indian agricultural sector is now in a state of turbulence, as argued below, and it is extremely difficult, if not impossible, for most players to decide on their optimal strategy. According to Emery and Trist, it is only through the eventual development of a shared code of practice that this situation can be resolved.

In the scenario project described here, we explored four different scenarios, each with its own unique value set stabilizing the Indian turbulent agricultural business environment and allowing its players to transition into a more placid 'protected island' in which they can develop a viable strategy.

Origins of the project

For many years, the World Bank has been involved with the government of India in funding agricultural development. Recently, this has taken the form of the National Agricultural Technology Project, the most current in a series of projects that have been spectacularly successful in making India essentially self-sufficient in feeding its population. To consolidate the gains of this programme and to face contemporary challenges facing the industry, the government of India and the World Bank agreed to undertake a new National Agricultural Innovation Project (NAIP). The scenario project discussed here is part of the development and negotiation of the NAIP.

The agricultural sector in India is subject to dramatic change. Some factors such as population growth, improved incomes and shifting dietary patterns are diversifying demand patterns. Agriculture is also increasingly demand and market driven. At the same time, the national resource base underpinning agriculture in India is under serious threat. While it is clear that agricultural systems need to reform, it is less evident what viability entails now and in the future.

The environment can be argued to be turbulent as many new and stronger interrelationships in the contextual environment are becoming salient to the players. Examples of trends being driven by these new relationships include increased and unexpected new demands on limited resources (e.g. water, agricultural land, other), new exposure to global forces as India opens its borders to international competition, and the increasing exposure of traditional regulatory structures to newly emerging powerful players (see below). These forces are linked in complex ways that are only partly understood. For example, increased exposure to global forces is affecting the traditional regulatory structure and stimulating new players to develop fundamentally new regulatory structures.

Such relationships can be usefully studied using scenario planning. This approach was used in order to address many of the uncertainties and to inform the negotiations going on in parallel with regard to the NAIP. The project also aimed at enabling participants to develop a shared perspective.

Participants and their interests

The main stakeholders in the project were the government of India (including the Ministry of Agriculture and the India Council for Agricultural Research) and the World Bank. However, from the outset, it was decided that this project needed to become a 'strategic conversation' (van der Heijden, 2005) among a wide range of interests in rural and agricultural issues. It was agreed that in order to be successful, the project required the participation of high-level officials, farm leaders, senior leaders from the private and public sectors, non-governmental organization leaders, donor representatives, experts on agricultural development and a number of 'generalists'. The scenario-building process was managed jointly by the World Bank's Agriculture and Rural Development group and the India Council for Agricultural Research.

A group of some 30 people then engaged in developing the scenarios. In addition to agricultural experts, the group included economists, experts in law, rural development, international trade, sustainable development, information systems, socio-economic change, water management and women issues. A few journalists with a special interest in this area were invited to participate.

The scenario process

The complete process covered an elapsed time of 22 months, from September 2004 until July 2006. It was designed as an iterative approach, in which sense-making of collected data alternated with in-depth research of the arising issues. In broad terms, the project comprised the following steps:

- interviewing across a wide range of stakeholders;
- first scenario-building iteration;
- scenario presentations to stakeholders (for critique and learning);
- formulation of key research question;
- research with experts;
- second scenario-building iteration.

Implications were starting to come out loud and clear from the second iteration, informing the shaping of the NAIP project. When the negotiations concerning NAIP were brought to a successful conclusion, the formal part of the scenario project was also brought to an end. Since then, several stakeholders have used the results to engage a wider audience in consultations in order to explore future policy issues.

The event that shaped the outcome most was the first scenario workshop, in which some 30 participants jointly developed the first set of scenarios. A fairly conventional approach was adopted, consisting of brainstorming for driving forces, followed by categorizing, prioritizing and clustering, leading to identification of two key scenario dimensions as the basis of a two-by-two matrix, allowing the development of story lines in each of the four resulting quadrants.

In light of the need for a wide-angle view specified for the project, the team selected two key scenario dimensions at a high conceptual level, one relating to the Indian economy and one relating to the social structure of Indian society. The economic forces were labelled as ranging from 'controlled' to 'commercialized', and the societal forces were labelled as ranging from 'cohesive/concern for equity' to 'individualistic/personal resilience'. These then gave rise to a matrix structure in which four scenarios could be fitted, as shown in Figure 6.1. Participants then

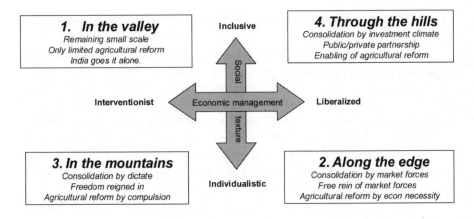

Figure 6.1 Scenarios framework

identified and examined a large number of possible future events and allocated the most salient to one of the scenarios. From these they then developed story lines that provided a causal explanation for the underlying developments in the logic of the relevant quadrant. Causal loop influence diagrams were drawn up to articulate the underlying dynamics of the scenarios, ensuring internal consistency over time of the story lines and highlighting the key strands in each.

The emerging key issue: Scale

The core team then developed a presentation of the results of the workshop and delivered this in formal and informal settings to a wide range of people and institutions in India. Audiences were invited to think critically about what was being said and to give their opinions, particularly on elements that they considered doubtful for whatever reason. These points were carefully collected by the core team, to be used as input to the research phase of the project and the second-generation scenario building.

During this consultation phase, one particular message emerged increasingly clearly. This was related to the level of productivity of agriculture in India. With the closer integration of the Indian economy with the rest of the world and the increasing importance of India's competitive position, the main emphasis in agriculture would gradually shift from self-sufficiency to productivity, building India's competitive advantage. National productivity in India is overwhelmingly influenced by agriculture upon which more than two-thirds of the population relies for their living. And current agricultural productivity is comparatively low, mostly due to low farm productivity. For example, McKinsey and Company (Beardsley and Farrell, 2005) estimates that current levels are lower than 20 per cent of farm productivity in Europe and the US, and less than half the productivity level of Brazil's.

Farming in a state of criticality

McKinsey and Company blames the poor productivity performance of India's agricultural sector on what it calls 'harmful government regulations'. India has a comparatively elaborate and complex set of rules regulating agriculture, mostly designed to keep the majority of its farmers from poverty. During the consultation phase, the team learned that poverty is a consequence of low productivity. And the main reason for the low productivity in Indian agriculture is lack of scale.

Farmland is privately owned in India. The average farm measures less than 1.5ha, two-thirds are 1ha or less. What is more, year-on-year average farm size is still coming down, with some holdings being split when ownership moves from one generation to the next. As a consequence, the great majority of farmers are poor and cannot invest in improving their productivity. The industry is stuck in a vicious circle from which it is extremely difficult to escape. With so many living on the edge of viability, the government has no alternative to stepping in whenever unforeseen circumstances drive segments of the farming population below the breadline. The system seems in a constant state of criticality (Bak et al, 1988). The alleviation of one problem, such as the recent escalation in energy prices, leaves the sector only to await the next problem. Over the years this has led to an expanding patchwork of regulations, subsidies and support arrangements which, once created, are extremely difficult to remove. A regulatory structure has rigidified and seems stuck in its place, with more and more farmers relying on the government for their survival.

This feedback proved a challenging situation for the scenario planners. While attempts were made during the workshop to come up with imaginative breakthrough stories, most commentators had problems with the plausibility of the resulting scenarios. On the other hand, most people agreed that if nothing changes, India cannot continue with its current project to open up to the rest of the world and take off economically. This was also considered unpalatable by most commentators, driving home the conundrum facing the country.

The debate is an important one for the country, its agricultural interests and its policy-makers as the long-term economic performance of the country as a whole depends upon it. To facilitate this 'strategic discussion', the scenario team adopted a number of key insights from this consultation phase and reformulated the scenarios to fall in line with the most strongly dominant ideas. The need to improve productivity through scale enlargement as a precondition for economic take-off was put to centre stage. The resulting stories are a careful balance between the dynamic needs of the future and maintaining plausibility in a current system that does not seem to have much room for manoeuvre.

While the scenario group managed to hold on to the overall structure originally developed in the first-generation scenario workshop (including the scenario names; see Figure 6.1), the stories themselves became substantially modified during the consultation phase.

Storytelling in India: Second-generation scenarios

In this section we report on the final set of scenarios that resulted from this process. The World Bank (Rajalahti et al, 2006) has published a report on this project in the public domain that contains a detailed description of the final result. We summarize it here.

Following the decision to put economies of scale at the centre of the scenarios, the set as a whole was reconfigured as follows. 'Valley' is the scenario in which current rigidities prevail and operational consolidation does not happen, as a result of which productivity does not improve and economic growth fizzles out. The other three scenarios describe different paths towards consolidation of the farming sector, in three fundamentally different ways: through market forces in the 'edge' scenario; through government dirigisme in the 'mountains' scenario; and through enabling policies and investment climate in the 'hills' scenario. A short vignette of each scenario as it emerged from the discussions is offered below.

Valley

In this scenario, the benefits of economic growth continue to bypass the two-thirds of the population depending upon agriculture for their living. With the increasing gap between rich and poor, the current pockets of unrest start to escalate. While the state of unsettlement continues, the call for a more equitable division of wealth starts to dominate political discourse. Protectionism is seen as the way forward as it is becoming accepted that India must give priority to protecting small-scale local activity, even if it is uncompetitive on a global basis. The desire to maintain order in society results in a societal preparedness to accept a significant degree of government intervention in its economic affairs. The price paid is a considerable slowing down of economic growth. India goes it alone.

Having considered the scenario in which India fails to get to grips with the big issues in the agricultural scene, we then developed three other scenarios in which the major issue is overcome, albeit in three different ways.

Edge

This scenario assumes that economic development becomes the number one priority, and significant inequity is allowed to exist as a powerful incentive for farmers to increase their productivity. The scenario explores how far such a view could be taken before inequity becomes intolerable enough for the dominant opinion in the country to cause the state to intervene and to moderate the worst excesses of market power. The question explored is how far things are allowed to develop before government intervention becomes inevitable to alleviate the suffering of those at the bottom of society who cannot keep up. This is a story about the societal limits to market-driven development and growth.

Mountains

In this scenario we explore the potential consequences of major upheavals and crises in the contextual environment, such as the geopolitical sphere (conflicts with Pakistan and China), climate change (escalating disasters), the world economy (worldwide crisis), and so on. In this scenario, Indian society calls for a return to 'strong government' as its reaction. Enhanced productivity is seen as the way of surviving in this uncertain world and the key in the context of this project is consolidation of farming in order to enhance economies of scale. It becomes legitimate for government to forcibly move people out of agriculture into more productive activities, preferably in a local rural setting, but, if necessary, also by migration into urban centres. After a period of very serious difficulties, central government takes hold of the situation and turns things around. The scenario explores the costs and the potential positive effects of such a strong government.

Hills

In this scenario, concern for cohesion and equity remains strong, but it is balanced with the desire to create incentives for productivity improvements through market forces. This scenario explores the potential of combining government intervention with freeing up market forces. The two objectives seem contradictory, particularly if the system experiences unexpected external shocks, and choices have to be made. In this scenario cohesion wins out in such circumstances; but in the long run a powerful base for a successful market economy is created. Central in this story is the management by government of the internal investment climate.

In a way, all of these scenarios skate along the edge of what is, or is not, acceptable in Indian society, both in terms of equity and government intervention. These are not very well-defined boundaries and the idea of storytelling through scenarios is powerful in terms of the possibility that it offers to explore such issues (see also Chapter 11 in this volume). We found that, listening carefully to comments on our scenarios, there seemed to be some degree of consensus among our commentators on what were plausible and implausible stories, even if people seemed hard put to venture into defining such limits without this story-based structure.

The scenarios interpreted as causal textures:
Values developing in the Indian turbulent environment

Emery and Trist argue that in a turbulent environment, as was experienced at the current time in Indian agriculture, people can cope by adhering to codes of behaviour based on shared value sets. If the four scenarios presented are alternative ways out of the current dilemmas, the question arises: what value sets emerge in each of these and how effective might these be in moving the sector away from turbulence into a more placid environment?

The 'valley' scenario illustrates an Indian economic system that becomes entirely overwhelmed by turbulence and, as a consequence, finds it impossible to get to grips with the big agricultural issues staring it in the face. It sees no alternative than to disengage from the global system and essentially gives up economic take-off as a consequence. By closing off the system, turbulence is shut out and internally a more placid environment is created ('placid random', with an element of 'clustered', as some resources would be located in identifiable parts of the field). The value set giving rise to such a strategy is based on the idea of sacrificing wealth for equity (justice-based ethical reasoning).

The 'edge' scenario contrasts with 'valley' in that it recreates a 'placid' environment, on the edge between 'placid random' and 'placid clustered', for a system that is open to the world. This sounds like a contradiction in a world where people see turbulence in the colloquial sense all around them; but Emery and Trist show how an open and free market can approximate a placid environment, with market forces and price-setting capturing salient L22 relations and therefore localizing the contextual environment. This therefore requires an accelerated removal of current regulations and interventions in the economy, and agriculture, in particular, and relying on market forces to regulate the economy. The value set driving this in this scenario is based on the idea of faster progress through self-reliance and personal choice in preference to cohesion and equity (utilitarian ethics). Exploration of this scenario proves useful in showing the major value issues arising and the consequent limits to what appears at first sight to be getting the best of both worlds: rapid development and a placid environment. The social acceptability of such a scenario became a major issue in the subsequent scenario discussions.

The 'mountain' scenario illustrates recreating a 'placid clustered' environment for an open system through the exercise of power. Central power removes turbulence by allocating to everyone their rightful place and due in a controlled environment (rights-based ethical reasoning). A value set that makes that possible in the Indian political context could only emerge in the face of major catastrophe. Therefore, this scenario is the story of major and escalating disasters, including the effects of escalating climate change. The value set is based on bundling power in the collective in the face of unexpected and unmanageable conditions.

The 'hills' scenario illustrates recreating a 'disturbed–reactive' environment through policy-making based on increasing value-sharing. It is disturbed/reactive in that players need to deal with comparable competitors in order to get to their 'high ground'. Policy-making at various levels is based on creating 'campaigns', not only by market participants as a business strategy, but also by government in order to create an attractive investment climate in which these business strategies can be made to work. The main value pursued here is the right for everyone across the population to have opportunities and incentives to develop and grow (community-based ethics). In the context of agriculture, the value focuses on policies to create remunerative alternative employment in the rural areas through the development of an attractive positive investment climate. The underlying shared value is the desire to pull together in the interest of avoiding the worst excesses of under-privilege and acknowledgement of everyone's personal responsibility in this as a distinctive Indian approach to the situation.

In summary, each of the four scenarios explores a different value set. In broad terms:

1   valley: justice-based ethics sacrificing wealth for equity;
2   edge: utilitarian ethics sacrificing equity for self-reliance and personal choice;
3   mountains: rights-based ethics centralizing power in the light of major catastrophe;
4   hills: communitarian ethics decentralizing individual responsibility for the joint project.

The results of the scenario project strongly suggests that, following Emery and Trist's argument, Indian society will eventually evolve a set of institutionalized behavioural codes based on traditional Indian values, but remoulded for the global environment of the 21st century.[1] Forging the shared codes will lead to active adaptation. Strategic conversation will help this process along. The four value systems in the four scenarios are outcomes of possible, but different, co-evolutionary processes, based on maintaining traditions and disengaging from the world (in 'valley'), or adopting imported value systems developed elsewhere in other circumstances (in 'edge' and 'mountains'), or developing India's distinctive response to the challenges of the turbulent environment (in 'hills').

In his 2007 Independence Day speech, the Prime Minister of India cautioned Indians against hubris. 'India cannot become a nation with islands of high growth and vast areas untouched by development, where the benefits of growth accrue only to a few', said Prime Minister Singh. The tone was far more cautious than the previous year. Instead of praising the erection of 'vast industrial estates and special economic zones', as he did in 2006, he simply advised that 'we must not be overconfident'. He promised new investments in rural development, and pointed to the challenge of 'how to industrialize and move people out of the lagging agricultural sector'. 'The transition from an agrarian society to an industrial economy has always been a difficult one', Prime Minister Singh said. 'But industrialization offers new opportunities and hope, especially for people in rural areas displaced by agrarian change' (*New York Times*, 16 August 2007).

With the strategic conversation intermediating between any scenario project and possible outcomes, it will always be near to impossible for scenario planners to causally trace direct or indirect results from their work. Even so, the scenario-planning group could not help being struck by the sentiments expressed in this speech, which seemed to reflect the issues as surfaced in the scenario conversation.

During the consultation process, there could be no doubt that most people's current value preference aligned with the 'hills' scenario. However, this is also the most demanding model for the future, where accelerated learning from experience needs to take place. Accelerating this process involves widening the range of what is perceived in the environment by expressing developments and explanations in common terms, such that they become comparable. This requires an ability to look at an issue from various different perspectives simultaneously. This is not how the strategic conversation normally approaches issues, which is more akin to as quickly as possible homing in on one specific way of considering a situation. This results in a narrowing of the observation field, leading to a locking in on one single way of interpreting what is going on. An example of this is the apparent reluctance in India of discussing policy issues relating to 'consolidation in agriculture'. During the consultation phase of the scenario project, we found that this is experienced by many participants as an attack on small farmers, something that most participants don't want to be involved in. On the other hand, the economic logic in favour of consolidation is strong, creating a tension in the minds of participants, sometimes leading to a process of denial. The tension may be particularly salient because we are considering a turbulent policy environment, requiring developments in a shared 'code of conduct' based on an alignment in society around a new value set that cuts across traditional power positions, often based on long-established relationships. The agricultural lobby is powerful in most countries. It is not surprising that in a country such as India, where more than two-thirds of the population live in rural areas, this is clearly evident.

The experience of the scenario research group was that introduction of alternative perspectives through the scenario approach through which various ways forward became visible seemed to defuse this tension in the stakeholder consultation group. This made it possible to introduce the issue in the strategic conversation, create an in-depth dialogue and reach conclusions that would otherwise be difficult to develop.

Conclusions

The following conclusions summarize the discussion above.

Relating to the content of the project

1   It became clear during the project that the way forward is not predetermined; the trajectory for the Indian agricultural sector remains unclear and is still to be forged. The current trajectory is unsustainable; thus, something will happen to alter it. The environment is complex and very salient, creating the 'high relevant uncertainty' that Emery and Trist said characterizes the turbulent field.
2   India needs to deal with the turbulence in its agricultural business environment, which could potentially derail the economic take-off that the country is currently experiencing.
3   Moving to a more placid environment requires the emergence of a new shared value set/code of behaviour fit for the 21st century. The project revealed several value sets that could come into being, based on experience in India and elsewhere. It is unlikely that models developed elsewhere will serve the needs of the country without major adaptation; but they need to be studied. Updating of its own value set will require a process of accelerated learning and intense negotiation.
4   Whatever value set emerges, it will only be effective if it accommodates the need for large-scale agricultural consolidation, which is now urgent.

Relating to the context of the project

1   This project, although not originally conceived in a 'causal texture' context, nevertheless can be successfully interpreted *ex post* using Emery and Trist's depiction of the turbulent field and how to deal with it. In doing so, it renders support for the causal textures theory. Adding the conceptual tool of causal textures and adaptive responses deepens the learning derived from the scenario exercise. It helps to explain why scenarios are valuable – they enable visualization of paths to a more sustainable (i.e. more placid) future.
2   A scenario-planning approach can be an effective way of exploring the value-based issues associated with Emery and Trist's concept of turbulence.
3   Can scenario planning on its own inspire actors to take action to alleviate the experience of turbulence and transform it into a more placid texture? It remains a moot point. But at least it can make a useful contribution in starting to move entrenched mental models.

Note

1   Theoretically, the survival of the agrarian sector is not a foregone conclusion. McCann and Selsky (1984) would offer a fifth scenario: increasing disorder that threatens the existence of Indian agriculture as a sector (millions die, social upheaval, etc.). Unlike in 'mountains', the state does not intervene and the sector advances into a hyper-turbulent environment. However, such a scenario would be considered totally implausible by most, if not all, contributors to the research phase whom we met. In scenario methodology, this would invalidate it and it would be dropped.

References

Bak, P., Tang, C. and Wiesenfeld, K. (1988) 'Self-organized criticality', *Physical Review A*, vol 38, no 1, pp364–374

Beardsley, S. and Farrell, D. (2005) 'Regulation that's good for competition', *The McKinsey Quarterly*, no 2, pp49–59

Emery, F. (1976) *Futures We Are In*, Martinus-Nijhoff, Leiden

Emery, F. and Trist, E. (1965) 'The causal texture of organizational environments', *Human Relations*, vol 18, pp21–32

McCann, J. and Selsky, J. (1984) 'Hyperturbulence and the emergence of type 5 environments', *Academy of Management Review*, vol 9, no 4, pp460–470

Rajalahti, R., Van der Heijden, K., Janssen, W. and Pehu, E. (2006) *Scenario Planning to Guide Long-Term Investments in Agricultural Science and Technology*, World Bank, Washington, DC

Van der Heijden, K (2005) *Scenarios: The Art of Strategic Conversation*, 2nd edition, John Wiley and Sons, Chichester, UK

7

Swarm Planning: A New Design Paradigm Dealing with Long-Term Problems Associated with Turbulence

Rob E. Roggema

Introduction

In this chapter I discuss the role of spatial design in The Netherlands in its struggle with the consequences of climate change as an example of coping with turbulence.

The world is facing substantial and uncertain climate changes. The processes that influence these changes are contextual, diffuse and can only be understood over the longer term. It is a typical example of what Emery and Trist (1965) have called turbulence (see Chapter 2 in this volume). Coping with turbulence asks for a new planning strategy to anticipate future developments, while at the same time retaining a flexible stance to cope with irreducible uncertainty.

The urge for a new planning paradigm is nothing new. Spatial design methods tend to respond to the changing requirements of society. The requirements of today involve an environment of increasing contextual complexity, in which it has become difficult to define the interventions needed to achieve goals. With the traditional and often single-discipline design methods available, we are unable to give sufficient answers to challenges of longer timeframes and higher complexity associated with turbulence. Climate change is an example of this. This chapter discusses the question of how to define or invent a new design approach able to meet these current needs. I will illustrate conclusions reached by referring to a case study of tackling the issue in the province of Groningen, The Netherlands.

A short history of spatial design paradigms

The history of spatial planning in The Netherlands shows a clear sequence of views emerging in response to the needs of the times (Emden, 1985). Over time, planning paradigms change, steered by trends and developments in society. This section explores the connection between spatial design and the dynamics of the 'environment', following Emery and Trist's (1965) categorization of causal texture and the issues involved in predicting future connections. The different eras described here are placed in the Dutch context of design. They do not represent eras in other countries and/or other times. For instance, one can imagine that developments in France or North America show the same sequence, but are, due to specific local situations and history, placed in different timeframes. The different eras are distinguished by their varying textures. And these textures create different contexts for designers, who wish to adopt the appropriate design paradigms to deal with the different textures.

Placid, randomized planning: End of the 19th to the beginning of the 20th century

A placid, randomized environment is defined as follows (Emery and Trist, 1965): 'The simplest type of environmental texture is that in which goals and noxiants ("goods" and "bads") are relatively unchanging in themselves and randomly distributed' (see Chapter 2). At the end of the 19th century, spatial design tended to be a somewhat random affair, in which some centres of excellence could be distinguished, but where most of the time there was no design at all (Neuwirth, 2005). In order to tackle increasingly severe problems in cities (e.g. pollution and disease), the urge to make laws and regulations (1901 Housing Law; 1904 Education Law) increased. Society, on the whole, was prepared to accept that an elite made the decisions for the rest of the population.

By the end of the 19th century, modern comprehensive planning emerged for the first time in The Netherlands. Apart from comprehensive planning of trade and military cities such as Elburg (end 14th century) and Bourtange (late 16th century), centralized and comprehensive spatial design was uncommon.

The Baronielaan in Breda (see Figure 7.1) is an early example of modern comprehensive planning: the development of a whole street as one project (Duijghuisen, 1990; Sectie D, 1997). The development of the Vondelpark in Amsterdam and its surroundings presents strong similarities with this development. During this period, the first urban designs for entire cities were initiated. The city of The Hague hired Berlage as its 'city architect'. He drew up a carefully designed urban pattern for the entire city. The design was equally and randomly spread over the area bounded by the city borders without specific clustering. It marks the end of an era and a transformation to the next phase in design.

Placid, clustered planning: 1920 to 1950

Chapter 2 gives the following definition of a placid, clustered environment (Emery and Trist, 1965): 'which can be characterized in terms of clustering: goals

Source: Duijghuisen (1990)

Figure 7.1 Baronielaan, Breda, The Netherlands

and noxiants are not randomly distributed but hang together in certain ways'. This causal texture became relevant when planning and design started to gain importance. The Garden Cities Movement (Howard, 1902) initiated thinking about how and where people should live. Centrally planned villages were placed in concentrated, fully self-contained areas, where health and well-being played a major role (see Figure 7.2) in designs based on the best available techniques. The design principle adopted was to construct an end-state image of a harmonious and healthy society of the future. A placid causal texture ensured the best location for urban developments.

Disturbed–reactive planning: 1960 to 1970

A disturbed–reactive environment is defined as follows (Emery and Trist, 1965): 'it is an environment in which there is more than one organization of the same kind... The existence of a number of similar organizations now becomes the dominant characteristic.' At this stage of the history of spatial planning, an

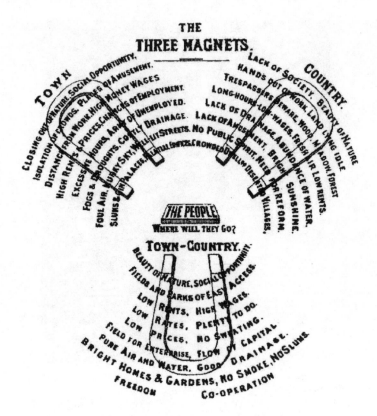

Source: Howard (1902)

Figure 7.2 The three magnets: Ebenezer Howard's garden cities of tomorrow

increasing number of influential stakeholders (action groups, social housing corporations, etc.) comment critically on the centrally planned future. During the early stages of this period, a strong belief in technocratic end-state images of a wealthy future evolved in the form of high-rise building parks with separation of functions. The International Congress of Modern Architecture (CIAM) – an international city planners' movement, which dates back to the 1920s – became the leading voice in the world of urban designers and planners. Rebuilding Holland after World War II came to a climax in the development of the Bijlmer, an extension of Amsterdam, where extreme separation of functions is designed in (see Figure 7.3). But a new development saw people starting to react against these designs, which found less and less support in the community. In response to that, planners started to build scenarios to widen the bandwidth of future predictions. In the end, however, the planning system still comes up with a fixed design for

Figure 7.3 Bijlmer, Amsterdam

the future, not paying sufficient attention to future needs, aims and ambitions in society.

Turbulent planning: 1980 to 1990

A turbulent environment is defined as follows (Emery and Trist, 1965): 'The dynamic properties arise not simply from the interaction of the component organizations, but also from the ground itself. The "ground" is in motion.' During this period, everything was in a state of flux as a consequence of the democratization of the urban design process. Everyone with an interest, or even without, participated in deliberations about the future. Parties talked endlessly about details, down to the colour of the flowers in the nearest flowerpot. The aim of design was to shape an environment as close as possible to the wishes of the people. This led to what became known as the *Bloemkool* (cauliflower) neighbourhoods: designs with endlessly winding roads in which the streets are intended to be places in which to live and play instead of traffic conduits. This bottom-up process gives priority to making everyone happy over giving areas a distinct identity. Politics became a talking machine aimed at producing compromises. The design environment was characterized by a lot of uncertainty, based on contrasting opinions, which needed to be taken seriously, but could not always be united.

Vortical planning: 1990 to 2010

The vortical environment is defined as follows (Babüroğlu, 1988): 'the prevalence of stalemate, polarization and monothematic dogmatism ... leads to a frozen or a clinched order of connectedness as well as that of unevenly dynamic turbulent conditions'. Nowadays, severe problems characterized by their unprecedented complex contextual nature, such as climate change, call for immediate action in order to solve problems occurring in the (far) future. However, existing political structures and decision-making systems find their origin in earlier, more placid, environments. The habit that systems have of reproducing themselves, the repetitive patterns of working methods, accepted political behaviour and power-based systems are ill prepared to respond to the needs of the new turbulent environment. It seems almost impossible to step out of this cluster of characteristics. It appears that everyone is sucked into a vortex of unwritten rules and role assumptions, unable to escape.

As predicted by Emery and Trist's (1965) causal texture theory, spatial planning in this period sees a more collaborative stance, agreements are made between developers, governments and other parties, and local governments start to work together – in content, process and realization – with key players, strategists or opinion leaders. The main concern is reaching a compromise about the content, responsibilities, investments and achievement of projects. These public–private partnerships give rise to what becomes known as 'area-oriented planning'. In this activity, certain unwritten values and rules guide the participants. The underlying agreement, which fixes the existing power balances, leads to repetitive processes, similar solutions and non-transparent decision-making. Participants are sucked into this vortex. This has serious consequences:

- Action is often taken too late due to slow decision-making. Therefore, anticipating expected situations is difficult (see Chapter 8 in this volume for a similar situation in southern Sweden).
- Existing and well-known political systems are the standard. People know how these systems work, so they continue to use them. These systems inevitably produce average solutions and proposals.
- People inside this arena become immune to signals from outside. The average opinion, resulting from trying to find compromises, tends to crowd out innovative and original solutions.
- These systems tend to reproduce themselves and become even stronger when threatened by external threats – for instance, climate change.

This way of solving problems, focused on reaching agreements, precludes tackling major problems and loses sight of the complete picture. As a result, the system becomes reactive instead of anticipatory or adaptive. And, even worse, because the whole picture is too complex for individual people to overview, they focus on only a segment of information as the basis for their decisions: the start of new problems (see Chapter 5 in this volume on how these tipping points come about).

At the same time, the new intractable and interconnected problems that the world faces have a long time horizon. Emery and Trist (1965) suggest that they are the result of a new set of indirect and unpredictable interactions in the contextual environment. The traditional set of political constellations does not have the power or the insight to anticipate the coming complex difficulties related to this. Consequently, attention tends to concentrate on single issues, such as income politics or specific conflicts and wars. As a result, taking the right measures now to adapt to the new issues such as climate change in the future is difficult. A new paradigm will, and has to, emerge in which the fixed constellations are broken. In this paradigm, a collaborative approach cannot be the whole story. Design within a vortical texture is also topical: coming up with the right impulse at the right moment (again, see Chapter 5).

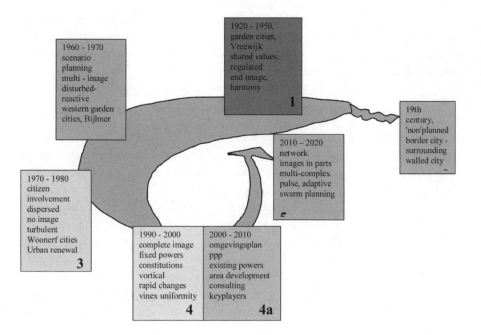

Source: Roggema (2005b)

Figure 7.4 The spiral of planning

The 'spiral of planning' (see Figure 7.4) shows a clear parallel between the findings of Emery and Trist (1965) and the developments in society and spatial design. In response to the contextually complex problems that the world is facing, requiring focus on future actions, a new design paradigm – adapting to current developments in society – is likely to emerge. Extrapolation of the spiral into the future will give an insight into the characteristics of this future design paradigm. The traditional paradigm with its centrally controlled and fixed picture of the future will be left behind and will be replaced with one that contains more room for specific area-oriented developments, where the influence of people is able to give rise to a more flexible paradigm. The future complexity of society and its problems requires a planning paradigm of a higher order in which a spatial intervention is able to change the entire regional spatial system, which we have called the swarm paradigm (Jacobs and Roggema, 2005). Before we discuss this in more detail, we consider recent developments in spatial design methods in the Dutch province of Groningen, providing us with a real-world background against which the swarm paradigm may be explained and understood.

Climate change scenarios: The Groningen case study

We now have a number of different types of climate change scenarios available to examine. On the one hand, scientific scenarios aim to predict the future within certain boundaries, and, on the other hand, more qualitative climate change scenarios are intended as a basis for policies and decisions on spatial measures. The Groningen example will illustrate how the latter can be used.

Scientific scenarios: KNMI

The Intergovernmental Panel on Climate Change (IPCC) collects recent scientific data every five to ten years and publishes it in a periodic assessment. The Fourth Assessment (IPCC, 2007) was finalized in 2007. The Netherlands are represented in the IPCC by the Royal Dutch Meteorological Institute (KNMI) and the Dutch Environment Assessment Agency (MNP). The IPCC scenarios are translated for The Netherlands by the KNMI into four climate scenarios for the year 2050 (KNMI, 2006). The scenarios – moderate, changed moderate, warm and changed warm – describe the changes in temperature (1°C to 2°C) and the possible fluctuations in air patterns, which might lead to wetter winter periods and dryer summer periods (see Figure 7.5). Corresponding with these scenarios are significant changes in sea level (between 15cm and 35cm in 2050) (Dorland and Jansen, 2006).

On the other hand, the future may be rather different. David Carlson, scientific director of the International Polar Year (IPY), considers such a different

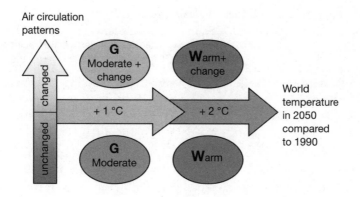

Schematic overview of the four KNMI'06 climate scenarios.

Source: KNMI (2006)

Figure 7.5 Four climate scenarios for The Netherlands

future plausible. In an interview with a national newspaper (Carlson, 2006) he states that it might be possible that the upcoming century will see the sea level rise by 10m, caused by an accelerated melting of glaciers in Greenland and Western Antarctica.

Robustness scenarios: Groningen

To discuss future trends affecting the province of Groningen, climate change scenarios are used in a different way, focusing on the definition of an integrated spatial policy.

Starting point: Two scenarios

To start with, the KNMI scenarios were combined into one warm scenario with changed air patterns. A second scenario is based on the accelerated melting of the land ice in Greenland and Antarctica (Roggema, 2007). This scenario is found to be less realistic by the IPCC; but polar research scientists (Carlson, 2006; Hacquebord, 2007) consider the latter scenario closer to reality than the KNMI scenarios. Both scenarios are defined for 2050. Table 7.1 summarizes the key indicators.

Table 7.1 *Scenarios for 2050*

	Royal Dutch Meteorological Institute (KNMI) scenario	Accelerated melting land ice scenario
Precipitation: spring and autumn	+20%	+30%
Precipitation: summer	–20%	–40%
Precipitation: winter	+15%	+30%
Temperature	+1.5°C	+3.0°C
Sea-level rise	+35cm	+150cm

Source: Roggema (2007)

Implications for Groningen

Climate change has been, until now, researched at the global and national level. At the regional scale, uncertainties are huge and research is just being started. For the province of Groningen, three key factors, crucial for spatial functions, are researched: precipitation, temperature and sea-level rise.

The summer will become much drier. The peat colonies, in particular, will have to face water shortages. During these dry periods, it will be necessary to supply water to dried-out areas. Higher temperatures and an increase in evaporation will drive up water demand in summer even further. On the other hand, occasional rains will be much heavier. In autumn and spring, precipitation will increase. In the northern parts of the province, in and around the city of Groningen and in other urban areas, this will cause urban floods. The surplus of rainwater may be discharged towards storage areas. This requires space.

An important question will be whether agriculture and nature can withstand the dry summer period. Will potato production be able to reach the necessary level to supply the local starch industry, which is prominent in the area? The absence of water is a main factor; but the lengthening of the growing season – due to early higher temperatures – needs to be taken into account. Will nature be able to overcome the dry summer? The wet to dry gradients will especially create vulnerability at the edges of brooks and small and isolated ecological reserves. Rising temperatures, however, will offer opportunities for leisure and tourism.

The sea level is rising in both scenarios, and the extent to which this occurs will depend upon the speed of the melting processes of land ice. Potential impact upon the landscape if the sea enters the land undisturbed is shown in Figure 7.6.

In reality, the landscape contains several obstacles (e.g. roads and small dikes), which will reduce flooding of the land. On the other hand, the impact maps of Figure 7.6 do not take into account the circumstances under which a breech of the water defences would normally take place – combining spring tide with heavy rain and wind. In the highest parts of the province, the risk of flooding is minimal. Only if sea level rises more than 3m will these areas be in danger. The northern

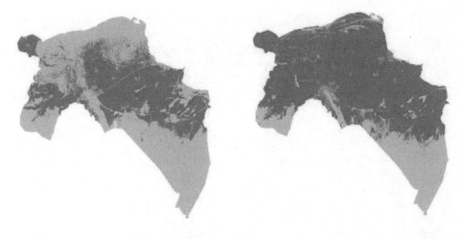

Note: Darker grey indicates flooded areas.
Source: Roggema (2007)

Figure 7.6 Potential impact of sea-level rise on the landscape in Groningen
(left: 35cm; right: 155cm)

parts of the province can withstand sea level rises of 1.5m. The industrial areas of Eemshaven and Delfzijl are (even in the more extreme scenarios) relatively safe due to their (artificial) higher altitudes. The lower and wetter parts of the province show a spatial connection between Lauwers Lake and Dollard. This connection might be crucial for ecological zoning because nature has the best chance to survive in these robust and wet areas.

Another effect of sea-level rise could be the disappearance of parts of the Wadden Sea sandbanks to the north. Rapid sea-level rise leads to the inability of the sedimentation process to supply sandbanks, which quickly become submerged (De Boo, 2004). It is estimated that 40 per cent of sandbanks could disappear 40 years from now.

Idea map of climate-adapted Groningen

Climate analysis leads to an idea map of a more adaptive Groningen. In Figure 7.7, the adaptation is spatially translated (Roggema, 2007). The map is a spatial image of climate design principles. The realization of functions that are valuable to the economy, such as housing, industry and infrastructure, at the safest locations (i.e. higher altitudes) is an important underlying principle. If housing or other functions are to be located in lower areas, the newest innovative techniques (floodable houses, floating houses, new artificial hills or *wierden*, or living on super dikes) will have to be used. On the other hand, the province will profit from warmer and dry summers by creating housing and recreation near nature reserves, on islands and along the coast. To cope with increased rainfall during autumn

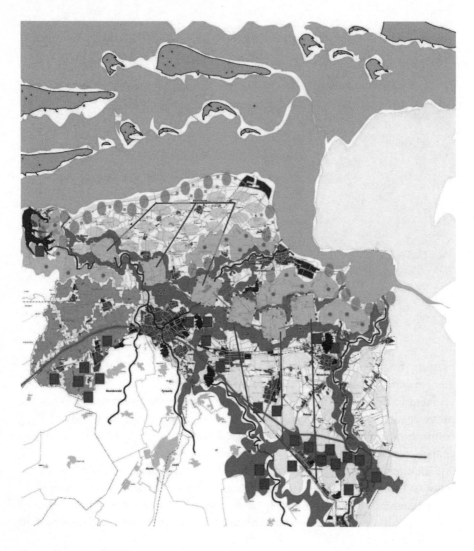

Source: Roggema (2007)

Figure 7.7 Idea map of climate-adapted Groningen, The Netherlands

and spring, water storage needs to be organized. A system that provides nature and agriculture with water during the dry summer will have to be implemented. Finally, space is required for various other functions, such as aquaculture along the saltier coast, inundation and robust ecological zones.

In autumn, winter and spring, existing brooks will discharge the surplus of rainwater into the storage reservoirs in the central lower area. Here, a robust

Source: Roggema et al (2006)

Figure 7.8 New Wadden islands in front of the northern coast

ecological network offers space for species that are pushed away from other climate zones in order to survive. The reservoirs provide agriculture with enough water in summer, making use of the existing canal system.

The coastal zone will become saltier, which makes this area suitable for aquaculture. Near Lauwers Lake, Dollard and around Delfzijl, space is created where seawater is allowed to inundate and can be periodically stored. A brackish environment emerges.

Accelerating sea-level rise places the ecosystem of the Wadden Sea at risk. To prevent the natural environment from disappearing, an offensive coastal defence system is introduced. As part of this future, new islands are created in the North Sea (Alders, 2006; Roggema et al, 2006) to protect the hinterland against heavier storms and to allow the landscape to develop by downgrading the intensity of the waves. At the same time, the islands offer an excellent opportunity to achieve luxurious living space in recreational and tourist areas. The new islands will create a lagoon, where sand easily moves through a sedimentation process and the existing sandbanks are able to catch up with the speed of sea-level rise. The sandbanks will continue to fall dry and the Wadden Sea will retain its semi-natural environment.

The introduction of new islands is an example of the new planning paradigm. It is an answer to long-term and complex problems. The islands function as an intervention that might change the whole ecosystem of the coast and the sea, affecting life in water and on land, as it makes use of the natural processes of water, wind and sea.

This is an example of swarm planning, a new paradigm that differs fundamentally from the current paradigm, in which solutions are one-dimensional, such as the heightening of dikes.

Swarm planning

Developments in society

Today a broad range of information is continuously available to everyone. An increasing number of interactions is possible and continuously occurs. These interactions determine the direction that society is taking, although it is difficult to predict how things will evolve. Issues such as climate change, which will have a major impact upon people's lives, are an illustration of how an increasing series of complex interactions, which influence each other, lead to high-impact problems: floods, drought, bushfires, deserts, melting permafrost, etc. The exact relation and effects of these interactions cannot be assessed by any single individual. People are gradually beginning to understand how a single intervention can affect the entire system, requiring multilayered thinking.

Design approach

A combination of continuous and ongoing interactions, multilayered thinking and knowledge of invisible connections will be required to deal with climate change because the indirect consequences of any intervention need to be foreseen such that the total system is able to adapt in time. The creation of new islands exemplifies this: they change the existing system, creating emerging circumstances for spectacular living, high-quality nature and coastal protection. By influencing a crucial part in the system at a carefully selected high-leverage point, the entire area changes and future effects of climate change can benefit spatial quality. Extraordinary creativity of a specialist nature (Ridderstråle and Nordström, 2004) is required to find these crucial interventions. These bright and above-average ideas will be able to help us change the way in which we live in order to adapt to climate change. If we do not anticipate long-term developments and stick to the way we usually act, finding compromises and devising substandard solutions, unsolvable problems will appear.

Innovation shift

Because society evolves, it is reasonable to assume that the planning paradigm will adjust as well. The shift that is taking place can be described as an innovation

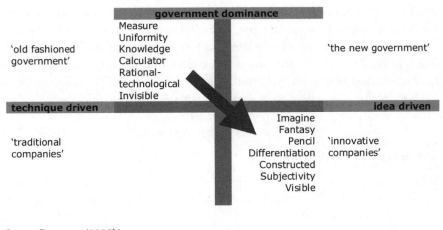

Source: Roggema (2005b)

Figure 7.9 Innovation shift

shift (see Figure 7.9). A government with strong established procedures and rules will become inert. In these circumstances, it is hardly possible for creativity and new solutions to emerge. We need to consider what can be done technologically as traditional solutions reach their limits. An innovation shift (Roggema, 2005b) brings a new arena, where exceptional talents and imaginative creativity are the main values. The role of the government is still important but has lessened – essentially in order to stimulate the emergence of ideas and to guide a network-based organization in which the idea-creating processes are embedded. Small innovative companies – able to operate flexibly, and reacting directly to fuzzy questions while distinguishing themselves with brilliant skills in solving such problems creatively – will become crucial for progress (Florida, 2005).

Swarm planning

In order to prepare society, with its endless interactions, for the future, it is necessary to bring the regional spatial design system to a higher level of complexity so that it is able to adapt better to future and unforeseen changes. In the long term, a region of higher complexity is better capable of adjusting itself to new circumstances than an inert one. In order to reach this higher level of complexity, new crucial interventions must be discovered that can change the entire regional spatial system and make it more robust. A new design paradigm, which focuses on these interventions, is therefore required. This new design paradigm can be called swarm planning (an analogy of a swarm of birds).

A swarm is transforming constantly, influenced by external impulses and directed by only a few, very simple, rules. The swarm is changing its pattern suddenly by apparent impulse: it alters its form and direction. The question is which interventions bring the swarm to a higher lever of complexity, which can be characterized as above average and which as 'multilayered thinking'. In order to consider this it is helpful to look at complex systems, especially those that are 'close to chaos' (see Chapter 5 in this volume).

Typology of complex systems

Which kind of systems are the 'playground' for new ideas on the edge between chaos and effective interventions? Systems in general can be subdivided into four categories (Wolfram, 2002):

1 closed system;
2 linear feedback systems;
3 systems randomly open to assimilation; and
4 non-linear adaptive systems.

Roo (2006) describes class IV systems (non-linear adaptive systems) as able to behave in order to maximize benefits of stability while retaining a capacity to change (Mitchell Waldrop, 1994). The question is how to interpret design projects in terms of complex systems. Roo (2006) suggests that the following aspects are relevant to create class IV systems:

• They contain a large number of interactions.
• Simple rules underpin complexity.
• Adaptation, self-organization and co-evolution are apparent.
• The design transforms and retains the project.
• Design principles are characterized by robustness, emergence and fitness for purpose.

In addition, experience shows that the subject of design is often sensitive to impulses and tipping points.

The question at this stage is which planning approaches would be most effective if the future consists of class IV system behaviour manifest in a large number of interactions. The insights of organization dynamics can be useful here. Homan (2005) suggests that improving the overall fitness of an organization requires the following conditions:

• Large groups of individual elements lead to the emergence of collective patterns under certain conditions (e.g. the amount of connections, quality of relations and network).

- There is enough diversity, but not too much to start autocatalytic processes.
- Idea interaction (Homan calls it idea sex) between different elements may lead to creative jumps where new structures and information are created.
- Co-evolution of local systems leads to the emergence of collective patterns, enhancing the overall fitness of the system.
- Complex systems manifest several co-existing patterns (patches), rather than one overall pattern or a large variety of local systems.
- Local ideas function as nuclei, eventually influencing and patronizing large parts of a complex system.

The common characteristic in the conditions described are large numbers and many interactions. There needs to be a substantial pool of elements. The chance that elements will interact is then more probable and new processes emerge increasing the overall fitness of the system.

What is missing so far is a trigger setting these processes in motion, such as a focal point that enforces the pool of interactive elements and starting the process of changing the system. These points, where 'dovecotes flutter', ultimately make things happen. Every element in the system orientates itself to these points, and by doing so the system as a whole changes. The result is an innovation coming out of a bunch of ideas. An impulse needs to be added in order to reach a tipping point.

Tipping points

The tipping point is that magic moment when an idea, trend or social behaviour crosses a threshold, tips and spreads like wildfire. The possibility of sudden change is at the centre of the idea of the tipping point. Big changes occur as a result of small events. The situation is similar to the phenomenon of an epidemic.

Epidemics follow three rules (Gladwell, 2000):

1   the law of the few: a small part of the whole does all the work (80/20);
2   the stickiness factor: the message makes an impact – it is impossible to forget;
3   the power of context: sensitivity to the environment; influence of the surroundings.

By applying these rules to planning and design, the question of when a design becomes a success, reinforcing the required changes, can be understood. First of all, the law of the few tells us that a successful design will originate from a small group of individuals. The design is not what the majority expects. In order to change things, the design will be above average (Ridderstråle and Nordström, 2004; Roggema, 2005b).

Second, the stickiness factor suggests that a successful design sticks in one's head. Once having seen the image of the design, it is not forgotten. Roberts (2005) calls it a visible love mark. A good example of this is the design for the wall in Almere Poort (see Figure 7.10) (MVRDV et al, 2001).

Finally, the power of context in relation to design processes tells us that a design with high impact provides the solution to a commonly felt problem. If a fundamental change is required, such as climate change necessitates, a widely shared context of deep trouble improves the chances of change. A sense of real urgency is required for fundamental change, and a crisis will provide the energy to jump to the new situation (Timmermans, 2004). If the existing system is inadequate, a crisis is required to jump to the next level of complexity required to upgrade the system (see Figure 7.11) (Geldof, 2002). These crises can be seen as the tipping points in design processes.

Source: MVRDV et al (2001)

Figure 7.10 The wall in Almere Poort, The Netherlands

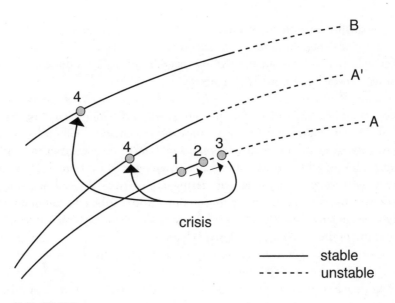

Source: Geldof (2002)

Figure 7.11 Crisis enforces the jump to a higher level

A new design paradigm

Translated in planning design terms, the effective spatial intervention creates a tipping point, orientating all spatial, societal and political elements in such a way that the entire region changes. Contemporary planning approaches do not provide this and, therefore, in the light of the problems posed by climate change, a new way of design is required. As we suggested earlier, the new spatial design paradigm is called swarm planning (Roggema, 2005b). In this paradigm, the role of spatial design is seen as introducing essential impulses to influence the whole system, like a swarm of birds reshapes itself constantly under external influences. Spatial design will no longer be concerned with the whole picture, but will focus on those essential design interventions that enforce the region to reshape itself. The metaphor is not any longer the blueprint, but acupuncture.

Thus, for a swarm-planning approach (Roggema et al, 2006) to be successful, two aspects are essential: the (spatial) characteristics of the region and the availability of extraordinary ideas. Complex systems theory suggests that the swarm paradigm will work where the following conditions are met:

- a large group of individual elements (people, buildings);
- many connections (virtual, roads, rail, water);

- high-quality relations (fast, intense);
- high-quality network (flexibility, intensity);
- enough, but not too much, diversity (neighbourhoods, groups);
- several co-existing patterns (patches).

If these circumstances entail idea mergers between different elements, this will lead to creative jumps, and new structures and information will evolve. A small group of extravagant and creative people will enforce this and transform it into a catchy idea, which influences and shapes large parts of the region. If a sense of urgency exists (e.g. regarding climate change), a suitable trigger brings the idea to a tipping point and collective patterns emerge out of the co-evolution of local systems, leading to an increased overall fitness of the system, which is able to adapt more easily to the new world of climate change.

This paradigm is not yet common; but the first examples in spatial design are there. The way in which interventions are planned in the 'Blauwe Stad' in the remote parts of Groningen Province (van der Meer, 2003), the projection of new islands along the northern coast of The Netherlands, the impact that the Öresund Bridge has on accessibility, economic welfare and images of Malmö and Copenhagen, or the way in which Mendini (Poletti, 1994) changed the entire inner city in Groningen through the Groninger Museum project are early examples of swarm planning.

'Blauwe Stad'

The eastern part of the province of Groningen has traditionally been the poorest region in The Netherlands, with pervasive high unemployment, low levels of education and poverty. People, who could, left the area. This provides a good example of swarm planning. In this case, the swarm consists of the people living in the area. They were dissatisfied with their situation – or, in swarm language, with the shape of their swarm. It was commonly felt that something needed to be changed. This change was created through an impulse provided by one deputy of the regional government. The project concerned establishing a completely new village – Blauwe Stad – around a new lake, which had been shown to attract well-educated and wealthy people from outside the area. The project acts as an impulse as the new village makes itself felt across the entire area, with new amenities, restructured villages and new transportation developing around the Blauwe Stad.

The Groninger Museum

The 'Verbindingskanaal' is a waterway at the edge of the city centre of Groningen, located between the central station and the inner city. The fastest way to reach

Source: R. Roggema

Figure 7.12 The village of Blauwe Stad established in the landscape of eastern Groningen, The Netherlands

the inner city was traditionally to go around the canal. As a result, the area at the city side of the Verbindingskanaal became neglected, attracting hooligans and criminals. In this case, the swarm consists of the buildings, functions and routes in this part of the inner city. Most of the elements in the area were neglected, malfunctioning and of low quality. The shape of the swarm dissatisfied large groups of people, users, policy-makers and politicians. Once again, one deputy of the municipality provided the important impulse. He enforced the building of the museum right in the middle of the Verbindingskanaal. A new and much shorter connection was introduced between the station and the inner city. Many people began to use this connection and in few years' time the neglected area was transformed into a very popular neighbourhood, where lots of high-quality shops emerged. In this way, the museum transformed the entire inner city.

The solar polder

The Dutch supply of natural gas is produced in Groningen Province. The gas network and knowledge about gas in Groningen is exceptional. Even so, by 2040, most gas reserves will be depleted. In this case, the swarm consists of the current energy constellation – energy companies, existing network and market policies – which does not want to change its way of acting. This network is strong and tends to be repetitive in its behaviour. This will eventually be problematic as fossil fuel reserves diminish. In order to prevent the province from becoming dependent

Source: Poletti (1994)

Figure 7.13 The Groninger Museum positioned in the Verbindingskanaalzone:
before (top) and after (bottom)

Source: R. Roggema

Figure 7.14 The Groninger Museum in the Verbindingskanaal

upon the import of energy, plans have been developed to create a so-called 500ha 'solar polder' in the eastern part of Groningen – once again, an initiative of one deputy of the regional authority. By making use of current knowledge and the existing gas network, this will enable energy to be supplied to most people and industries within the province. The introduction of solar energy will change the entire energy supply. First, it will cut through the existing industry structure of gas and oil companies, without changing the distribution network. Second, it will attract specialized research companies to the province. The introduction of the solar polder will stimulate the technological development of solar power, resulting in a decisive advance compared to other sources. Once the tipping point has been reached, solar power may well become the most important energy source in the future, at least in this part of the world.

Steer the swarm

Because of the inability of traditional spatial planning to create and reinforce effective interventions that are capable of changing the regional system, a new steering principle needs to be developed. This issue is explored in some depth in the environmental spatial plan of Groningen Province (Roggema and Huyink, 2007), leading to the decision to develop a range of approaches in order to influence the spatial system. In doing so, it is hoped that the best regime with the most satisfactory outcome will emerge. The aim is to end up with a regime that is able to change the direction of the 'swarm' towards a high standard of spatial

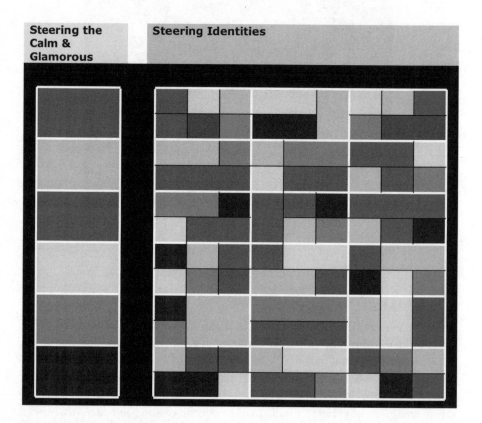

Source: Roggema and Huyink (2007)

Figure 7.15 The Dutch painter Mondrian, combining regimes and identities

quality. The most appropriate approaches may differ from area to area, depending upon their identity, and the availability of a number of approaches to choose from in combination with the unique characteristics of the area will make it possible to help the area adapt to uncertain future developments, such as climate change, as illustrated colourfully by the well-known Dutch painter Mondrian.

Conclusion: The benefits of swarm planning

The world has firmly entered the era of global turbulence. This has serious consequences for how people and organizations need to conduct their affairs. Countries and regions must expect significant and unforeseen structural change in the future. In order to cope with this, they need to develop a degree of adaptability that is of a different order of magnitude than is manifest today. This is particularly true for spatial design, which anticipates the uncertainties of the (far) future.

Over time, designers have shown themselves able to change their paradigm in response to the needs of the moment. Such a change is necessary today. Swarm planning will be able to help regions in this task. The application of swarm planning in Groningen, The Netherlands, has shown how it is capable of making vulnerable regions more robust and flexible, allowing them to manage turbulent and unexpected changes in a spatial manner as energy and climate change.

Swarm planning rises above the spatial design idea of prescribing, in detail, what should be done with every inch of the area. Instead, it provides an opportunity for finding those special interventions that change the region and creates space for surprises to be dealt with in time. This allows designers to continue connecting with the profoundest desires of citizens: the search for beauty, safety, comfort and the absence of worry about their children's future (Roggema, 2005a).

I have found it interesting to compare the idea of adaptability through swarm planning with Emery and Trist's (1965) ideas of coping with turbulence. They emphasize the need for common values and collaboration in order to build institutions that cope with the new uncertain environment. Yet, experience in spatial design has shown that common values and collaboration cannot provide the full answer. The lesson of swarm planning is that there is a crucial role to be played by invention, creativity and original ideas, which require the active contribution of single individuals and/or small groups with divergent, even maverick, views at the right place and at the right time. As demonstrated in this chapter, the most spectacular examples of spatial planning in coping with new and unanticipated change all arise as a result of the initiatives of single individuals who did not subscribe to the common view.

I see a strong analogy with Prigogine's idea of 'dissipative structures' (see Chapter 5 in this volume). At the point of bifurcation where structure is created, one single small fluctuation causes the whole field to transform in one direction or another. Swarms act in a similar way. At the point where things really matter – at the point of bifurcation – the future is made by individuals, not collaborators.

References

Alders, H. (2006) 'De waterkolom als veiligheidspartner' ['The water pillar as safety partner'], Paper presented at Pinpoint Conference, Den Haag, 21 October 2006

Babüroğlu, O. (1988) 'The vortical environment: The fifth in the Emery–Trist levels of organizational environments', *Human Relations*, vol 41, no 3, pp181–210

De Boo (2005) 'Verdronken Wadden', in *NRC*, 20 March 2005, Rotterdam

Carlson, D. (2006) *International Polar Year 2007–2008*, Volkskrant, Amsterdam

Dorland, R. van and Jansen, B. (eds) (2006) *De Staat van Het Klimaat 2006*, PCCC, De Bilt/Wageningen, The Netherlands

Duijghuisen, M. (1990) *Geschiedenis van Breda, III Hoofdlijnen en Accenten 1795–1960*, Boekhandel Gianotten, Breda, The Netherlands

Emden, S., van (1985) *Stedebouw in Nederland, 50 jaar Bond van Nederlandse Stedenbouw-kundigen* (edited by F. De Jong), Walburg Pers, Zutphen, The Netherlands

Emery, F. and Trist, E. (1965) 'The causal texture of organizational environments', *Human Relations*, vol 18, pp21–32

Florida, R. (2005) *The Flight of the Creative Class*, Harper Business, New York, NY

Geldof, G. (2002) *Coping with Complexity in Integrated Water Management*, Universiteit Twente, Enschede, The Netherlands

Gladwell, M. (2000) *The Tipping Point*, Back Bay Books, New York, NY

Hacquebord, L. (2007) personal communication, Arctic Centre, University of Groningen, Groningen, The Netherlands

Homan, T. (2005) *Organizational Dynamics*, Sdu uitgevers, Den Haag, The Netherlands

Howard, E. (1902) *Garden Cities of Tomorrow*, Swan Sonnenschein & Co Ltd, London

IPCC (2007) *4th Assessment: The Physical Science Basis, WG I, Summary for Policymakers, 2007 and Climate Change Impacts, Adaptation and Vulnerability, WGII, Summary for Policymakers*, IPCC, Cambridge University Press, UK

Jacobs, D. and Roggema, R. (2005) Term invented during searching conversation, Brainstorm, July 2005, Groningen, The Netherlands

KNMI (2006) *Climate Scenarios for the Netherlands*, KNMI, De Bilt, The Netherlands

Mitchell Waldrop, M. (1994) *The Edge of Chaos: About Complex Systems*, Uitgeverij Contact, Amsterdam/Antwerpen, The Netherlands

MVRDV, KCAP and Roggema, R. (2001) *Working City, Development Plan Working Locations, Almere Poort*, Department of Urban Development, Municipality of Almere, Almere, The Netherlands

Neuwirth, R. (2005) *Shadow Cities*, Routledge, New York, NY

Poletti, R. (1994) *Atelier Mendini Groninger Museum*, Fabbri Editori, R.C.S. Libri and Grande Opere, S.p.A., Bergamo

Ridderstråle, J. and Nordström, K. (2004) *Karaoke Capitalism*, Pearson Education Ltd, Harlow, UK

Roberts, K. (2005) Interview in *De Volkskrant,* 15 October 2005, Amsterdam

Roggema, R. (2005a) 'New strategies for energy-inclusive design in Energy Valley', Paper presented at the Green Cities Conference, San Francisco, CA, 7 July 2005

Roggema, R. (2005b) 'Hansje Brinker take your finger away', *Oxford Futures Forum,* Templeton College, Oxford, UK

Roggema, R. (2007) *Spatial Impact of Adaptation to Climate Change in Groningen,* Province of Groningen, Groningen, The Netherlands

Roggema, R. and Dobbelsteen, A., van den (2006) 'How was becomes', in C. Brebbia, M. E. Conti and E. Tiezzi (eds) *The Management of Natural Resources, Sustainable Development and Ecological Hazards: The Ravage of the Planet,* WIT Press, Southampton, UK

Roggema, R. and Huyink, W. (2007) *Atlas Groningen, Analytical Document – Environmental –Spatial Plan,* Province of Groningen, Groningen, The Netherlands

Roggema, R., Dobbelsteen A., van den and Stegenga, K. (2006) *Pallet of Possibilities, Grounds for Change,* Province of Groningen, Groningen, The Netherlands

Roo, G. de (2006) *Understanding Planning and Complexity: A Systems Approach,* AESOP Working Group on Complexity and Planning, Cardiff, Wales

Sectie, D. (1997) *100 jaar Baronielaan,* Zandbergse boekstichting, Breda, The Netherlands

Timmermans, W. (2004) *Crises and Innovation in Sustainable City Planning,* Wessex Institute of Technology, UK

van der Meer, K. (2003) *Urban Design: Blauwe Stad,* Province of Groningen, Groningen, The Netherlands

Wolfram, S. (2002) *A New Kind of Science,* Wolfram Media, Champain

8

Designing More Effective Political Governance of Turbulent Fields: The Case of Healthcare

Niklas Arvidsson

Introduction

This chapter addresses the role of how governance is designed in relation to situations where turbulent systems face the possibility of becoming hyper-turbulent (McCann and Selsky, 1984). I illustrate this situation and how it might be addressed by studying the design of governance in a healthcare field in a Swedish region. Since political influence over healthcare is high – especially in a country such as Sweden, but also, generally, in Organisation for Economic Co-operation and Development (OECD) countries – I focus my discussion on the role of political governance in turbulent contexts. The case and the recommendations on how to design governance modes to address it lead me to propose that centralized and detached political governance designs, manifested in policies and regulations, become an important driver of turbulence and thus cannot be a way to address it. Just as Emery and Trist (1965) suggested over 40 years ago, I believe that traditional governance alternatives can reinforce the turbulence towards which these very governance options are directed.

This implies that a different governance design to address the contexts that surround today's Western economies is called for. Governance must attend to systemic, field-level issues more broadly, instead of focusing on apparently stable and controllable sub-systems. My research suggests that understanding causal textures in turbulent fields appears to be crucial in designing more effective political governance. These arguments are consistent with Emery and Trist's (1965) causal textures theory, which suggests that second-order unintended consequences creating turbulent environmental causal textures emerge from 'normal' decision-making and acting.

I argue in this chapter that turbulence calls for a different form of governance, and that, as proposed by Emery and Trist (1965), without changes in the values driving human activities, the consequences of regulative acts will lead environments to become even more turbulent. If members of a field are able and willing to adapt to changing conditions by recalibrating, transforming or even replacing their values, turbulence will be addressed and may disappear. If not, the field may partition itself into small enclaves where some are able to adapt while others are not, which means that turbulence is addressed only by the lucky few (McCann and Selsky, 1984).

My illustrative case – the healthcare field in a Swedish region – was in a turbulent causal texture at the end of the 1990s as political governance had made adaptation to a highly uncertain contextual environment impossible. I show how this led the field to face the risk of reaching hyper-turbulence where organizational failure increases rapidly, rendering turbulence endemic (McCann and Selsky, 1984). My main contribution is to illustrate and propose an alternative and, in many ways (for that field), new conception of how governance design can be linked to policy-making in order to more effectively address turbulent environments.

After having introduced the background to my approach in the preamble, this chapter explores the ideas on governance design presented above in three steps:

1   First, I argue that turbulent causal textures make it critical to bring a systemic model of governance to the policy-making table, and to invite stakeholders to become involved in regulatory affairs around that table. My case shows the benefits when actors are engaged as more than just voters in democratic systems. I argue instead that stakeholders fully involved in the early stages of governance dialogues leading to new policies, rules and laws is an effective way of addressing turbulence. This has to do not only with effectiveness, but also with fairness (see Chapter 13 in this volume). The setting of the governance model in this way is a necessary, but insufficient, step to address turbulent conditions.

2   Next, I argue that governance designs relying on a future orientation are more capable of addressing turbulence than governance designs using case-based historic experiences and current convictions. This sets a more inclusive than exclusive tone for attracting the multi-stakeholder format needed to enhance future effectiveness.

3   Then, I illustrate aspects of this ('new') governance design that uses environmental scanning linked to the creation of future images of an ideal healthcare system that responds to plausible future contextual conditions elicited through scenarios – the idealized design (Ackoff, 1974) – in the most southern region of Sweden.

Preamble

As this book emphasizes, two important tools emerged during the 1960s to expand management knowledge. The first, seeing how in turbulent causal textures the environment becomes an actor in it its own right, was a way of including what had been previously excluded. The second, scenario formation, was a means of negotiating with future environments. Both advanced the means of dealing with uncertain change. Fred Emery and Eric Trist articulated the clearest model of the first (Emery and Trist, 1965) while Wack (1985a, 1985b), Schwartz (1992) and van der Heijden (1996, 2005) successfully developed and applied the second. The first conceptualized what had not previously been seen, while the second clarified how its role in the future would help the present. Both were instruments for negotiating with future realities in the present. Each was typically used alone, which may be why both fell short in delivering on their promises.

I think that joining them together, as this book does, gives the causal texture conceptualization a practical implication and makes the practice of future analysis more conceptually rigorous and robust. To achieve this in my chapter, I describe, illustrate and discuss how a scenario-based methodology leading to an idealized design of a future regional healthcare field was used to debate, analyse and improve the current field when facing the risks of becoming hyper-turbulent. Interestingly, some of the most important manifestations of the changed system were manifested in new values and standpoints regarding critical components that shaped behaviour. The new values enabled the system to tackle hyper-turbulence.

Scenarios and scanning for turbulent uncertainties can be described as a means of accomplishing two distinct, yet complementary, agendas in system governance. First, they act to involve the people who are to change their behaviour, thus realizing the intention of transformation in the strategy-making learning process. This not only improves the chance of achieving the intent, but also engages the knowledge, experience and interests of these individuals – enriching the quality of the output. Second, they stretch into and probe future developments that are unknown, but seem ambiguously knowable, thereby avoiding myopic learning (Levinthal and March, 1993).

A very intriguing aspect of the causal texture view of environmental sensing, which I rely on here, is that it addresses the risk of myopic learning by capturing field-driving forces that were initiated by our past actions (see Chapter 12 in this volume). Other approaches to enhancing the thinking about the future – such as the Delphi method, dialectic reasoning and forecasting – have not proven to be as strong in this regard since they focus much less on using differences of opinion on the future to better understand the present. I therefore want to stress the benefits of using future analysis based on contextual analysis engaging a multitude of stakeholders. Its main advantages lie in its ability to identify strategic issues systematically, its broad approach to problem-scoping, as well as its focus on exploring uncertainty (Schoemaker, 1993). The idealized design exemplified by scenarios in the healthcare case presented in this chapter transpired as a result of appreciating the importance of signals from the future.

I find that this approach can reinstate a field's lost ability to adapt to turbulence and thereby avoid hyper-turbulence since it provides a response to political governance that avoids key traps in group processes, such as the risks of analytical blind spots and myopic thinking frames (Schoemaker, 1993). The approach strives to frame political governance operations with a focus on the long-term effectiveness of the governed system itself, and does so by realizing change of supporting values.

Limitations in traditional political governance

The practice of governance manifested in policies and regulations has gone from its origins as a societal safety net during the late 19th century (Ewald, 1986) to becoming a less-than-ideal arena for stimulating behavioural change in our societies (Thorngate, 2001). Laws widely debated and narrowly passed all too often end up with unintended results that fail to be seen as socially legitimate (Gangl, 2003). This is largely due to how the larger field in which regulation is embedded, including the domain of governance, continues to be deeply shaken by unexpected contextual events. Human affairs can be argued to have moved beyond the dreams of Greek causality. And the dependable hierarchy of chains of command has become suspect by non-governmental organizations (NGOs), as well as by younger generations in many societies. Paradoxically, individuals now have powers never seen before in human history due to higher education and access to global information, as well as global media space.

As regional integration and globalization grow, laws formulated by and emanating from nation states no longer allow for governance of issues to be bounded by a single nation's or region's interests. Environmental pollution, resource management in the energy field and labour market regulation, as well as healthcare system needs, require political governance that acknowledges supra-national interests and organic change. On a general level, policy-making is today often stretched to the point where the benefits of central control – predictability and accountability – do not exceed the costs of little or incorrect information or of societal resistance to accept the implications of policies (McCaffrey et al, 1995). There is, thus, potential value in more participative approaches to policy-making in turbulent environments – sometimes also spanning national and industry definitions. In our case, this means that the project defined the participants not by their industrial links – e.g. pharmaceutical industry, biotech or a public municipality – but, rather, from the fact that they in some way contributed to creating better health for local citizens.

I understand that policy-makers have a responsibility to create effective policies which govern social behaviour in a desired direction. Some behaviours and actions should be stimulated while others are to be avoided. In order to achieve this, the policy analyst may take different and complementary stances. Thorngate (2001) suggested a most cherished stance is that of the policy analyst as neutral and rational, providing insightful analyses and policy recommendations based on reliable and valid information. A second possible stance is for policy-makers to take on the role of a doctor, prescribing how policy should be formulated and implemented. Such policy-making acts more as decision-making than as providing information to be used when formulating decisions. Thorngate's (2001) third stance is that policy-makers may, instead, choose to act as mercenaries, guided by a higher vision or understanding, where their main responsibility is to convince others to follow a given path or ideal. This third stance is particularly frequent when policy-makers have a vested interest in the matter at hand (Jenkins-Smith and Weimer, 1985; Pettigrew, 2003; Maak, 2007). The ultimate objective for all three stances, however, is to improve policy, where the best way to measure the success of policy analysis is a function of how much attitudes in society are formed or changed (Sabatier and Jenkins-Smith, 1993). To further a discussion of effective political governance, I propose a way of combining these three stances and thereby propose a fourth.

Whichever stance analysts take is conditioned by the fact that policy analysts and policy-makers think and behave like most people – and are subject to the same social and psychological limitations (Thorngate, 2001). Analysts, too, are not perfectly rational, nor free from biases. Their motives may shift during the analytic process and may include personal ambitions as well as official objectives. They may be influenced by social pressures to conform to what they believe others want (Milgram, 1965), especially when information about the subject matter at hand is scarce (Festinger, 1954). Analysts and decision-makers are often treated as an elite group in society, which underpins their perception of themselves as a small and privileged group, increasing the probability of harmful groupthink (Janis, 1972). Other social factors such as persuasion and fatigue may also impact upon policy formulation: 'Social psychology perspectives on policy-making lead to the conclusion that policy analyses usually form a very small part of policy-making processes. It may be the most rational part. But social and psychological factors still seem to play a far more dominant role in policy-making' (Thorngate, 2001, p108). From available research, I can thus conclude that governance will tend to become more biased by single lobbyist groups' interests and individual preferences if the information-seeking and decision-making processes used exclude important stakeholders. In the case of healthcare, it may be pharmaceutical companies that perform such a role. So, logically, I believe in the fourth stance on governance where policy analysts and decision-makers act as designers, providers and operators of a governance system or process. It is this fourth stance that I elaborate upon in this chapter.

Stakeholder engagement in governance and realization of intended results

When those who are to be governed by policies are excluded from the governance-making process, adherence to its outcome is problematic (Mvungi et al, 2005; Videira et al, 2006; Steyaert et al, 2007). For example, in a study of commercial fishermen's responses to changes in fisheries policies, it was found that how perceptions of policy-making processes are managed is an important factor in explaining resilience to change. Social resilience was improved (Marshall, 2007) if:

- social knowledge was co-produced through involvement in the decision-making process;
- a sense of equity or fairness (see Chapter 13 in this volume) was secured; and if
- an ability to influence the speed of implementation was acknowledged in the formation of policies (Marshall, 2007).

The importance of procedural justice for establishing law-making legitimacy was also found by Gangl (2003) in a study of US Congress law-making. These studies indicate the importance of stakeholder engagement when realizing the intended objectives from policy-making in a number of different fields – arguably also in the field of healthcare, which we discuss in depth later.

In addition, final outcomes are improved by stakeholder engagement. In a study of a stakeholder approach to policy-making for watershed management, Leach et al (2002) found that the open and collaborative process had significant effects on the final outcome, particularly in addressing problems on a local or regional scale, such as which projects will be pursued and how they will be monitored. As they put it: 'partnerships apparently have the most positive effect on the most serious problems in the watershed, which suggests that partnerships devote more efforts to serious problems' (Leach et al, 2002, p665). It was shown that partnerships and the collaborative process helped political governance in terms of solving imminent problems in the regional context. These results were stronger the longer the partnerships had existed.

The importance of stakeholder involvement and societal development is also manifested through the deployment and reinforcement of social capital (Putnam, 2000). When actors meet and work together they develop relationships that build social capital, which stimulates the creation of new knowledge (Nahapiet and Ghoshal, 1998). This does not happen by itself. It requires designing for institutional and leadership involvement – the type of governance that the fourth type I mentioned above entails. Responsible leadership (i.e. focusing on relations and morale) in a global stakeholder society helps to create social capital among stakeholders (Maak, 2007) – which retro-feeds back into the more effective policy-making loop and produces better governance (Putnam, 2000). The engagement by stakeholders in political governance consequently not only improves access to information, but also creates a social platform for future learning.

However, stakeholder participation *per se* does not address turbulence. I argue that it is more important that participation rests upon active engagement which mobilizes the stakeholders' capabilities and interests to co-produce knowledge. This co-production of knowledge has made a real difference in natural resource management (Steyaert et al, 2007), as well as in irrigation agriculture (Mvungi et al, 2005). The importance of effective knowledge co-production design was also seen in a study of stakeholder participation in the reform of European water policy (Videira et al, 2006). While knowledge co-production was important in all of these cases, many potentially important stakeholders were not involved. It was primarily representatives of the state or local authorities, as well as NGOs who participated, and the issues discussed were largely of a technical nature. Moreover, the actual processes used to create participation (i.e. public hearings and public comments), were found to be inadequate as they primarily aimed to conform to the European Union's (EU's) participatory principle[1] but did not allow active engagement of concerned stakeholders (Videira et al, 2006). Thus, if stakeholder involvement is to be effective in terms of influencing final policy-making, distanced participation by only a few actors is not enough. The process and ambitions of broader and deeper participation, as well as the types of participants, are of vital importance – especially in turbulent fields. A socio-ecological governance approach to US healthcare based on a field-focused holistic and collaborative approach proved to be an important way of managing hyper-turbulence (Selsky et al, 2007). As pointed out by Beierle and Cayford (2002), the choice or design of policy-making methodology may create positive side-effects in terms of strong social capital and improved opportunities for effective partnerships in future policy-making. Tavits (2006) found that social capital increases the level of political sophistication and facilitates cooperation within society, helping people to voice their policy demands better, thus improving political governance in turbulent situations.

Stakeholder engagement in policy analysis and decision-making adds more perspectives in governance-making processes. An earlier, wider and more active engagement of stakeholders provides more information and reduces the risk of single-actor biases. Yet, the risk remains that policy-making which includes more interests will turn into a political power struggle, where the vested interests of each party involved may lead to forming coalitions and to a strongly politicized process. This is where there is an obvious need for designing governance mechanisms that can openly challenge powerful interests – for instance, pharmaceutical companies or political actors – over the long run (see, for example, Pettigrew, 2003). To avoid such politicized risks, I argue that designing for the inclusion of more stakeholder groups with diverse interests engaged as active co-producers of the governance structure and processes, in governance guided by the future, contributes more effectively to tackling turbulence.

The importance of future-oriented analysis

Scenarios create a process that is conducted by analysis and shared understanding of contextual factor analyses (Schoemaker, 1993). A basic principle of scenario planning is that it involves a learning process based on cooperation and disagreement between individuals, leading to co-producing and internalizing a shared meaning and understanding, as well as articulation of potential differences in opinion (Schwartz, 1992; van der Heijden, 1996). If done properly, the process tends to force the collaborative analysis to redefine or reframe political arguments based on shared understanding of contextual information. The focus on contextual factors (i.e. social, economic, political, technological, environmental and legal forces) aims to prevent and supersede short-term private interests and ambitions of involved partners. If searching for an understanding of how new policies for energy systems may be formed and realized, one would be guided by using scenarios as contextual factors, such as green technologies, the greenhouse effect, emissions regulation, global transportation and travelling, societal values, and global politics around the Kyoto Protocol. This outside-in approach improves the governance process as contextual factors are beyond the control of each individual stakeholder, and considering them jointly in this way avoids many psychological traps – such as overconfidence and tunnel vision (Schoemaker, 1995) – in decision-making processes. In the case of the Skåne region in this chapter, the outside-in approach came in the form of patient – or, rather, customer – focus.

For many people, a drawback when using scenarios is that they increase anxiety since they underline that there are no easy answers to a contentious (Rittel and Webber, 1973) or complicated (Ackoff, 1974) situation in a turbulent context. Since scenarios may not single out one ideal and preferable policy, creating, instead, a learning process through which improved policy-making may emerge, they do cause anxiety. For policy analysis and decision-making, this anxiety is positive as it provides an opportunity to test different conclusions and calls for action in the psychological safety that long-term futures provide. Scenarios will help the process by providing relevant, novel, challenging, coherent and plausible alternative stories of how the future context may look. These stories are, in turn, used to inform governance with regard to policy analysis and current decision-making.

I argue that future-oriented stakeholder engagement may improve political governance's ability to respond to Ostrom's (1990, p7) call for studies that 'address the question of how to enhance the capabilities of those involved to change the constraining rules of the game to lead to outcomes other than remorseless tragedies'. Instead of being stuck in a prisoner's dilemma where a superior power – whether it is the district attorney or the policy-maker – sets the rules of the game, my chapter aims to describe a policy approach in which concerned individuals may actually co-create the rules of the game before (or simultaneously) playing it. Instead of rules set by detached politicians and influential lobbying groups, there is collaboration between a multitude of large and small stakeholders who set rules and play the game, in this way potentially avoiding Ostrom's (1990) remorseless tragedies.

To illustrate how a future-oriented stakeholder-intensive approach may change the scene in a heavily politicized and traditional industry, I now turn to the case of healthcare in southern Sweden.

The case of healthcare in southern Sweden

During the late 1990s, the Swedish healthcare field was in a state of turbulence due to its inability to adapt to changes in the highly uncertain contextual environment. A government report warned that the Swedish healthcare system would not meet its responsibilities without structural renewal (SOU, 1996); but the solutions that were called for (e.g. new forms of ownership, profit-driven incentives and increased competition; SOU, 2002) did not materialize. Costs for healthcare in Sweden increased by more than 5 per cent annually between 1997 and 2000, while productivity deteriorated (Jönsson et al, 2004), which was dealt with through inadequate rationalization and downsizing. Turbulence was seemingly driven by the lack of structural renewal that had been called for.

In addition, significant degrees of innovation in, for instance, information technology (IT), biotechnology, medical equipment and pharmaceuticals had opened up a new scene of opportunities and demographic changes with a large proportion of people born during the 1940s approaching retirement. These forces together had created a need for systemic transformation (Levin and Normann, 2000). The political governance – or, rather, lack thereof – had at the same time not instilled an effective ability enabling the field to adapt to these changes by the much needed structural renewal that had been called for. The field's governance was actually reinforcing its own state of turbulence and was in need of renewal. Two consultants, Bert Levin and Richard Normann, therefore designed and launched a collaborative project for a southern region within Sweden – Skåne – that could help the field to adapt to the turbulence that poor governance and unexpected change had created. In 1999, political reforms at the national level had also given more political freedom to the region to address it own problems. My role in relation to this work was to co-edit a book on healthcare systems in which the Skåne case is a central component (Normann and Arvidsson, 2006). The clients in this work consisted of a number of public and private actors (see below) who shared an interest in a well-functioning healthcare system in Skåne.

The Skåne healthcare project started out by accepting that systems result from a long history, and with the insight that if one wants to challenge the current features of the system, it is difficult to do it from within the system's own premises. The system characteristics in themselves tend to reinforce the status quo and hinder radical change. In order to counter these articulated systemic problems, the project started by analysing the contextual drivers of change on the system from a historic perspective to enable an insightful dialogue on the possible future development of the regional healthcare system. This process identified critical key uncertainties and created an opportunity for scenario analysis, manifested, for instance, in discussions regarding future healthcare needs by patients. The scenarios dialogue also created a conversation on which critical components a well-functioning future healthcare system had to incorporate. The analyses and discussion of key uncertainties in scenarios thus became a tool that framed and produced an idealized design of a regional healthcare system in Skåne.

The idealized design deliberately disregarded the administrative organization in place at that time. This meant, for example, that the project group intentionally disregarded circumstances fundamental to some sub-systems, such as distribution of work between the law-making national state, the region/county council with responsibility for care of the ill, and the municipalities with responsibility for home nursing and old-age care. Another synergistic objective was that the working process in itself countered risks of a lack of stakeholder engagement in existing collaborative processes.

The Skåne region was, during the late 1990s, responsible for the healthcare of 1.2 million Swedish citizens, where responsibility for different activities such as old age, healthcare and financing were distributed between local, regional and national authorities. The project constituted a collaborative approach including representatives – politicians, administrators and professionals – from municipalities and regional and national authorities, as well as trade unions, companies and other organizations in the field of healthcare. Participating organizations (i.e. the group of actors who jointly served as clients and co-producers of new insights) included Astra Zeneca (a pharmaceutical company), Praktikertjänst AB (a private healthcare provider), Försäkringskassan Skåne (a state-owned labour and health market insurance company), Region Skåne (the regional municipality), KF Business Development Health (a cooperatively owned food retailer), Kommunförbundet Skåne (the county municipality), Landstingsförbundet (the regional municipality managing healthcare), Läkarförbundet (a trade organization for physicians) and Länsförsäkringar Skåne (a private insurance company).

The participants were heavily engaged in these projects from their inception in spring 1999, as well as during the post-project realization of the systemic ideas, which is still ongoing as of 2008. It is, for instance, manifested in the ambition of realizing '*Skånsk Livskraft*' (the Living Strength of Skåne)[2], which describes how healthcare in the region is reorganized around the needs of 'customers' and the organizational structure of each particular form of care. The idealized design was developed in 2000 with a ten-year perspective and a systemic level, which meant that it had to be realistically true in 2010. A ten-year timeframe was chosen since political elections were held every fourth year and the project wanted to span two election cycles. The quality of the idealized design was judged to be acceptable through criteria developed by Levin and Normann (2000) (i.e. in terms of usefulness, accuracy, avoidance of minimal critical denominators and insight). The project strived to make the idealized design actionable and realistic, internally consistent and realistically different from the current state of affairs. It was meant to be inferred from disagreement and not based only on a narrow common ground that everybody could agree upon, enabling participants to deduce new insights on healthcare systems in order to lessen relevant uncertainties for all involved stakeholders. The overriding ambition was to prevent the systemic design from being subject to hyper-turbulence.

The project designed and convened open discussions of many ideas and questioned taken-for-granted opinions – which, in many cases, had not before been articulated and/or had remained subconscious. This approach produced a set of characteristics that the participants agreed should be a feature of healthcare systems (see Normann and Arvidsson, 2006). The characteristics describe the extent to which the participants – stakeholders in the healthcare system – managed to challenge their own preconceived ideas of healthcare that prior to the project were taken for granted. Monetization of healthcare was, for instance, almost impossible to discuss during the 1990s in Sweden. But the idealized design project helped everyone to see it as inevitable. The possibility of private ownership of healthcare providers was also, all of a sudden, possible to discuss. Nevertheless, some characteristics such as fairness and open access to healthcare for all were not discarded; instead, participants noted that monetization and fairness were not – *a priori* – incompatible, but could be characteristics to be harmonized with each other. Another characteristic – labour market regulation for people older than 65 – had previously not been seen as an integrated component of the healthcare system; but the participating actors now started to regard it as an important factor in an effective healthcare system. Thus, a major contribution of the project was its effectiveness in co-producing new values among the stakeholders vis-à-vis critical contextual factors.

The collaborative project also freed stakeholders' thinking and helped participants to identify and recognize two new characteristics that they believed had to be central in an ideal healthcare system. First, the main producers of health are individuals themselves – not physicians and nurses. At that time, individuals represented a sleeping resource in Skåne that could make the entire health field more efficient (i.e. by using lesser amounts of public resources) and more effective (i.e. by increasing the health of citizens at the same time). Second, as acute care, elective care and basic care differ in terms of which roles individuals are able to play, where the care ideally is done, who can perform the care and who should finance it, participants found it advisable to acknowledge these differences in order to ensure effectiveness. They realized that each form of care needed its own particular form of logic in order to function efficiently. These differences were identified in the dialectic and collaborative future-oriented work project that Levin and Normann (2000) designed and facilitated, leading to the idealized design of the Skåne healthcare field.

Despite the positive results on how to improve the system, participants were frustrated during the work. This can be expected given the ambition to critically debate contextual factors that earlier had been taken for granted or ignored, and may even be interpreted as a positive sign of a learning struggle, rather than as something to be avoided. The idea behind the project that Levin and Normann (2000) designed and deployed was to acknowledge uncertainty instead of hiding and ignoring it. In my experience, anxiety is part of the game when objectives include challenging what is taken for granted and seldom discussed, sometimes even not articulated at all.

The ambition of scenario analysis – in this case, ultimately manifested in an idealized design that could better address plausible future contextual conditions – was not to get existing authorized institutions to implement the design as such. The model, instead, provided a systemic foundation for future collaborative work, enabling strategic conversation (van der Heijden, 1996) to be carried out from a systemic perspective and a holistic view. One of the main results was, therefore, a new way of structuring a collaborative learning process behind political governance where the idealized design became a tool to stimulate and debate ideas.

During this change project, the idealized design attempted to provide a guiding vision, developing knowledge about the future in order to produce even better visions. A logical next step, once the idealized design had been established, was to identify existing restrictions between the system of that time and the idealized design in order to see which could be overcome in order to revise the design accordingly. The revised design then turned into an ambitious but attainable model for healthcare and old-age care for the year 2010. It became a long goal, and starting from this goal a programme of actions was then elaborated upon and implemented. The work in the Skåne region has manifested itself in several ways, including efforts to structure different types of healthcare around specific care logics, as well as efforts to make citizens actively engaged in the creation of their own health (see, for example, NUTEK, 2007).

The Skåne case illustrates the importance of design governance to understand how a future healthcare system aims to provide value to its stakeholders, and to effectively challenge what previously was taken for granted. Furthermore, as the case shows, governance designs that ensure the system is invested with self-developing and self-regulatory properties, ascertaining long-term innovation and reconfiguration capabilities (Levin and Normann, 2000), implies that governance is subjected to competitive pressures. In such governance designs, it becomes possible to question and challenge governance structure, functioning and effectiveness. The proposed idealized design of the Skåne region manifested an important change in this direction by arguing that care purchases should be allocated to the citizens and not, as had been the case until then, to medical expertise and public administrators. Interestingly, a paradox seems to be that the governance principles of a field that reduces turbulence must ensure their own survival by allowing and stimulating pressure on them from outside that system. If such pressure does not exist, the governance system will avoid uncertainty, pretend that it does not exist and act to co-produce more of it, causing the field in which it is embedded to become turbulent.

Conclusion

I have shown that there are inherent biases in social processes aiming to govern political systems by implementing policies and regulation. This is especially risky when facing a turbulent situation that may transform itself into hyper-turbulence due to inappropriate approaches of its political governance. In order to minimize this risk, I suggest that a different, more inclusive, governance stance based upon a design focus which counteracts and avoids some of the traps is worth deploying.

The approach I suggest rests on two steps. First, political governance is designed to include stakeholders and their competences, as well as their vested interests. Paradoxically, the exclusion of a multitude of stakeholders will increase the risk that governance holders focus on a particular vested interest since the potential for a single stakeholder to monopolistically influence the information process increases. As increasing numbers of stakeholders are included in the governance process, more and diverse information will be used, and vested interests will counter each other more effectively. Second, a future-oriented approach included in governance design appears to contribute to avoiding the risk that vested interests in the status quo will monopolize and harm the governance process. By using long-term possibilities and understanding drivers for change in the contextual environment, I argue that a more effective governance mode leading to changed societal values and behaviour is realized.

To illustrate this, I provide the case of how a scenario-based project leading to an idealized design of a healthcare system in Sweden changed the principles underlying political governance. It led the stakeholders to overcome psychological barriers and reluctance to change that was actually co-creating turbulence. By adopting a future analysis manifested in an idealized design of a healthcare system, political governance designed to address turbulent fields can engage participative stakeholders, as well as a future orientation of the larger system, to make an effective difference.

Notes

1   This principle is embraced in several regulations concerning the environment as, for instance, The Environmental Impact Assessment (EIA) Directive concerning the environmental impact of certain public and private projects and The Strategic Environmental Assessment Directive having the ambition to investigate environmental consequences of certain plans and programmes before they are adopted.
2   See www.skane.se.

References

Ackoff, R. (1974) *Redesigning the Future*, Wiley, New York, NY

Beierle, T. and Cayford, J. (2002) *Democracy in Practice: Public Participation in Environmental Decisions*, Resources for the Future, Washington, DC

Emery, F. and Trist, E. (1965) 'The causal texture of organisational environments', *Human Relations*, vol 18, pp21–32

Ewald, F. (1986) *L'Etat Providence*, Grasset, Paris, France

Festinger, L. (1954) 'A theory of social comparison processes', *Human Relations*, vol 7, pp117–140

Gangl, A. (2003) 'Procedural justice theory and evaluations of the lawmaking process', *Political Behavior*, vol 25, no 2, pp119–149

Janis, I. (1972) *Victims of Groupthink*, Houghton Mifflin, Boston, MA

Jenkins-Smith, H. and Weimer, D. (1985) 'Analysis as retrograde action', *Public Administration Review*, vol 45, pp485–494

Jönsson, B., Arvidsson, G., Levin, L.-Å. and Rehnberg, C. (2004) *Hälsa, Vård och Tillväxt – Välfärdspolitiska Rådets Rapport 2004*, SNS Förlag, Stockholm, Sweden

Leach, W., Pelkey, N. and Sabatier, P. (2002) 'Stakeholder partnerships as collaborative policymaking: Evaluation criteria applied to watershed management in California and Washington', *Journal of Policy Analysis and Management*, vol 21, no 4, pp645–670

Levin, B. and Normann, R. (2000) *Vårdens chans – En modell för morgondagens vård och äldreomsorg*, Ekerlids Förlag, Stockholm, Sweden

Levinthal, D. and March, J. (1993) 'The myopia of learning', *Strategic Management Journal, Special Issue: Organisations, Decision-Making and Strategy*, vol 14, pp95–112

Maak, T. (2007) 'Responsible leadership, stakeholder engagement, and the emergence of social capital', *Journal of Business Ethics*, vol 74, pp329–343

Marshall, N. (2007) 'Can policy perception influence social resilience to policy change?', *Fisheries Research*, vol 86, pp216–227

McCaffrey, D., Faerman, S. and Hart, D. (1995) 'The appeal and difficulties of participative systems', *Organisation Science*, vol 6, no 6, pp603–627

McCann, J. and Selsky, J. (1984) 'Hyperturbulence and the emergence of type 5 environments', *Academy of Management Review*, vol 9, no 3, pp460–470

Milgram, S. (1965) 'Some conditions of obedience and disobedience to authority', *Human Relations*, vol 18, pp57–86

Mvungi, A., Mashauri, D. and Madulu, N. (2005) 'Management of water for irrigation agriculture in semi-arid areas: Problems and prospects', *Physics and Chemistry of the Earth*, vol 30, pp809–817

Nahapiet, J. and Ghoshal, S. (1998) 'Social capital, intellectual capital, and the organisational advantage', *Academy of Management Review*, vol 23, no 2, pp242–266

Normann, R. and Arvidsson, N. (2006) *People as Care Catalysts: From Being Patient to Becoming Healthy*, John Wiley and Sons, Chichester, UK

NUTEK (2007) 'Vård och omsorg – En framtidsbransch', *Nya Fakta & Statistik, Framtidens Näringsliv*, no 6, July, pp1–8.

Ostrom, E. (1990) *Governing the Commons: The Evolution of Institutions for Collective Action*, Cambridge University Press, Cambridge, UK

Pettigrew, P. (2003) 'Power, conflicts, and resolutions: A change agent's perspective on conducting action research within a multiorganisational partnership', *Systemic Practice and Action Research*, vol 16, no 6, pp375–391

Putnam, R. (2000) *Bowling Alone: The Collapse and Revival of American Community*, Simon and Schuster, New York, NY

Rittel, H. and Webber, M. (1973) 'Dilemmas in a general theory of planning', *Policy Sciences*, vol 4, pp155–169

Sabatier, P. and Jenkins-Smith, H. (eds) (1993) *Policy Change and Learning: An Advocacy Coalition Approach*, Westview Press, Boulder, CO

Schoemaker, P. (1993) 'Multiple scenario development: Its conceptual and behavioural foundation', *Strategic Management Journal*, vol 14, no 3, pp193–213

Schoemaker, P. (1995) 'Scenario planning: A tool for strategic thinking', *Sloan Management Review*, vol 36, no 2, pp25–40

Schwartz, P. (1992) *The Art of the Long View: Scenario Planning – Protecting Your Company against an Uncertain Future*, Century Business, London, UK

Selsky, J., Goes, J. and Babüroğlu, O. (2007) 'Contrasting perspectives in strategy making: Applications in 'hyper' environments', *Organization Studies*, vol 28, no 1, pp71–94

SOU (1996) *Betänkande av kommittén om hälso- och sjukvårdens finansiering organisation*, Statens Offentliga Utredningar (government report), p163

SOU (2002) *Vårda vården – samverkan, mångfald och rättvisa*, Statens Offentliga Utredningar (government report), p23

Steyaert, P., Barzman, M., Billaud, J.-P., Brives, H.., Hubert, B., Ollivier, G. and Roche, B. (2007) 'The role of knowledge and research in facilitating social learning among stakeholders in natural resources management in the French Atlantic coastal wetlands', *Environmental Science and Policy*, vol 10, pp537–550

Tavits, M. (2006) 'Making democracy work more? Exploring the linkage between social capital and government performance', *Political Research Quarterly*, vol 59, no 2, pp211–225

Thorngate, W. (2001) 'The social psychology of policy analysis', *Journal of Comparative Policy Analysis: Research and Practice*, vol 3, pp85–112

Videira, N., Antunes, P., Santos, R. and Lobo, G. (2006) 'Public and stakeholder participation in European water policy: A critical review of project evaluation processes', *European Environment*, vol 16, pp19–31 van der Heijden, K. (1996) *Scenarios: The Art of Strategic Conversation*, John Wiley and Sons, Chichester, UK

van der Heijden, K. (2005) *Scenarios: The Art of Strategic Conversation*, 2nd edition, John Wiley and Sons, Chichester, UK

Wack, P. (1985a) 'Scenarios: Uncharted waters ahead', *Harvard Business Review*, September–October, pp73–90

Wack, P. (1985b) 'Scenarios: Shooting the rapids', *Harvard Business Review*, November–December, pp131–142

9

To What Extent Do Venezuela's Causal Textures Allow Scenarios to Work towards Social Dialogue?

Martin Thomas

Introduction

The basis of scenario thinking and the causal textures framework have been described in Chapter 2. In this chapter I explore whether scenarios can be usefully employed in Venezuela. I also suggest that an analysis of the causal textures at play helps practitioners to understand the sort of scenarios that may be appropriate. I undertook a series of research interviews in Venezuela in 2004 after the recall referendum which confirmed President Chávez's continued tenure. These interviews underpin the analysis in this chapter. The country as a whole – Venezuelan society, its politics and its economy – is taken as the unit of analysis in the context of its transactional environment.

The chapter starts with an overview of Venezuela and of causal textures, and then describes the research methodology used. Findings include a table of causal structures, a description of the prerequisites for successful scenario exercises, a summary of the interview results and a categorization of Venezuela's causal texture. I then consider the learning consequences of different causal textures and reflect upon appropriate uses of scenarios in differing degrees of disturbance.

Venezuela[1]

Venezuela's rich deposits of oil were first discovered in 1916. It became a founder member of the Organization of Petroleum Exporting Countries (OPEC) in 1960 and is still the only member of OPEC in the Americas. Oil attracted foreign investment as well as an inflow of immigrant workers, many of whom remained and settled. The paradox of the 'oil curse' is that it offers easy income to some, but seldom reduces wealth inequalities. It also casts a shadow over the agricultural sector and non-oil enterprises that all seem unattractive by comparison. Venezuela is no exception. Its political history shows a positive correlation between political stability and the world price of oil.

Indeed, high oil prices bring double benefits to Venezuela. Most obviously, its oil export sales are at higher prices: less obvious is the resource value effect. Since much of Venezuela's oil requires high extraction costs, potential reserves were excluded from exploitable reserves when the selling price per barrel was expected to continue to be around US$20. However, if the end-2007 prices of US$100 are expected to persist, huge Venezuelan potential reserves become economically viable. This increases the leverage that the country has in world trade. Most of Venezuela's oil traditionally went to the US; but the current government has been developing new markets to reduce this market share.

The first democratic elections in Venezuela in 1945 were won by the Accion Democratica (AD) party. The period between 1945 and the mid 1990s was dominated politically by AD and the Christian Democrats (COPEI) and was characterized by *coups d'état*, military rule, increasing social inequalities and popular discontent, extensive corruption, an oil price boom, a currency collapse, a structural adjustment programme and subsequent riots.

The 1993 elections saw the end of the period of political dominance of AD and COPEI, and in 1998, Hugo Chávez was elected president with a 56 per cent majority. Venezuelans sought new representation and two new parties, Movimiento V. R. and Proyecto Venezuela, emerged strongly. According to political analyst Marina Ottaway (2003), once in power, President Chávez bypassed the state institutions and appealed to populist support for a political clean-up. His style of erratic semi-authoritarianism (with direct military involvement in politics) eroded business confidence in Venezuela, the Latin American headquarters for many multinational businesses.

Chávez focused on a reform of the constitution and won 92 per cent support for a constituent assembly – the Assemblea Nacional Constituyente (ANC) in July 1999. A legislative emergency was declared, allowing the ANC to fire judges and reform the judiciary. In December 1999, 71 per cent voted in favour of expanded presidential powers and allowed for the first time the re-election of the president. The result was a more strongly centralized presidential system with fewer checks and balances. But even those constitutional constraints that remained were resisted by Chávez. Ottaway (2003) says that Chávez convinced the national assembly to authorize him to legislate by decree; but his vetting of judges suggested he was after political control, not judicial efficiency.

Chávez's *Plan Bolivar 2000* brought the military into a development role. Chávez appointed many military officers to political positions. His vision of rapid radical change tolerated no liberalism; results dominated process. However, the democratic heritage of a strong and independent press, unions and business all resisted this encroaching authoritarianism. As Chávez could not control these institutions, a schism developed and he began to harass them. Under the November 2001 economic reform programme, 49 decreed new laws raised business ire. Moreover, these measures, together with threats to nationalize banks, tended to discourage private investment. A national 12-hour strike in December 2001 was followed by a march in January 2002 for Chávez's ouster. He remained, surviving both a *coup* attempt in April 2002 and a 64-day strike that aimed to topple the government.

Opposition parties pinned their hopes on a recall referendum; but when it was eventually held in August 2004, it only strengthened Chávez's position. This completed the fragmentation of the opposition parties, which pulled out of the 2005 elections, handing Chávez an 88 per cent victory but with 75 per cent abstentions. In the run-up to a December 2007 referendum, Chávez proposed 69 amendments to the constitution, including further transfers of power from the legislative to the executive branches of government and the removal of constraints on the re-election of the president. It was also proposed that foreign currency from oil sales should bypass the Central Bank. Restrictions were introduced on media freedoms. Land expropriations were approved and implemented. Foreign investments in the oil sector were further restricted. However, the referendum's outcome was a rejection of the proposed constitutional reforms, showing that the democratic process was, indeed, working in Venezuela.

Political scientist Susanne Gratius (in Piccone and Youngs, 2006) summarizes well:

> *Rather than an absence of elections, the main political problems in Venezuela – after the recall process – relate to the lack of checks and balances, the concentration of power, authoritarian practices, political polarization and the weakness of the opposition. The roots of the current political struggle are found in the previous failure of an elitist democracy, corruption and social exclusion. In order to avoid future violence, Venezuela needs a new political pact between all political and social actors, including the military.*

Causal textures

Emery and Trist (1965) suggested a typology of *organizational* environments that identified four 'ideal types', approximations to which exist in the 'real world' of most organizations. They gave them descriptive names and assigned them codes numbered I to IV in ascending order of disturbance. McCann and Selsky extended this in 1984 to include hyper-turbulence, a transitional step to the vortical environment (Babüroğlu, 1988), now widely accepted as type V. Table 9.1 sets out a summary of this framework.

Table 9.1 *Causal textures: Environments and organizations*

Type	Environment	Characteristics	Successful strategy	Organizations	Learning consequences
I	*Placid randomized* (Emery and Trist, 1965)	Economist's classical market. Static	*Tactics* (= strategy) 'Optimal strategy is just doing one's best on purely local basis'	Distributed	Optimal position is learned by trial and error
II	*Placid clustered* (Emery and Trist, 1965)	Economist's imperfect competition. Stable	*Strategy* dominates over tactics. Keys are distinctive competencies and 'optimal location'	Central control and coordination grow central hierarchies	Knowledge of the environment becomes critical to success
III	*Disturbed reactive* (Emery and Trist, 1965)	Economist's oligopolistic market. More than one big player seeking same pot of resources. Dynamic	*'Operations'* (campaigns of tactical initiatives) between strategy and tactics. What is key is the capacity to move more or less at will to make and meet competitive challenge	Flexibility needs decentralization. Premium on quality and speed of decision at peripheral points. Interdependence emerges	'One has to know when not to fight to the death'. Dynamic stability is obtained by a coming to terms between competitors
IV	*Turbulent fields* (Emery and Trist, 1965)	Not just the interaction of organizations: 'The ground is in motion'. Increased reliance on R&D to build learning capability. Interdependency between economic and other social spheres	*Values* become 'power fields' overriding both strategy and tactics. Effective emerging values create ethical codes that enable simplified action to diverging causal strands. 'Institutionalization' (embodying society's values) becomes strategic objective	Individual organizations cannot adapt alone. Collaborative relationships between dissimilar organizations. Organizational matrix helps to attenuate the effects of turbulence. Values must be shared between all parts of the matrix for this to be effective	1 Increase in 'relevant uncertainty'. 2 Unpredictable results of actions; may not fall off with distance, but is amplified. 3 Emergent environmental forces may attenuate strong action. Changes in values take about one generation to develop

Table 9.1 *Continued*

Type	Environment	Characteristics	Successful strategy	Organizations	Learning consequences
Transitional	*Hyper-turbulent* (McCann and Selsky, 1984)	Partitioned 'enclaves' attract scarce resources. 'Vortices' are left without resources or skills needed to adapt to the environment	*Adaptive capacity* to deal with the 'relevant uncertainty' is the determinant of short-term success (enclave formation). Social triage – deliberate partitioning of the field	Field partitioned by triage policy into enclaves and vortices, with minimal interaction between them	Decoupling of interdependencies. Dysfunctional vortex relationships threatening to affect enclaves
V	*Vortical* (Babüroğlu, 1988)	Failure of active adaptation. Reversion to maladaptation: 1 monothematic dogmatism; 2 stalemate; and 3 polarization	*Double-loop learning* to develop new skills and more resources are needed for long-term removal of vortices. Collective and external strategy is required, and, possibly, temporary or permanent *surrender*	Apparently sealed off from the environment, but not really. Parts effectively immobilize each other	Decline of vortices depends upon external forces, as internal adaptive capacity is inadequate. Surrender may lead to re-emergence

In the 'Characteristics' column of Table 9.1, one sees that the framework starts with static conditions in type I, moves through stability in type II and dynamic in type III, to the 'ground being in motion' in the turbulent field of type IV. Then partitioning, enclave and vortex formation start to lead on to the paradox of type V in which there co-exist both unpredictable change and crystalline rigidity in the vortical environment.

In the next column, successful strategies to cope with these conditions show a different progression. Tactics are good enough in type I (perfect market), while strategy and optimal location are key to success in type II. In type III, the competitive challenge requires operational skills and by type IV, values are needed as a collective defence against the unpredictability of the turbulent fields. In hyper-turbulent conditions, adaptive capacity is key and collective strategy proves too demanding a challenge for the scarce resources. Consequently, social enclaves form from among the 'haves' and social vortices from among the 'have nots'. In the highly challenging conditions of the vortical environment in type V, internal resources are not enough to break out of the enclaves. Babüroğlu

(1988) suggests that the way out is for the actors in the field to develop new skills and bring in resources from outside the enclave(s) in order to address the situation with a collective strategy that includes all actors plus outsiders. However, according to Babüroğlu (1988), there may be no escape from type V other than surrendering to the possibility of collapse.

Organizational forms that typify each causal texture are shown in the next column. These vary from widely distributed in a field (type I) to centralized (type II) and to interdependent (type III). Once turbulence appears in type IV, collaborative relationships between dissimilar organizations are expected to help. Failures of such relationships tend to produce social enclaves in conditions of hyper-turbulence, and if the high level of disturbance is not quelled, an immobilized gridlock of self-serving enclaves results under the vortical conditions of type V.

Learning consequences are shown in the final column. These move from trial and error in type I to knowledge of the environment in type II, then to learning to come to terms with others in type III. Turbulent fields require organizations to learn new values. Hyper-turbulent and vortical causal textures demand an ability to learn new ways from others, and include discovering new ways of learning and accessing help from outside the entity or field itself. In the extreme case of surrender, the essential learning is how to restart if the field has been annihilated, but the entity has survived: 'One "lets go" and surrenders to a larger system in order to search for a new identity or configuration' at the appropriate time, Babüroğlu (1988, p169) argues.

In the polarized conditions prevalent in Venezuela, consensus with regard to the classification of its causal texture should not be expected. There is wide scope for subjective interpretations and little by way of internationally recognized metrics. However, it is desirable to get an accurate diagnosis of a situation's causal texture because each one suggests a different adaptive strategy. Inappropriate strategies can be counterproductive. My method of research (see below) delivers a reasonable body of information from which to produce a balanced assessment of the Venezuelan situation. The fact that people from both extremes of Venezuelan society consider it biased suggests to me that views from all sides have been reasonably well balanced. I therefore offer that assessment as a working hypothesis in order to provide a foundation for comments later in the chapter on the suitability of scenarios to meet Venezuela's needs.

Method

The purpose of the project was to explore the viability of a scenario exercise as a means of structuring a social dialogue across the whole of Venezuelan society. During the mid 1980s, Clem Sunter's High Road and Low Road scenarios of South Africa had shown how scenarios captured the imagination of leaders facing great change (Ilbury and Sunter, 2001). A decade later, the Mont Fleur scenarios demonstrated how the involvement of future leaders in building the scenarios and testing the resilience of their existing strategies in the context of each scenario could shape decisions (Kahane, 2004). Scenarios also provided excellent material for the further communication of the decisions in their contexts to a wider South African audience and beyond. For this project, the questions were whether this could be a useful route forward for Venezuela, and if not, why not? And could the causal texture of Venezuela's environment contribute to an understanding of the situation?

The research I undertook as part of an MSc degree in change management in September of 2004 set out to address these questions. In order to avoid forcing any causal texture onto the Venezuelan situation, I designed the research process using Glaser and Strauss's grounded theory for an initial analysis (Glaser and Strauss, 1967). I also established a framework of criteria by which to classify the causal texture of Venezuela and its transactional environment.

Drawing upon the high-level contacts of some thought leaders in the country, a programme of interviews was arranged with business, church, university and political party leaders as widely representative as possible of the whole of Venezuelan society.

Initial interviews were conducted with five internationally recognized authorities on scenario thinking, an international shuttle diplomat and the Venezuelan ambassador to a European Union (EU) country. Then, in Caracas, 26 interviews were held during September 2004. Of these 26 interviewees, 7 were supporters of Chávez, 16 were supporters of opposition parties and 3 were '*ni-nis*' (non-committed). Of the Chávez supporters, three were currently in post and two were former ministers.[2] However, in order to capture the views of people other than the highly educated elite who constituted the bulk of the thought leaders, I arranged two more sets of interviews in La Vega, a relatively poor '*barrio*' of Caracas. The first was with a group of students (all male) from the provinces currently studying in the capital. The second was an informal impromptu meeting also in La Vega on a wet Sunday afternoon, mostly attended by females of all ages. Some 18 more voices were captured via these meetings. All 18 seemed to be supporters of Chávez.

Three working documents were produced from the research process (as well as Table 9.1):

1   prerequisites for scenarios, drawing upon the interviews with leading practitioners;
2   *The Chorus of Voices*, classifying the interview materials according to topics that emerged from them;
3   a categorization of the Venezuelan situation by causal texture from interview materials.

The following section reports the findings from this process.

Findings

Prerequisites for successful scenario exercises are fivefold

The will to listen

All of the scenario experts agreed that listening was key to the success of scenario exercises. There needs to be a genuine will for reflective dialogue on the part of all participants. Kahane (2004) explains that this requires a search for deeper truths behind the words used both within one's self and within others.

Convening power

Convening power is essential to starting a national scenario-based dialogue process. Continuing leadership is also needed to protect it and to defend its cause throughout the process (see Chapter 13 in this volume). The interviewees were divided as to whether the convenor for the Venezuelan process should be a global authority or a prominent Venezuelan national.

An ability to meet

Well-known scenario thinker Hardin Tibbs pointed out that a somewhat turbulent environment is more conducive to scenario work than a stable environment since change is already a reality. However, when participants fear for their lives as a result of meeting for the scenario work, many naturally choose not to do so.

Time and resources

Maintaining a balance between time and resources, on the one hand, and the ambition of the exercise, on the other, is a way to avoid unfulfilled or unrealistic promises.

Technical competence

Technical competence to run and manage the process – challenging assumptions and administering it – is vital. However, this skill can be bought in from abroad if not available locally.

The Chorus of Voices

This was a collection I organized by topic of the views expressed in the larger set of interviews about Venezuela's context, and the appropriateness and feasibility of a national scenario exercise.

In summary, I found from the interviewees in 2004 that the success or failure of a national scenario dialogue initiative in Venezuela depended upon the support of the president, but as his leadership was considered unpredictable by many, credible convening power appeared to be absent. Venezuela appeared to be a country in which saying one thing and doing something else were accepted to the point of being expected. Trompenaars (1993) identified Venezuela as an extreme case of 'particularism' in which protecting a friend justifies telling a lie, albeit at the cost of eroding the currency of truth. If dissembling is the norm, it makes it difficult to grow trust since dialogue partners cannot be relied upon. Corruption also seemed to be widespread and worsening in 2004 (the 2007 World Bank Institute rankings show Venezuela to be consistently among the lowest 20 per cent of countries worldwide with regard to the control of corruption). The ethical loss to society appeared to me to be more significant than the financial loss to the economy. It undermined the trust that is essential to dialogue and impeded the open leadership of change. The media and political parties acted to pull the polarized country in two opposite directions. The mutual respect to be engendered in scenario work would be easily undermined by the aggressive media coverage with its extremes of 'us and them'.

The interviewees generally agreed that dialogue would help the country to heal wounds at many levels. Most interviewees saw this need; but it was unclear to them whether President Chávez understood it. Views from the government officials interviewed on the usefulness of a scenario exercise ranged from the disparaging to the fully supportive. Opposition people and those committed to neither side generally felt that any means of dialogue would be welcome, but only if the president were supportive of it. However, the opposition's action was not coordinated or consistent with its words since some proponents of dialogue were reluctant to follow up on openings for scenarios from government officials when they were offered. It seemed to me at the time (and I still believe) that dialogue would need to begin at sub-national or sectoral levels if scenarios were to take root in Venezuela. Several interviewees mentioned that scenarios are perceived to be a technique of the business sector. The challenge of introducing the concept at national level and at the same time addressing some of the major issues facing the country is perhaps too much to expect as a first step. An example of a sectoral initiative is that in March 2007 Venezuelan futurist José Luis Cordeiro presented some energy scenarios for Venezuela in the context of the United Nations *Global Energy Scenarios* for 2020.

Suzanne Gratius (cited in Piccone and Youngs, 2006), reached a similar conclusion:

> *For the international community, Venezuela is a challenging case. There is no easy solution to the phenomenon of electoral semi-authoritarianism. Difficult to classify, the Chávez regime 'is a rather unique and complex phenomenon' requiring a combination of measures that would take into account country specific political conditions. From the outside, the only viable strategy in Venezuela seems to be the promotion of regular contacts with, as well as between, the main political and social actors of the country. After the December 2005 parliamentary elections, the government may be more inclined to a consensus-building policy with other political and social actors... This might encourage national dialogue on the main*

national themes. The recently started dialogue between the government and the Catholic Church and the country's main business organization, Fedecámaras, are hopeful signs for a necessary process of national reconciliation. The international community should support these efforts and try to extend the government's agenda to the political level.

Categorization of the Venezuelan situation by causal texture

In the Venezuelan research I found attributes of several causal textures, including all of the characteristics associated with the vortical environment (see Table 9.2).

Table 9.2 *Summary of the main characteristics of vortical environments*

Monothematic dogmatism	Committed to one theme and cannot go beyond it Dogma becomes the norm for telling right from wrong Self-contained absolute truth for eternity
Stalemate	Means dominate ends; unable to pursue logical objectives Parts oppose each other; do not join to serve the whole Goal moratorium Productivity trap
Polarization	Maladaptive social enclaves provide norms and values Homonymy = sense of belonging Group identity strengthened by conflict between groups Us and them => god and devil extremes (in versus out groups)

I concluded in the research paper produced from this project in 2004 that, on balance, Venezuela presented an extreme vortical case. It showed the three paradoxes of vortical environments (Babüroğlu, 1988) – namely, the co-existence of:

- crystalline rigidity together with unpredictable change;
- clinched connectedness and chaotic fluctuations;
- stalemated systems that are highly differentiated and highly integrated at once.

In Venezuela in 2004, many interviewees felt a strong undercurrent of change that was seemingly frozen on the surface. Dialogue between government supporters and opposition parties was a near impossibility as recrimination over the strike of 2002 to 2003 was still a live and divisive issue.

Babüroğlu (1988) says that the inability to pursue logical ends, parts opposing each other, goal moratorium and the productivity trap are all characteristics of a maladaptive response called stalemate, which seemed to characterize the system in 2004.

I believe that since 2004 the prospects of complete political and economic stalemate have attenuated. The increasing price of oil has certainly enabled the government to avoid facing the economic accountability issues that would have surfaced had the price returned to the mid US$20s per barrel, as expected at the time of the research. The December 2007 referendum result clearly shows that democratic voting is functioning. Indeed, one commentator on a draft of this chapter expressed the opinion that Venezuela in 2007 presented an example of a disturbed–reactive causal texture in that the situation was 'oligopolistic and dynamic'. I reject this as it appears to me that the country is in the throes of paradigmatic change in its economic, social and political policies. Consequently, there is a complete absence of the dynamic stability characteristic of type III causal textures.

Another possible interpretation of Venezuela's environment's causal texture during 2004 draws attention to its hyper-turbulent features. The defining characteristic of this transitional state is that the cohesion and interdependency that were characteristic of the turbulent field start to give way to more self-centred tendencies to defend local interests, even at the cost of other members of the system or the whole system. This seemed clearly to describe the situation in Venezuela where many interest groups across the social and political spectrum have formed enclaves. Enclave interests predominate over objectives of the whole country. A prime example is the political scene where individual party interests have been driving the agendas of all opposition parties, almost all of which withdrew from the 2005 elections, handing the electoral victory on a plate to the supporters of President Chávez. The entire democratic process has been damaged as a result of the pursuit of enclave interests, where the adaptive capacity fell short of what the context demanded. Perhaps the political power shown by students in 2007 may characterize them as an emerging enclave.

Venezuela in 2007 appeared to come closer to hyper-turbulence than the vortical situation I found in 2004. However, classifying a complex national political, economic and social system and its environment in terms of a causal texture is only a first step in a learning process.

Learning consequences of different causal textures

Perhaps more important than seeking consensus on the 'correct' causal texture for the Venezuelan situation is seeking understanding of possible solutions from the theoretical concepts.

Emery and Trist (1965) pointed out that at type II (placid–clustered environment), knowledge of the environment would be critical to the success of the system in question. It seems that different perceptions of the environment by various factions in Venezuela continue to keep the opposite poles in the country apart. The continuing polarization of the media feeds these different perceptions. At an international summit of Hispanic heads of state in late 2007, Chávez expressed his view that the previous Aznar government in Spain was 'fascist'; opposition parties saw it as more democratic than the elected Venezuelan government. Scenario work offers the opportunity to 're-perceive' the environment and understand the perceptions of others. As noted above, the scenario experts I interviewed believe a crucial determinant of scenario success is a willingness to listen.

At type III (disturbed–reactive environment), the critical knowledge required is an understanding of when not to eliminate the adversary. Emery and Trist (1965) say that 'stability can be obtained only by a certain coming-to-terms between competitors, whether enterprises, interest groups or governments'. There were few signs of such agreements, either implicit or explicit, between competing factions in Venezuela at the time of the research. Indeed, both political extremes seemed determined to eliminate the other and both were failing to learn to come to terms with others of differing opinions.

At type IV (turbulent field environment), 'what becomes precarious ... is how organizational stability can be achieved. In these environments, individual organizations, however large, cannot expect to adapt successfully simply through their own direct actions' (Emery and Trist, 1965). In other words, the interdependencies among economic and other social actors become complex and saturated. This, in turn, requires a collective effort to learn new values. Emery and Trist (1965) argue that social values become the new 'power fields' that allow organizations to adapt effectively to the turbulence in their environments through collaborative endeavours. They also warn that new values take a lifetime to learn, recognizing that values contain both rational and irrational components.

Venezuela in the first decade of this century has characteristics of all three of these causal textures (types II, III and IV) and their learning needs. Chávez has introduced the formerly marginalized into the heart of political life with a new set of social values. Many of those values would probably be shared by a majority of the population, but a forum for sharing them is lacking. So long as the highly polarized media are the only channels open to mass communication, the 'us versus them', 'in and out group' division is perpetuated that typifies yet another causal texture – namely, the partition of a field in hyper-turbulent conditions. Venezuela needs a means of communicating across the social and political spectra. The 2004 research project identified this need and proposed scenarios as a possible way forward. In the trauma of the post-strike situation in 2003 in which the Venezuelan economy had been paralysed for 64 days, there initially appeared to be no desire on the part of the government to collaborate with opposition parties or people. Trust was at the lowest levels imaginable. Once again, scenario thinking could have contributed towards offering a way forward for the country or for parts of it. However, there was no suggestion from the research work that scenarios or any other social dialogue process could lead to a collaborative approach between the polarized factions of Venezuelan society. The best that could have been achieved would have been some mutual appreciation, perhaps the initiation of the sharing of new values. Indeed, when a highly placed representative of the government offered to support the scenario initiative, the only precondition being that it respected the then new constitution, apparent supporters of dialogue from the opposition were reluctant to participate for fear that the process might be manipulated to meet the ends of the government. They also feared for their personal safety if they were to participate. This appeared to me to present an example of insufficient adaptive capacity. Enclave objectives were dominating the needs of the whole and the environment was not conducive to the dialogue it seemed to require so desperately.

Under the hyper-turbulent conditions described by McCann and Selsky (1984), differences in how actors perceive and deploy their adaptive capacity are the crucial determinant of how well they will cope. This dictates what the people need to learn. Articulating the learning needs (whether they are learning for collective strategy formulation or learning how to appreciate differences that separate factions operating in a hyper-turbulent context) are critical considerations when determining the scope, nature and ambition of a scenario exercise at national level. The implication of the disturbed–reactive causal texture is that interdependence between the main actors becomes important and needs to be acknowledged and dealt with. The main actors in Venezuela could not envisage this at the time of the research project. On the contrary, there were sufficient signs of social triage for it to be classified as hyper-turbulent if not vortical. Consequently, the dialogue of scenarios was needed to enable members of all polarized factions to understand the views of others, to develop new skills and to look at ways of doing things differently. Since more of the same sort of behaviour seemed unlikely to address the increasing divisions within Venezuelan society, and no short-term solution appeared available, the proposal for scenarios of appreciation was put forward as a small, but potentially productive, step in the right direction.

In 2006, Suzanne Gratius (cited in Piccone and Youngs, 2006) argued that 'the international community should redirect democracy promotion strategies in Venezuela from an electoral to a bilateral and multilateral dialogue approach'. In other words, Gratius sees dialogue as the key requirement for democracy to prosper in Venezuela – a more important target of international support than the election process hitherto seen as the top priority. This corroborates both the need for dialogue expressed at the time of the research project and its continued validity.

Appropriate uses of scenarios

Scenarios have proven track records as excellent vehicles for social dialogue if they are appropriately scoped and properly structured. As discussed in Chapter 2, scenarios may be considered useful to decision-makers operating in turbulent environments. However, my research project and my work with scenarios in practice have led me to consider that scenarios might be used in different ways in different causal textures. I outline this notion below as a practitioner's working hypothesis and recognize that it calls for further exploration.

In Figure 9.1, I propose a scheme that identifies the purpose of scenarios most likely to be achieved in the various causal textures. The horizontal axis uses the appreciate, influence, control (AIC) framework developed by William E. Smith in 1980 (see Smith and Davis, 2004). It is concerned with organizing the relationship between purpose and power. For example, the most that can be *controlled* by the members of any organization is what happens within the organization or system itself. People and groups outside the organization may be capable of being *influenced* by that organization if they are in its immediate transactional environment. But beyond that, entities in the contextual environment can only be *appreciated* as they are beyond the power field of the organization's influence.

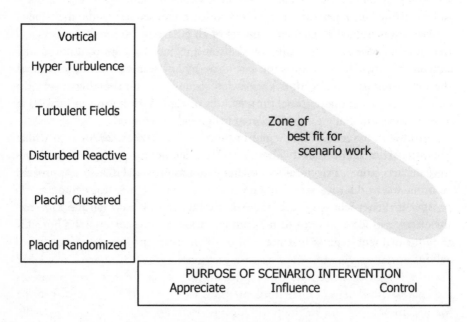

Figure 9.1 Causal textures and purpose of scenarios

Whereas at relatively low levels of disturbance it is possible to envisage scenarios designed to allow actors to control the system, higher levels of disturbance in the causal texture make control by any single organization or actor impossible. Scanning the successful strategy and organization columns of Table 9.1 shows that actors have less direct control as the causal texture of the organization in its environment becomes increasingly disturbed. In the placid–random condition of type I, tactics are appropriate behaviour; while decision-making is decentralized and decision-takers are in full control of their own organization's actions. In type II, strategy replaces tactics and centralized hierarchies come into play to take the strategic decisions. This involves separating strategic decisions from the action and direct control of 'line' managers. Under the disturbed–reactive type III causal texture, other organizations come into play as interdependence between organizations emerges. This means that strategy becomes another step removed from action and line control. In fact, control no longer resides within the system itself in the sense that successful strategy relies upon an organization's success in influencing others. Actors in the transactional environment become critical to success and can be expected to influence the organization. It would be possible to involve some third parties in a scenario exercise in such circumstances in order to encourage the sharing of understanding and the formulation of mutually acceptable strategies.

Emery and Trist (1965) make it clear that in turbulent fields (type IV), values become power fields. Values cannot be imposed (particularly not upon people in the transactional and contextual environments), and so influence is exercised via people's adoption of new values or their expression of existing, latent values. Thus, under these conditions, mutual influence replaces command and control, and scenarios designed to maximize the adoption of commonly held values may well be successful. Since these values must be shared by all actors in the environment, control is wrested from the organization itself. Indeed, it may be argued that this is exactly what happened with the South African scenarios. Both Sunter and Kahane used scenarios to convince the leaders of political polar opposites to appreciate the position of the others and to adopt new values that would embrace the whole of the racial spectrum of the country. Such cohesive values were new to both the Afrikaner regime and to the African National Congress (ANC); scenarios were instrumental in their adoption.

When turbulence gives way to hyper-turbulence, collaborative endeavours are abandoned as organizations focus their scarce adaptive capacity on the ends of their own 'enclave'. While it may be argued that scenarios of control may be appropriate *within* enclaves, the transactional context of hyper-turbulence implies immense uncertainty due to the impact of highly turbulent forces on the enclaves themselves. Therefore, an appreciation of what is going on in the wider context may well be the most appropriate purpose for scenarios, possibly addressing the emerging gaps between the enclaves. The energy scenarios of 2007 in Venezuela may be examples of appropriate appreciative purpose. In the type V vortical environment, appreciation of the other is what is needed to relax the dogma that keeps the parts polarized and the system in stalemate. Babüroğlu (1988, 1992) points out that a little learning may be enough to melt the ice of the apparently frozen system, but also acknowledges that abandonment may be the only available strategy.

Indeed, one of the recommendations of the 2004 research in Venezuela was that some initial steps towards dialogue should be set up, particularly scenarios of appreciation, in certain sectors of Venezuela, such as energy or education. International development planner Francisco Sagasti pointed out in the interview for this project that in the case of national scenarios for Peru, it took ten years of such small-scale preparation before the country was able to contemplate a fully fledged national scenario exercise. This appeared to the proponents of scenarios in Venezuela in 2004 to be too distant a time horizon. In appreciate, influence, control (AIC) terms, their ambition was beyond their power field and was therefore unachievable in Venezuela in 2004.

In national scenario processes, country scenario facilitator Barbara Heinzen considers that more than half the time is usually needed to explore the driving forces that have brought the country to its current situation in terms that are meaningful to participants from a wide variety of backgrounds. Vickers (1995) would see this as a means of establishing a 'reality judgement'. Recognizing where we are and what has brought us here (even though we agree to see history through the different lenses that we each use) constitutes a major first step. The Truth and Reconciliation Commission allowed this to happen in South Africa with stunning new perceptions of reality in all parts of society as a consequence. Scenarios can start this process in a workshop setting and provide the seed corn for a wider broadcasting. For example, an understanding of the historical impact of oil on Venezuela and other oil-rich countries, for better and for worse, would enable a widespread understanding of the status quo by all parts of Venezuelan society. This may be a critical prerequisite to agreeing future action or understanding possible futures.

Scenario thinking creates a 'space' for dialogue, and scenario exercises provide an infrastructure for communication among the various enclaves or factions in society. The history of the world shows that events have rarely unfolded according to expert predictions. Those who adapt to the improbable emergent reality most quickly are the long-term winners. Darwin came to this conclusion in the evolution of species. Stuart Kauffman reached the same conclusion in his Complex Adaptive Systems Theory, with reference to organizational behaviour (Kauffman, 1995). Scenario thinking enables people and organizations to contemplate the way in which different futures may look by examining the limits of what might plausibly occur in extreme circumstances.

Conclusion

Venezuela as a system appears to be undergoing tectonic shifts in social, economic and political spheres. The rules of the game are in flux, including constitutional changes with far-reaching consequences. Oil income at record high levels is funding temporary solutions to structural problems. The demands on resources are extreme and people are unable to accommodate the changes needed in a polarized society with few mechanisms for dialogue. If Venezuela is to move forward, it will have to look within itself to find the adaptive capacity, even given the big external driving forces that have been buffeting it (and will continue to do so). It seems to me that modest steps are needed to build communications and cooperation. Scenarios can help social dialogue; but a desire to heal the deep wounds has to come from within Venezuela. If the dialogue process is imposed from outside, scenarios would almost certainly be inappropriate since they would become a forum for negotiations among the parties, not a vehicle for enriching or enlarging perceptions.

The jargon of business to which scenarios have been tethered from their origin gives scenarios a veneer of capitalism that makes them unwelcome in certain quarters. I found this to be the case among some people interviewed in Venezuela. A new vocabulary is needed to accommodate the social aspirations for all. The exploration of multiple possible futures offers a cognitive tool for many different causal textures so long as the ambition of the exercise is commensurate with the context. An understanding of the causal texture of the environment and the system in question can help to ensure that this is accomplished. The debate surrounding it is essential to expanding the use of such classifications and understanding their implications for mounting scenario exercises.

The South African experience shows that scenarios offer an evolutionary process to achieve sustainable change that would otherwise be considered revolutionary. If used appropriately in Venezuela, multiple futures analysis could yet prove to be instrumental to the cause of the Bolivarian Revolution or to any other approach to the lasting good of the country, its people and its institutions.

Notes

1 Material in this section is drawn largely from Ottaway (2003) and Gratius (in Piccone and Youngs, 2006).
2 The apparent imbalance in numbers is not significant in grounded theory since topics become 'saturated' once a view has been expressed more than once. Further repetitions of the same view do not add to its weight.

References

Babüroğlu, O. (1988) 'The vortical environment: The fifth in the Emery–Trist levels of organizational environments', *Human Relations*, vol 41, pp181–210

Babüroğlu, O. (1991) 'Is the end of free fall free fall?', in F. Geyes (ed) *The Cybernetics of Complex Systems,* InterSystems Publications, Salinas, CA

Babüroğlu, O. (1992) 'Surrendering to the environment in educational system design', in C. Reigeluth, B. Banathy and J. Olson (eds) *Nato ASI Series,* Springer Verlag, AH Dordrecht, The Netherlands

Emery, F. and Trist, E. (1965) 'The causal texture of organizational environments', *Human Relations,* vol 18, pp21–32

Glaser, B. and Strauss, A. (1967) *The Discovery of Grounded Theory*, Aldine, Chicago

Kahane, A. (2004) *Solving Tough Problems,* Berrett-Koehler, San Francisco, CA

Kauffman, S. A. (1995) *At Home in the Universe: The Search for Laws of Self-Organization and Complexity*, Oxford University Press, Oxford, UK

Ilbury, C. and Sunter, C. (2001) *The Mind of a Fox: Scenario Planning in Action,* Human and Rousseau, Tafelberg

McCann, J. and Selsky, J. (1984) 'Hyperturbulence and the emergence of type 5 environments', *Academy of Management Review*, vol 9, no 3, pp460–470

Ottaway, M. (2003) *Democracy Challenged*, Carnegie, Washington, DC

Piccone, T. and Youngs, R. (2006) *Strategies for Democratic Change: Assessing the Global Response,* Democracy Coalition Project, Washington, DC

Smith, W. and Davis, E. (2004) 'Transforming organizations and leaders: The AIC process – a five dimensional power systems framework', www.odii.com/aic-process.html, accessed February 2008

Trompenaars, A. (1993) *Riding the Waves of Culture*, Brealey, London,UK

Vickers, G. (1995) *The Art of Judgment: A Study of Policy Making*, Sage, London, UK

Part III

10

Managing Disruptive Change and Turbulence through Continuous Change Thinking and Scenarios[1]

John W. Selsky and Joseph E. McCann

Introduction

Scenario building is more than a prelude to strategic planning – these two practices play different roles. Traditional strategic planning is often associated with goal-directed deterministic thinking and execution. In contrast, scenario building explicitly offers potential for imaginative and systemic thinking. The latter kind of thinking is likely to prove more valuable in the increasingly volatile world of global commerce and industry (Normann and Ramírez, 1993; Flood, 1999; Beck and Holzer, 2007). This is the world of the turbulent environment.

Turbulent environments are characterized by rapid change, surprising connections of events and frequent shocks. For example, the impact of one of the most shocking events of the recent past, the attacks of 11 September 2001, has been profound. Pursuing a vision and goals under such conditions requires broad skills on the part of organizations and their members, including imagination and holistic thinking as well as rational planning. 'Nine-eleven' seems to have signalled a big shift in the attention of both executives and organization researchers.

Driven largely by the dynamic nature of high-technology businesses, management and strategy scholars during the past decade have given considerable attention to the rapid pace of change and responses to it, such as flexible organizational structures and 'boundary-less' designs that break down internal silos, foster cross-functional solutions and enable an organization to keep up or set the pace of change in its industry. However, the focus now seems to be shifting to a new set of key drivers of change – shock, surprise, crisis, discontinuity, chaos – which are difficult, if not impossible, to anticipate. Scholars have begun to search for effective responses that organizations might mobilize to such threats to avoid 'collisions' and remain resilient. In short, resilience, along with agility, has become essential for absorbing and responding to disruptive change.

The purpose of this chapter is to explore these new key drivers. We first situate disruptiveness in terms of Emery and Trist's (1965) causal textures of the environment, as discussed in Chapter 2. We distinguish among three kinds of disruptiveness – operational, competitive and contextual – and demonstrate that managers need to cope with each kind in a different way. We argue that *contextual* disruption is increasingly salient for managers today and suggest two avenues for managers to enhance their capabilities in coping with it. First, they need to shift their thinking about change from an 'episodic' model to a 'continuous' model (see also Chapter 5 in this volume). Second, they need to use scenarios to develop a robust foundation for improvising effective collective action. We suggest that doing these two things can help managers to deepen their appreciation of contextual disruption and develop new capabilities to cope with future turbulence.

We cite data from an online global survey on change, agility and resilience that we conducted in 2006 on behalf of the American Management Association (AMA) and Human Resource Institute (HRI) (AMA/HRI, 2006). The survey yielded 1378 usable responses from senior and human resource managers in 803 private-sector firms out of the approximately 8000 members worldwide of these two associations. We extracted sub-samples of 494 'higher performers' and 326 'lower performers'[2] to contrast their views about change and reinforce the importance of building adaptive capacity.

Disruptiveness and environmental textures

As discussed in Chapter 2, studies in the fields of scenarios and causal textures distinguish between the transactional and contextual environment. Managers play the game of producing goods and services through dealings with other organizations in their transactional environments. They organize these dealings through strategies designed to deliver success in the industry(ies) chosen. Each organization creates and maintains its own transactional environment; this is the arena of its operational and competitive processes. Organizations align themselves with others in certain 'value constellations' (Normann and Ramírez, 1993, p66), in which 'suppliers, business partners, allies, governments and other economic actors work together to co-produce value' with customers. The transactional environments of firms in the same industry or value constellation routinely overlap to some extent. The larger contextual environment (the 'L22' relationships discussed in Chapter 2) encompasses all overlapping transactional arenas and is the source of forces that create broader challenges, such as technology advances, changing economic conditions and political trends, and shifts in societal values and attitudes (e.g. about the natural environment).

In Emery and Trist's (1965) terms, environments can be distinguished in relation to their complexity and dynamism; this gives them the distinctive 'textures' discussed in Chapter 2. Building on their work, we propose that managers generally experience the complexity and dynamism of an environment in terms of its pace of change and its disruptiveness. The perceived frequency at which events and conditions change, as well as the potential for unique, unanticipated surprises, differentiates environmental textures and produces organizational challenges of various kinds. In this chapter we focus on the disruptive aspect of environmental change.

In the causal textures framework, *placid* environments are characterized by mineral disruption and a modest pace of change. *Disturbed–reactive* environments feature competitive manoeuvres among industry players based on generally acknowledged, relatively stable and predictable ground rules of competition. The competition and the disruption it causes may be intense, with rapid changes in research and development (R&D) cycles, product introductions and technology leapfrogging that provide opportunities for – and threats to – competitive advantage. In a *turbulent field*, environment-competitive gaming is intense and fast paced, *and* the ground rules of competitive action are disrupted by unexpected events and forces coming in from the contextual environment. The 'escalating scale and density of social interaction brought on by population growth and its demands ... and increasing, but uneven, technological innovation' are two driving contextual forces that have been making environments less stable and predictable, and promoting turbulence (McCann and Selsky, 1984, p461).

Finally, when pace or disruptiveness begin to exceed the adaptive capacities of organizations in that environment, the texture shifts again and a *hyper-turbulent* (McCann and Selsky, 1984) or *vortical* environment (Babüroğlu, 1988) may emerge (Chapter 9 discusses these excessively volatile textures with regard to the situation in Venezuela). An acute crisis such as a natural disaster or terrorist attack may escalate quickly, sending all affected organizations into a state of extreme uncertainty and disturbance to which they must respond in unaccustomed ways (Weick, 2003). If such a state of extreme uncertainty recedes relatively quickly, then the environmental texture will revert to the less turbulent pre-existing condition. But if the extreme uncertainty state becomes endemic, then the very existence of the field of organizations may be in jeopardy.

All causal textures of the environment feature change of some kind. Note that rapid pace and competitor-driven disruption are features of the *disturbed–reactive* causal texture. Effective businesses routinely cope with these conditions by outplaying their competitors. These conditions do not necessarily produce a turbulent environment (Selsky et al, 2007). In the turbulent causal texture, rapid pace combines with the broader (contextual) kind of disruption discussed below to produce intense conditions that challenge the normal competitive ways of adapting. In the next section we explore three different kinds of disruption, link them to environmental textures, and illustrate coping mechanisms that managers need to use to deal with each kind.

The salience of disruptive change

If organizations are faced with disruption all the time, then disruption may be considered routine; various kinds of events, issues, processes and ideas continually threaten to disturb the normal functioning of organizations. Yet, some disruption is far from routine. Strategy researchers have begun to recognize the shock potential of organization environments as a key contingency in adaptation and capability-building (see Bower and Christensen, 1995; Sutcliffe and Vogus, 2003; Sirmon et al, 2007). Clearly, disruption is a broad concept worth exploring.

Table 10.1 *Managerial experience of disruptive change over the past year*

	Overall results (percentage)	Higher performers (percentage)	Lower performers (percentage)
No	31.1	36.6	24.8
Only minor disruption and operational impact	28.5	29.5	19.9
Core operations were affected	17.7	15.8	17.8
A major business strategy shift was required	16.6	13.7	24.2
Overall mission and vision were challenged	3.0	2.1	5.6
Long-term viability and existence were/are threatened	3.1	2.4	7.7

Source: AMA/HRI (2006, p61)

We begin by asking how disruption impacts upon organizations. Disruptive events and processes may penetrate deeply or shallowly. In the global survey (AMA/HRI, 2006), we asked respondents: 'In the past 12 months, has your organization experienced disruptive change …?' Their responses, in Table 10.1, show that significant disruption – to firms' core operations, business strategy, mission and vision, or long-term viability – occurred in 40 per cent of the overall sample, but the difference between the higher (34 per cent) and the lower (55 per cent) performers is striking. However, we did not ask managers to identify the kinds or sources of disruption that affected them. We explore this area next.

Three kinds of disruption

We suggest that there are three broad kinds of disruption – operational, competitive and contextual (Bouchikhi and Kimberly, 2003). Managers need to cope with each kind in distinctive ways.

Operational disruption is the normal fluctuation in demand, supply and price for an organization's goods and services over time. This kind of disruption occurs in *placid* environmental textures. Scholars of organization design have offered structural solutions for this kind of disruption for many years. For example, organizational units such as sales, purchasing and human resource departments serve as structural mechanisms to 'buffer the technical core' and ensure smooth operations (Thompson, 1967). In addition, organizations routinely use rules, policies, chains of command and plans to cope with operational disruption (Galbraith, 1977).

Competitive disruption is characterized by jostling for superior position and sustainable advantage among players within and even between industries (see Bower and Christensen, 1995). This kind of disruption occurs in *disturbed–reactive* environmental textures. It continually threatens strategic plans and forces changes in basic business strategy due to the actions of competitors and changing industry conditions (see Michael Porter's, 1980, 1985, classic works on competitive strategy). 'High-velocity' industries with rapid product innovations present special competitive challenges (Brown and Eisenhardt, 1997).

Organizations cope with competitive disruption through competitive environmental scanning, traditional strategic planning and manoeuvring, judicious partnering with other firms, and development of unique capabilities. Managers may incorporate novel structural features and cross-functional teams to mobilize internal capabilities against those of competitors (see Nadler and Tushman, 1988). The tactic of 'hypercompetition' (D'Aveni, 1994, 1999) pushes the envelope of responses to competitive disruption by claiming that firms can prosper by continually disrupting the bases of competition in their industries and inventing new competitive rules. Some big players, such as Intel's former chief executive officer (CEO) Andy Grove, relish disrupting their industries by creating 'technological discontinuities' that they can both control and withstand better than others. Yet, other big players shy away from such aggressive manoeuvring and try to maintain an 'imperial order' within their industry (D'Aveni, 2002).

Competitive actions may fail to deliver the intended effects, and they may have unintended effects and consequences that make things worse for the initiator, for other players in the industry, or, indeed, for the industry as a whole or the wider society. The fact that competitive disruptions can spill out of the industry container and incite wider social effects and consequences has not been studied much by strategy scholars; instead, scholars of corporate social responsibility have taken up these issues. In addition, it is possible that the pace of change may accelerate to the point where it becomes disruptive and unmanageable for most players. That means that the pace of change and the disruptiveness of change may not be mutually independent dimensions of environmental texture. These 'loose ends' lead us to consider a third kind of disruption.

Contextual disruption is less predictable as it falls in the category of 'unknowns that we don't know'. As such, it poses potentially damaging consequences much more broadly – but also potential opportunities. These are the truly surprising exogenous changes that buffet all firms in an industry and disturb their well-crafted plans and strategies. This kind of disruption occurs in *turbulent* environmental textures; they are intrusions of the new and unexpected L22 relationships into the shared transactional space of organizations. We discuss contextual disruption at length because we feel this is – or should be – the area of greatest concern to managers operating in volatile industries today.

Contextual disruptions may come in the form of surprises, crises and disasters, whether natural or man-made (Beck, 2002; Nathan and Kovoor-Misra, 2002; Mitroff and Alpaslan, 2003; Cunha et al, 2006). They arise from a number of sources:

(a) *Novel conjunctures of seemingly unrelated parts of one or multiple systems.* Complexity theory tells us that whole systems with dense connections among the parts exhibit behaviours that cannot be predicted from understanding the parts and their direct interactions (Stacey, 2001; van der Heijden, 2005). An example is Perrow's (1984) study of the 1979 Three Mile Island nuclear accident and its aftermath, discussed in Chapter 2. Perrow examined how complexly connected technologies can produce what he called 'normal accidents' that can go on to severely disrupt entire societies (see also Perrow, 2007). Bonabeau (2007) notes that 'interconnected risk factors and cascading failures' make complex systems fragile, without even considering the effect of malicious intent (as in computer viruses or terrorist attacks on infrastructure). The tight connectivity of complex systems increases the likelihood that a disruption in one system or part of a system may jump a system boundary and produce 'synchronous failure' (Homer-Dixon, 2006, p127) or a cascading series of unexpected events (Farjoun and Starbuck, 2007).

(b) *Attempts at competitive disruption that spin out of control.* Unintended consequences have long been studied in economics, public policy and other disciplines, but not so much in strategic management. When new developments in multiple industries emerge and accelerate together, they can create unintended consequences that no single organization can manage. Examples include effects of pollution on the human food chain, unemployment caused by job exports to low-wage countries, and the sub-prime mortgage morass in the US with wide exposure of banks and investment firms worldwide.

The concept of the *risk society* (Beck, 2002; Beck and Holzer, 2007) offers a rich insight into unintended consequences. Beck's idea starts from the observation that all disruptions, apart from natural disasters, are self-induced in an endogenous, systemic way – that is, industrial societies using complex technologies always produce unexpected risk, along with a vast array of beneficial goods and services. These unexpected risks cannot be easily contained, and produce the potential for three main societal-level threats: ecosystem collapse, financial collapse and cultural-political collapse (see Diamond, 2005; Homer-Dixon, 2006). At the organizational level, the wealth produced in industrial societies tends to accrue to corporations, but so does the risk, and corporations must absorb that risk. Shell's infamous encounter with Greenpeace in the *Brent Spar* incident in 1995 is an apt example of how challenging it is to manage precisely the repercussions of even well-planned corporate decisions (see Watkins and Bazerman, 2003; and Chapter 14 in this volume).

(c)   *Intentional attempts to 'jolt' a field or industry.* These include external events such as major regulatory or technology changes that impact upon entire populations of organizations. A classic example is Meyer's (1982) study of how a completely unanticipated physicians' strike 'jolted' the California healthcare sector, destabilized long-standing arrangements among the industry players and forced them to adjust in unorthodox ways. Jolts 'disrupt organizational programs, create panic, energize members, mobilize advocates for change, and legitimate unorthodox moves' (Meyer et al, 2005, p460). Jolts also enable learning: they 'constitute natural experiments not only for organizational researchers, but for perceptive organizational actors as well' (Meyer et al, 2005, p460). Other examples of jolts, or what Homer-Dixon (2006) calls 'social earthquakes', include the creative destruction of firms and value that comes with radically new technologies as they reshape competition in an industry or even the industry itself (Bower and Christensen, 1995; D'Aveni, 1999).

System-wide jolts may have hidden dynamics that may be surprising when uncovered. Jolts are usually thought of as exogenous to a particular field, but a recent study by Canadian social critic Naomi Klein (2007) reveals that they may, in fact, be endogenous. The managers of state-owned enterprises in Chile after the overthrow of Allende in the mid 1970s, or in post-Soviet Russia during the early 1990s would have been surprised that their firms had suddenly been privatized. They probably would have perceived that jolt as an exogenous force – the aggressive intrusion of capitalism or globalization on their sheltered society. Klein's analysis shows that, in reality, the jolt was an intentional policy of the respective governments to shock the nations' economic and social systems and reconfigure them along neo-liberal lines. She calls this the 'shock doctrine'. This shows that synchronous failure can be intentional.

(d)   *Natural and man-made disasters.* Hurricanes, earthquakes and floods affect firms across the industrial landscape, sending entire sectors of an economy into temporary states of extreme uncertainty. As effects cascade, hidden connections between industries, the fragility of the natural–human interface (Weick, 2003) or the limits of organizational capabilities are often revealed

(Homer-Dixon, 2006; Farjoun and Starbuck, 2007). In this way, natural disasters can produce social and organizational disruptions of immense and long-lasting impact (e.g. the ongoing aftermath of Hurricane Katrina). A current example is climate change and the systemic problem of increasing demand for ecological footprint space. This category also includes such events as accidental releases of toxic substances and new organisms, as well as disease outbreaks that severely impact upon organizations and the economies of entire nations and regions. Man-made disasters such as terrorist attacks are different from the intentional disruptions discussed in (b) or (c) because of their pervasive, boundary-jumping character. Cunha et al (2006) call such incomprehensible surprises 'losses of meaning'.

We recognize that the four categories of contextual disruption described above may not be mutually exclusive. These are highly complex events/phenomena and can have several sources. For organizations trying to strategize and thrive, such disruptions will be seen as 'discontinuities' – events or periods of sharp or gradual unexpected disturbances to the normal flow of operations and the normal pursuit of strategic goals.

Different ways of perceiving disruption and different coping responses

It is sometimes difficult to maintain the distinctions we have drawn between competitive and contextual forms of disruptions, and among the various sources of contextual disruption. This is partly because different managers perceive their situations with different degrees of skill and accuracy. Cunha et al (2006, p319) define surprises that affect managers as 'any event that happens unexpectedly, or any expected event that takes an unexpected turn'. Similarly, for Farjoun and Starbuck (2007, p541): 'surprises occur when organizations try to exceed the limits of their capabilities'.

Our point is not the obvious one that surprises themselves are perceived differently, although that may be the case. Any competent firm's strategic plans will be able to take into account expected changes, but *not* the (unexpected) surprises (Watkins and Bazerman, 2003; Farjoun and Starbuck, 2007). Through luck or superior scanning skill, one firm may even anticipate an event such as a terrorist attack that its competitors miss. Instead, we are suggesting that what matters more is the differences in the *meanings* that different managers attach to surprises. 'Unexpected', 'sudden', 'capabilities' and 'limits' may mean different things to different players in an industry.

Why do these meanings differ? We argue that it is because of differences in adaptive capacity that managers think they have. Adaptive capacity is 'the amount and variety of resources and skills possessed by and available within a member's environment for maintaining its viability' (McCann and Selsky, 1984, p462). In terms of coping with the unexpected, those resources and skills include learning routines, knowledge management systems, and the ability to execute large change processes and to manage dynamic sets of external relationships. Adaptive capacity also includes the ability to mobilize 'collective' resources along with other players in the same field. Because adaptive capacities vary from organization to organization, disruptive change and, therefore, environmental turbulence is experienced unevenly (McCann et al, 2007).

An example is how different managers fix the boundary between predictability and uncertainty. This boundary is malleable (Watkins and Bazerman, 2003). Some managers may declare certain jolts, step-function shifts or oscillations to be unpredictable, frame them as 'non-linear' or 'discontinuous' and beyond the pale of traditional strategic planning, then react poorly. Others may find such changes within their learning capacity and respond proactively to take advantage of the newly seen opportunity. Thus, differences not only in how managers perceive environmental events and conditions but also how they make sense of them based on the adaptive capacities they think they have produce varying coping responses and, ultimately, performance differences among industry players. This is the key challenge of navigating the turbulent environment.

The AMA/HRI (2006) survey sheds some light on these differences in understanding the environment. In one question we defined disruptive change as 'severe surprises and unanticipated shocks that may significantly destabilize the organization'. When we asked respondents to assess the current disruptiveness of their organization's environment compared to five years ago, they responded as in Table 10. 2. This shows that 37 per cent of the overall sample recognized more disruptiveness. However, the performance of the firm matters. Whereas more than half of the lower performers recognized more disruptiveness, less than one

Table 10.2 *Managerial recognition of changes in disruption compared to five years ago*

	Overall results (percentage)	Higher performers (percentage)	Lower performers (percentage)
Fewer, less frequent shocks/surprises	18.8	24.5	12.2
About the same number and frequency of shocks/surprises	44.2	43.6	34.6
More shocks/surprises	28.9	25.7	39.2
Many more shocks/surprises	6.8	5.2	11.2
Very many more shocks/surprises	1.3	0.9	2.8

Source: AMA/HRI (2006, p61)

third of higher performers answered this way. Insights from the survey regarding adaptive capacity are provided in the next section.

Although the *pace* of change is not the focus of this chapter, respondents also perceived that it had escalated considerably compared to five years ago. More than 80 per cent recognized a faster pace of change, and the differences between higher and lower performers were not so pronounced as for disruptive change (AMA/HRI, 2006, p60). This suggests that the pace and the disruptiveness of change have different dynamics and gradients. If the global sample is representative, the majority of managers perceive change as normal and recognize that it creates opportunities, though a sizeable minority perceive it as threatening.

Coping with contextual disruption

We argued early in this chapter that competitive disruption can be addressed competently through traditional strategic planning and environmental scanning. In view of our argument regarding adaptive capacity, can contextual disruptions also be anticipated and planned for? This is a difficult question. If different managers make sense of their environmental challenges differently, then they may misconstrue them – for instance, by mistaking contextual disruption for competitive disruption. In doing so, they may try to cope through traditional strategic planning, competitive intelligence-gathering and other techniques, and be dismayed when these tried-and-true methods no longer work well.

For all four sources of contextual disruption identified above, the seeds often lie in emergent properties in the existing dynamics of a system that are not recognized as such (Emery, 1973). Scenarios offer the possibility of increasing awareness of these properties. Wack (1985) called attention to the 'predetermined elements' inherent in a situation that can be expected to produce future discontinuities from a past and current situation. For example, Chapter 12 in this book discusses a case of a group of British utility executives participating in a scenario exercise who came to a new realization of an unexpected major shift in UK power generation. Thus, astute insight into the existing dynamics of the system of which a manager is part may help her to appreciate the importance and potential impact of contextual (L22) links, and, in turn, anticipate future contextual disruptions.

We now turn to ways of sharpening these anticipatory insights. The question arises: how can managers deepen their appreciation and anticipation of contextual disruption? In the next two sections we offer two possibilities:

1   rethinking the nature of change; and
2   using scenarios in imaginative ways.

Shifting thinking from episodic to continuous change

Managers tend to perceive external change on a gradient from a manageable challenge to a grave threat. In the global survey, respondents reported their *experience* of change as shown in Table 10.3.

Table 10.3 *How managers experience change*

	Overall results (percentage)	Higher performers (percentage)	Lower performers (percentage)
Overwhelming – beyond our ability to manage	1.3	0.2	3.2
Wearing us down – too much for too long	7.5	3.4	12.9
A threat – destabilizes what we do	13.3	10.8	20.3
Normal – expected and manageable	53.4	53.4	45.0
An opportunity – we like things shaken up	24.5	32.2	18.6

Source: AMA/HRI (2006, p62)

The gradient is clearly skewed. It shows that three-quarters of the overall sample view change either as normal and expected or as an exploitable opportunity. However, this view differed depending upon the performance of the firm: 36 per cent of the lower performers were threatened, worn down or overwhelmed by change, whereas only 14 per cent of higher performers expressed that sentiment. Thus, consistent with our ideas about adaptive capacity above, the survey indicates that how managers experience change very much depends upon their ability to manage it to advantage.

In recent years, managers, consultants and organizational scholars have begun to shift the way in which they think about change (Weick and Quinn, 1999). The traditional model of 'episodic' change is characterized by an 'unfreezing' of normal operating conditions, a burst of change to a new set of conditions, and a locking in of those new conditions. In this model, organizational change is driven by the need to adapt, or adapt better, to changing conditions in the environment. This model, articulated by Kurt Lewin during the 1950s, has proved remarkably durable as a mental model for managers to think about how change occurs and how to design change interventions. However, in a more and more turbulent world it is increasingly ineffective in describing recent conditions and requirements confronting managers.

Some scholars and practitioners have begun to think in terms of a different model: one of 'continuous' change. In this model one thinks in terms of the relentless flow of organizational activity that is bracketed for a period of reflective rebalancing, after which the flow of action resumes (Weick and Quinn, 1999; McCann, 2004; Purser and Petranker, 2005). This is consistent with the perspective of complexity theory, which views change as the essence of reality (see Chapter 5 in this volume). The world is in – or, indeed, *is* – a process of continuous emergence. For our purposes, this means that whole systems and their environments co-evolve or emerge over time together as a single entity. In the continuous change model, organizational change is a 'pattern of endless modifications of work processes ... driven by organizational instability and alert reactions to daily contingencies' (Weick and Quinn, 1999, p366).

The challenge for managers faced with continuous change is its potential for *dis*continuity – more numerous and intense surprises and shocks to the orderly flow of operations than managers can absorb and respond to effectively (Purser and Petranker, 2005; Cunha et al, 2006). Meyer et al (2005) point out that many management researchers assume a model of system equilibrium, which implies adaptation, or 'fit' between an organization's properties and the demands of the environment. This notion is inherited from episodic change thinking. Meyer and his colleagues concluded that:

> ... 'adaptation' is an unproductive concept in nonlinear [or non-equilibrium] settings. When discontinuous changes ripple through an organizational field, there is no equilibrium to be sought, and the idea of organizational adaptation loses meaning. (Meyer et al, 2005, p457)

What replaces equilibrium and adaptation? They suggest *emergence* and *improvisation*. Emergence means that managers need to think and strategize in terms of whole systems in environments (i.e. fields) co-evolving over time, possibly changing form and character together. Improvisation means that, as part of one or more of these fields, a firm continually needs to be prepared to act heedfully in novel ways along with other players. We discuss emergence next and then improvisation in the next section.

The continuous change model leads to an intriguing implication for strategizing in terms of emergence. As Meyer et al (2005) dug into previous studies on externally induced organizational change they began to shift their thinking from episodic to continuous change. When they did this, they noticed that their unit of analysis 'shifted from focal organizations in exogenous environments, to be replaced by a set of nested units – organizations, that collectively constitute a population, amalgamated into an ecological community, embedded in a changing organizational field' (Meyer et al, 2005, p458). Thus, when managers are faced with extensive contextual disruption in a turbulent environment, appreciating continuous change should lead them towards a 'field' perspective in their strategizing rather than a single autonomous 'firm' perspective. A field perspective recognizes that turbulence affects entire fields of action and is not simply a property of any firm's transactional environment (Selsky et al, 2007). As discussed in Chapter 2, coping with turbulence involves seeing one's firm as part of a larger system and understanding one's role in it. This view fosters collaboration among players sharing a particular field.

This set of insights about continuous change and contextual disruption may help managers to understand turbulence better. For instance, profit pressures in the chemical industry may inspire the production managers of chemical plants to dump waste products illegally. The build-up of untreated chemical wastes in soils and groundwater may cause cancers in local residents years later. Lawsuits brought by cancer victims may then rebound back to the chemical firms themselves, while also affecting other organizations and groups. The chemical companies may declare the spate of lawsuits a surprise, a discontinuity that shows their environment to be turbulent because the lawsuits surely could not be predicted. In fact, the chemical companies and the law firms lodging the suits are parts of the same field in continuous change. From the perspective of contextual disruption, this set of events is a manifestation of what we described earlier as a 'novel conjuncture of seemingly unrelated parts of one or multiple systems'.

In sum, shifting mental models from episodic to continuous change leads to several understandings that can help managers to cope with high levels of contextual disruption:

- An awareness that one's strategic situation is (merely?) a part of fields (i.e. whole systems in environments) that are emerging over time. In a turbulent environment, contextual forces intrude upon the shared transactional space of firms in the same industry or value constellation. These forces drive the emergence of fields.
- An awareness that fields are in continuous change and that longing for, or trying to return to, a state of normalcy or stability is futile. Here the strategic task is to improvise effective action, as discussed below.
- An awareness that collaborative endeavours with other organizations must be a much larger part of strategy. This is in order to have much of a chance of dealing effectively with contextual disruption.

We show in the next section that using scenarios can build the capacity for cognitive openness needed to take advantage of these three insights.

Improvisation through scenarios

In this section we suggest, following Meyer et al (2005), that managers need to complement the awareness of emergence with enhanced capabilities for improvised action in order to deal with contextual disruption.

When faced with contextual disruption, openness in strategic thinking and response capability are crucial. Openness fosters the mentality needed for improvising novel responses; van der Heijden (2005, p34) points out that managers in turbulent environments instinctively know they should keep things fluid in order to provide more room to manoeuvre. Improvisation in strategic thinking and action occurs at the 'edge of chaos' or 'bifurcations' in Prigogine terms (see Chapter 5), where the need for structure and the need for flexibility are balanced precariously (Brown and Eisenhardt, 1998). Unlike *competitive* disruption in which sets of industry players may push each other to that edge in intense competitive moves and countermoves, *contextual* disruption may push entire fields of organizations to that edge of chaos with surprises, trend breaks, crises or disasters that render familiar routines, processes and relationships ineffective. Meyer et al (2005) found in their field studies that when 'non-linear changes' back organizations in a field up to this edge, they tend to improvise solutions together in rapidly forming networks. For example, in one case in the US healthcare field, they found that 'trans-industry linkages joined unlikely organizational partners in symbiotic relationships that breached and redrew industry boundaries'. Such openness to novel collective action is consistent with the continuous change model described above and with the features of the turbulent environmental texture.

As shown in Chapter 2, scenarios are at home in this world of continuous change and the turbulent environment. Scenarios are developed collectively to build shared images of possible futures of organizations in their contextual environments. We are interested in how scenarios can be used in conjunction with strategic planning to 'open ... up exploration of ongoing "surviving/thriving" rather than one-time only problem-solving' (Bradfield et al, 2005, p805). Scenarios nurture openness to change by allowing more complexity in future states of a system and the environment to be taken into account than traditional strategic planning. Enabling multiple perspectives on the future to be generated and evaluated simultaneously is crucial for managers in turbulent environments because it enables a richer set of response repertoires to be developed. In addition, the scenario-planning *method* structures the uncertainty that managers face from a contextual environment. It provides a sense of order, priority and significance that opens up choices, which differs from traditional strategic planning that is designed to eliminate choices. Scenario planning offers a structured way of capturing future contextual disruptions in whole systems in environments, instilling images previously not conceived of in the minds of participants (Schoemaker, 1993; Watkins and Bazerman, 2003; see also Chapter 12 in this volume).

Ramírez and van der Heijden (2007, p97) suggest that strategic planning and scenario planning are best used in tandem. The transactional environment has been taken to be the usual arena for strategizing, and the contextual environment the usual arena for scenario planning. In this 'wind tunnelling' model, scenarios serve the function of questioning the boundary between the transactional and contextual environments, and delivering imaginative information to strategic planning. However, Ramírez and van der Heijden (2007) also suggest that strategic planning has been tethered to assumptions of a disturbed–reactive environment. They suggest that by using scenario planning in a new way, it might pull strategic planning into being more useful in a turbulent environment. They suggest an intervention called 'staging inter-organizational futures' can help managers to identify parts of the contextual environment that are misconstrued as non-controllable, and add these into transactional space amenable to strategic planning. By using scenarios in terms of a staging event, the novelty, uniqueness or surprise associated with the extension of the transactional space can be harnessed to generate new strategic options for a firm's managers. Those novel options can then become strategic initiatives that force competitors and other stakeholders, such as regulators, to 'master their responses'. In this way, scenario thinking can help managers to break out of static strategic thinking about competitors, the environment and capabilities (Schreyogg and Kliesch-Eberl, 2007).

We extend Ramírez and van der Heijden's (2007) insight by noting that the transactional environment of a single organization has also been seen as the arena available for *developing adaptive capacity* to cope with disruption. Recall that how managers make sense of disruption in their environment can make a difference in their adaptive capacity. A strategic manager may relegate forces that she or he thinks are uncontrollable to the contextual environment; but further analysis may reveal that such forces might be influenced, especially through collective action. The shift described above towards thinking in terms of the shared transactional space of members of a field can aid this reassessment. In this sense, those forces become transactional and possibilities for *collective* adaptive capacity are opened up. Chapter 6 in this volume gives an example of how scenario planning helped stakeholders in the Indian agricultural sector to increase the adaptive capacity they thought they had. It enlarged their mental model of the situation, creating a tipping point in their understanding of the key variables involved. This helped them to mobilize new resources to cope with a problematic situation that they had come to realize they shared.

In this way the technique of staging inter-organizational futures can help managers to envision future disruptive events – and undesirable future states – for which they can prepare in collaboration with others in their field. Moreover, the staging technique shows where new roles, skill sets and perspectives need to be developed, in order to extend managers' range of influence to their larger industries and environments.

An example, relating to corporate social responsibility (CSR) is presented in Chapter 14. It is evident that societal expectations regarding CSR are changing rapidly. These expectations lie in the contextual environment. A public utility company experiences these expectations when some of its stakeholders mobilize to demand more CSR action from it. The company may respond on its own by acceding to the stakeholder demands or by resisting them. Or this may play out in a more collective way: the senior managers of many public utility companies may come to recognize CSR demands as a shared problem and act collaboratively, such as developing an industry-wide code of CSR conduct. As Prigogine describes, when a field is at a tipping point (or edge of chaos), one stakeholder may cause an avalanche that may change the contextual environment relationships fundamentally.

Building collaborative capabilities

Contextual disruption unsettles managers' common assumption of stability and equilibrium, both in the present and in the future. The assumption of stability in the *present* reflects episodic thinking about change, where change is seen as an unwelcome deviation from a routine equilibrium state. The assumption of stability in the *future* reflects the belief that the future will be an extrapolation of the present (Das, 2002; Purser and Petranker, 2005), a common fallacy in strategic planning (Das, 2002; van der Heijden, 2005). By using continuous change thinking and staging scenario work, when players in a field examine the possibility of future disruptive change, it can galvanize them to come together to create, foster or strengthen common ground. Similar to the planning technique of getting participants focused on a super-ordinate goal, a scenario practitioner may try to focus the players in a field on a super-ordinate *threat*, such as a financial collapse, an ecological catastrophe or a terrorist attack. The prospect of a future event that may severely disrupt all players in a field may prompt them to come together to deal with it collaboratively. For example, they might work to prevent the disruption from happening (e.g. the nuclear weapons club to prevent proliferation; the Montreal Protocol to prevent ozone depletion); to mitigate the consequences of the disruption (e.g. creation or bolstering of insurance markets; preventive medicine); or to develop new capabilities and skill sets to cope with similar disruptions (e.g. 'hardening' infrastructure).

In summary, by using scenarios to probe the boundary between the transactional and the contextual environments and to stage inter-organizational futures, the improvisational thinking needed to develop effective response repertoires can become a core competence for coping with disruptions from contextual environments.

Conclusion

In this chapter we have identified some key features of disruptiveness and linked three kinds of disruption to textures of the environment. We found that disruption is viewed with wariness or anxiety by some managers, as a source of strategic opportunity by others, and as a threat to firm existence by still others. Firm performance and perceived adaptive capacity are major reasons why managers view disruption differently and why it impacts upon firms differently. We have argued that *contextual* disruption is what managers need to be concerned about today because it arises in the uncontrollable part of the environment and has the potential to affect entire fields of organizations. Contextual disruption is the basis of the idea of the risk society (Beck, 2002) – the general potential of uncontained real risk that erupts periodically in surprising, critical incidents in unpredictable ways. But it also underlies the *perceived* 'risks that do not fit people's conceptual frameworks' (Schoemaker, 1993, p208).

The famous economist Kenneth Boulding (1984, p72) once observed: 'If nothing is happening it is fairly easy to predict the future.' When the environment is turbulent, contextual disruption is the norm: lots of things *may* happen, and prediction is dubious. In such conditions it is important that managers shift their thinking from viewing disruption as a deviation from normalcy or equilibrium, to viewing it as a normal condition of organizational life. This helps managers to appreciate the immanence of the uncertain future in their current practice. It also helps managers and consultants to rethink what adaptive capacity may mean, helping them to move beyond building and sustaining capabilities to counteract or dampen aberrations from normal operating routines, and towards improvising collective capabilities to embrace emergence of whole systems in environments. Managers can improvise more competently by using scenarios to complement their strategic planning. Traditional strategic planning is effective for operational and competitive disruption; but scenario planning provides a richer platform and better tools for contextual disruption.

'Is the world in disarray? Unfortunately, the answer is yes', said Mohamed ElBaradei, chief of the International Atomic Energy Agency, in a speech at an international security conference in February 2008. 'The world is going through a period of insecurity and instability; I think we all agree on that' (*Los Angeles Times*, 2008). ElBaradei sums up the anxiety of many that a quite plausible image of the world's future is one of accelerating contextual disruptions, both individually and in interaction, producing more shocks for people, organizations, fields of organizations and societal institutions. This state of affairs may be foreshadowed today by 'early signals', such as writings on 'world risk society' (Beck and Holzer, 2007), societal collapse (Diamond, 2005), catastrophe and renewal (Homer-Dixon, 2006), and in the 'scramble' scenario in the Shell 2008 long-term energy scenario set. The plausibility of such a future emphasizes the need for managers, consultants and scholars to work to ensure the transition from the risk society to resilient organizations and sustainable societies.

Notes

1   This chapter is part of the authors' programme of research on organizational agility and resilience. It draws on and extends previous published works; see McCann and Selsky (2003), AMA/HRI (2006) and McCann et al (2007).
2   Performance measures are based on self-reported comparisons with others in their industries in terms of market share, profitability and competitiveness.

References

AMA/HRI (American Management Association/Human Resource Institute) (2006) *Agility and Resilience in the Face of Continuous Change: A Global Study of Current Trends and Future Possibilities 2006–2016*, Report prepared for AMA/HRI (Researchers: J. McCann, J. Lee, C. Morrison, J. Selsky and M. Vickers)

Babüroğlu, O. (1988) 'The vortical environment: The fifth in the Emery–Trist levels of organizational environments', *Human Relations*, vol 41, pp181–210

Beck, U. (2002) 'The terrorist threat: World risk society revisited', *Theory, Culture and Society*, vol 19, no 3, pp9–55

Beck, U. and Holzer, B. (2007) 'Organizations in world risk society', in C. Pearson, C. Roux-Dufort and J. Clair (eds) *International Handbook of Organizational Crisis Management*, Sage, Thousand Oaks, CA

Bonabeau, E. (2007) 'Understanding and managing complexity risk', *Sloan Management Review*, vol 48, no 4, pp62–68

Bouchikhi, H. and Kimberly, J. (2003) 'Escaping the identity trap', *Sloan Management Review*, vol 44, no 3, pp20–26

Boulding, K. (1984) *The Economics of Human Betterment*, SUNY Press, Albany, New York, NY

Bower, J. and Christensen, C. (1995) 'Disruptive technologies: Catching the wave', *Harvard Business Review*, January–February, pp43–53

Bradfield, R., Wright, G., Burt, G., Cairns G. and van der Heijden, K. (2005) 'The origins and evolution of scenario techniques in long range business planning', *Futures*, vol 37, pp795–812

Brown, S. and Eisenhardt, K. (1997) 'The art of continuous change: Linking complexity theory and time-paced evolution in relentlessly shifting organizations', *Administrative Science Quarterly*, vol 42, pp1–34

Brown, S. and Eisenhardt, K. (1998) *Competing on the Edge: Strategy as Structured Chaos*, Harvard Business School Press, Boston, MA

Cunha, M., Clegg, S. and Kamoche, K. (2006) 'Surprises in management and organization: Concept, sources and a typology', *British Journal of Management*, vol 17, pp317–329

Das, T. (2002) 'Strategizing and time: Recognizing the future,' Paper presented at conference on Probing the Future: Developing Organizational Foresight in the Knowledge Economy, University of Strathclyde, Glasgow, Scotland, July

D'Aveni, R. (1994) *Hypercompetition: The Dynamics of Strategic Maneuvering*, The Free Press, New York, NY

D'Aveni, R. (1999) 'Strategic supremacy through disruption and dominance', *Sloan Management Review*, vol 40, pp127–135

D'Aveni, R. (2002) 'The empire strikes back: Counterrevolutionary strategies for industry leaders', *Harvard Business Review*, vol 80, no 11, pp66–74

Diamond, J. (2005) *Collapse: How Societies Choose To Fail or Succeed*, Penguin, New York, NY

Emery, F. (1973) 'The early detection of emergent processes', in F. Emery and E. Trist, *Towards a Social Ecology*, Plenum, New York, NY

Emery, M. and Purser, R. (1996) *The Search Conference*, Jossey-Bass, San Francisco, CA

Farjoun, M. and Starbuck, W. (2007) 'Organizing at and beyond the limits', *Organization Studies*, vol 28, no 4, pp541–566

Flood, R. (1999) *Rethinking the Fifth Discipline: Learning within the Unknowable*, Routledge, London, UK

Galbraith, J. (1977) *Organization Design*, Addison-Wesley, Reading, MA

Homer-Dixon, T. (2006) *The Upside of Down: Catastrophe, Creativity and the Renewal of Civilization*, Island Press, Washington, DC

Klein, N. (2007) *The Shock Doctrine: The Rise of Disaster Capitalism*, Metropolitan Books (Holt), New York, NY

Los Angeles Times (2008) 'UN nuke watchdog: Terrorists main risk', in *Lakeland (Florida) Ledger*, 10 February 2008, pA13

McCann, J. (2004) 'Organizational effectiveness: Changing concepts for changing environments', *Human Resource Planning Journal*, March, pp42–50

McCann, J. and Selsky, J. (1984) 'Hyperturbulence and the emergence of type 5 environments', *Academy of Management Review*, vol 9, no 3, pp460–470

McCann, J. and Selsky, J. (2003) 'Boundary formation, defense and destruction: Strategically managing environmental turbulence', Paper presented at Academy of Management national meetings, Seattle, WA, August

McCann, J., Selsky J. and Lee, J. (2007) 'Agility, resilience and organization performance during environmental change', Paper presented at Academy of Management national meetings, Philadelphia, PA, August

Meyer, A. (1982) 'Adapting to environmental jolts', *Administrative Science Quarterly*, vol 27, pp515–537

Meyer, A., Gaba, V. and Colwell, K. (2005) 'Organizing far from equilibrium: Nonlinear change in organizational fields', *Organization Science*, vol 16, no 5, pp456–473

Mitroff, I. and Alpaslan, M. (2003) 'Preparing for evil', *Harvard Business Review*, vol 81, no 4, p109

Nadler, D. and Tushman, M. (1988) *Strategic Organization Design*, Scott Foresman, Glenview, IL

Nathan, M. and Kovoor-Misra, S. (2002) 'No pain, yet gain: Vicarious organizational learning from crises in an interorganizational field', *Journal of Applied Behavioral Science*, vol 38, no 2, pp245–266

Normann, R. and Ramírez, R. (1993) 'From value chain to value constellation: Designing interactive strategy', *Harvard Business Review*, July–August, pp65–77

Perrow, C. (1984) *Normal Accidents: Living with High-Risk Technologies*, Basic Books, New York, NY

Perrow, C. (2007) *The Next Catastrophe: Reducing Our Vulnerabilities to Natural, Industrial and Terrorist Disasters*. Princeton University Press, Princeton, NJ

Porter, M. (1980) *Competitive Strategy*, The Free Press, New York, NY

Porter, M. (1985) *Competitive Advantage*, The Free Press, New York, NY

Purser, R. and Petranker, J. (2005) 'Unfreezing the future: Exploring the dynamic of time in organizational change', *Journal of Applied Behavioral Science*, vol 41, no 2, pp182–203

Ramírez, R. and van der Heijden, K. (2007) 'Scenarios to develop strategic options: A new interactive role for scenarios in strategy', in W. Sharpe and K. van der Heijden (eds) *Scenarios for Success*, John Wiley and Sons, Chichester, UK

Schoemaker, P. (1993) 'Multiple scenario development: Its conceptual and behavioural foundation', *Strategic Management Journal*, vol 14, no 3, pp193–213

Schreyogg, G. and Kliesch-Eberl, M. (2007) 'How dynamic can organizational capabilities be? Towards a dual-process model of capability dynamization', *Strategic Management Journal*, vol 28, pp913–933

Selsky, J., Goes, J. and Babüroğlu, O. (2007) 'Contrasting perspectives of strategy making: Applications in 'hyper' environments', *Organization Studies*, vol 28, no 1, pp71–94

Sirmon, D., Hitt, M. and Ireland, R. (2007) 'Managing firm resources in dynamic environments to create value: Looking inside the black box', *Academy of Management Review*, vol 32, no 1, pp273–292

Stacey, R. (2001) *Complex Responsive Processes in Organizations*, Routledge, London, UK

Sutcliffe, K. and Vogus, T. (2003) 'Organizing for resilience', in K. Cameron, J. Dutton and R. Quinn (eds) *Positive Organizational Scholarship*, Berrett-Koehler, San Francisco, CA

van der Heijden, K. (2005) *Scenarios: The Art of Strategic Conversation*, John Wiley and Sons, Chichester, UK

Thompson, J. (1967) *Organizations in Action*, McGraw Hill, New York, NY

Wack, P. (1985) 'Scenarios: Uncharted waters ahead', *Harvard Business Review*, vol 63, no 5, pp73–89

Watkins, M. and Bazerman, M. (2003) 'Predictable surprises: The disasters you should have seen coming', *Harvard Business Review*, vol 81, no 3, pp72–80

Weick, K. (2003) 'Positive organizing and organizational tragedy', in K. Cameron, J. Dutton and R. Quinn (eds) *Positive Organizational Scholarship*, Berrett-Koehler, San Francisco, CA

Weick, K. and Quinn, R. (1999) 'Organizational change and development', *Annual Review of Psychology*, vol 50, pp361–386

11

Scenarios that Provide Clarity in Addressing Turbulence

Rafael Ramírez

Introduction

Turbulent waters are like the contents of your blender after you have pressed button number 10^1 – they are anything but clear. The turbulent waters and swirls and eddies in an overgrown stream, tumbling down a steep mountain after a heavy rainfall, pick up sediments from the bottom and mix them with the mud the storm has collected. One cannot see the stream's bottom or the fish in it as one might in a still, shallow pond.

Scenarios seek to provide clear views of plausible futures and attempt to do so in the midst of turbulent waters. The main point I want to explore in this chapter is how finding clarity in turbulence is something that scenarios seek to secure, and how scenario work helps to obtain such clarity. In return, I suggest that attending to clarity improves the effectiveness of scenario work.

The chapter has two components. In the first part I overview some theoretical considerations on clarity and turbulence. In the second I describe a workshop I designed and convened that explored the way in which scenarios help to produce clarity and how attending to clarification improves scenario work. In the conclusion I wrap the first two parts together by showing that explicitly attending to clarity in setting expectations for scenario work helps users and facilitators to understand the roles that scenarios play in addressing turbulent environments.

Part one: Theoretical considerations

Clarity and turbulence

The connection between turbulence and clarity first became evident for me when a colleague and I (Ramírez and Vasconcellos, 1999), building on the work of Atlan

(1991), suggested that the complexity usually associated with turbulence may be better addressed through clarification than through simplification. Atlan (1991) had found that simplification works in addressing 'complicated' systems whose components are known, and where relations among these can be mapped. The degree of complication in such systems had to do with how simply one could map or model the system in question – the more elements in the map or model, the more complicated the system. But Atlan discovered that such conditions are not found in the 'complexity' of turbulent conditions, where some components remain unknown; the relations among them remain hidden and/or changed; the dimensions of both components and the relations among them are contingent upon other factors; causality is non-linear; and the systems they constitute are thus 'messy' (Ackoff, 1970) or 'wicked' (Rittel and Webber, 1973). In a similar way, Senge (1990, p71), in his popular *The Fifth Discipline*, distinguished between detail complexity (many interconnected variables) and dynamic complexity (cause and effect are subtle and 'effects over time of interventions are not obvious').

According to the *Oxford English Dictionary* (OED), 'turbulence' relates to 'violent or unsteady movement of air or water', and to 'conflict or confusion'. It is derived from the Latin '*turbulentus*', which is also the root for both turbid and trouble.

The label 'turbulent' for the type of environment Emery and Trist were conceptualizing in the mid 1960s struck them as the most appropriate name while they flew together through turbulent weather. Had they been in a boat instead of an airplane, we would today talk about 'troubled waters' instead of 'turbulent environments'. In fact, they believed the labels they gave to the four environments and, thus, the label turbulence were incidental (Trist et al, 1997, p49). Nevertheless, the metaphorical power of the turbulence label (Morgan, 1986) has resonated broadly with managers, strategy scholars and consultants (Amado, 1993, 1994).

It follows from the OED that the non-turbulent is peaceful, steady, conflict free and unconfused. In the way that Emery and Trist meant the term, turbulence was essentially a condition of high relevant uncertainty (Trist et al, 1997, pp50–51), meaning that the non-linear causality in the complex context of a system becomes the salient aspect in the perception of actors in that field.

Other chapters in this book discuss how scenarios help to secure 'common ground', where steadiness and shared values can be obtained (even transitionally – see Amado and Ambrose, 2001) to address turbulent conditions in the environment. In this chapter, I complement this task and focus instead on how scenarios attempt to clarify the confusion that relevant uncertainty entails by focusing on the sensed and felt cognition that aesthetic understanding consists of.

What is not confused is clear. This chapter thus concerns how scenarios, in addressing turbulence, obtain clarity.

Clarity

Clarity and its adjective 'clear' denote, says the OED, easy seeing, hearing, or understanding; lack of doubt; transparency. Thus, 'clearing the air' means 'improving a tense situation by frank discussion'; when 'the weather clears' it 'becomes fine'; and 'in the clear' means 'no longer in danger'.

Clarity – from the Latin *'claritas'* – denotes luminosity, limpidity, transparency.

For example, clear water in a pond allows the light through, helping us to see the fish in it, and the rocks and plants at the bottom.

Such limpid and transparent water is opposed to a fast-moving, turbid and opaque downpour flood with the unexpected swirls that 'turbulence' entails. Very turbulent water foams and becomes so white that nothing but the foam is visible – hence, the expression 'permanent white water' given by Pierre Wack (1984) to the turbulent environmental conditions that Shell would encounter after the Organization of Petroleum Exporting Countries (OPEC) was formed. The 'permanent' part of Wack's description referred to the feeling that the salient turbulent context would persist when compared to the relatively clear and certain conditions Shell had enjoyed in its context up to then.

Since clarity is closely related to luminosity, throwing light upon something clarifies it and enlightens our comprehension. It lifts the weight of darkness and thus provides a 'lighter' appreciation of what it helps us to see better. Clarity enables understanding by rendering that which is clarified transparent, by removing opacity and by providing the opportunity to see what turbulence attempts to hide from us.

How good fiction contributes to clarity in our minds

In her *Dreaming by the Book* (2001), Elaine Scarry, Harvard University professor in English and Aesthetics, explores how poets and writers help readers to construct clear images in their minds. She suggests that in reading literature, we form mental images that are not only 'vivid' but actually 'radiant'. As radiance is made possible by powerful light, she feels we become enlightened in reading this work, creating images that, in our minds, become alive – perhaps more alive in our minds, she suggests, than the images of live persons in our immediate surroundings with whom we actually relate.

I believe that effective scenarios need to be like good literature – they need to be read by users in ways that help their minds render futures 'more real than real'. By this I mean more real *imagined* futures than an actually real, existing present so that the futures are clarified in the mind in order to ensure that we attend to them (Ocasio, 1997). As van der Heijden (2005, pp113–114) observes, scenarios ('the strategic perspectives on the environment of a business idea') are 'expressed as internally consistent and challenging narrative descriptions of possible futures in this external world'. Scenarios tend to be presented and shared as stories. If Scarry (2001) is correct, effective scenarios will be like well-written fiction inciting us to imagine their subjects more clearly than we manage to think about the immediate reality around us.

In literature, knowledge, meaning and/or appreciation are co-produced between writer and reader. They engage with each other in a form of conversation (van der Heijden, 2005). This is also the case between scenario producer and scenario reader – the 'consumer' of the scenarios co-produces plausible futures helped by the 'supplier' of the scenario stories. Scenarios in this sense play the same role as novels. As Carlos Fuentes (1993, p28), a major Mexican literary critic, put it: 'What then is a novel, other than telling that which can not be told otherwise? A novel is a verbal search of that which awaits being written.' The novel, like the scenario, enables conversational relations between readers and the writer in reading and re-reading: 'Never again should we have only one voice or reading. Imagination is real and its languages multiple' (Fuentes, 1993, p21).

Scenarios as novels can thus be understood as searches, often expressed in writing as stories, even if often heavily illustrated, of that which is yet to be imagined. These fictions are relations between an enabler – the writer (or scenarist) – and the reader (or user of the scenarios), where the writer enables the reader to imagine (to form the clear, enlightening, even radiant mental images of what might happen, so that these clearly imaged futures take on a 'realistic' position in the attentive mind of the user).

Schwartz (1996, p26) states that:

> *There is a wonderful book by novelist John Gardner called* The Art of Fiction *in which he never describes exactly how to write a story. Rather, he says, here are some … techniques you can use, some helpful things … some of the methods by which you can practice writing. But there is no prescription for an effective story. Scenarios are much the same.*

In the same way, the profession of '*scenariste*' (scenario-maker in French film) describes itself as 'transitory and preliminary writing' (Monnier and Roche, 2006, p10) and scenarios as 'truthful lying' or 'a literary genre that does not exist' (p9). Thus, in documenting social realities, 'scenarios are both indispensable and problematic' (p73). Their job is 'not to create TV programmes but TV audiences' (p29).

Clarity and aesthetics

Churchman (1979, p192) suggested that clarity should be considered to be an aesthetic category. I understand aesthetics as the branch of Western philosophy that studies those forms of understanding, perception, conception and experience which we qualify (often after the fact) with adjectives such as 'beautiful', 'ugly', 'elegant', or 'repulsive'. Aesthetic knowledge depends largely upon sensing and feeling, upon empathy and intuition, and upon relating sense perception with conception.

There is growing evidence from cognitive psychology and neurobiology (Damasio, 2000) that aesthetic forms of knowing precede other forms and shape how these other forms of knowing operate. This had already been proposed by philosophers such as Cassirer (1964) and Langer (1942).

For these authors, the pattern recognition involved in sense perception precedes the formalization of these into concepts and their manifestation as words. I believe that this characteristic of preceding other forms of cognition has played an important role in extending the scope of aesthetics well beyond the domain of art. In mathematics, for example, 'the motivational aesthetic does not merely catch the mathematician's attention; rather, it serves the necessary role of framing the very way problems and initial conjectures are identified' (Sinclair, 2004, p277).

In the same way, Schlagg, who analysed and organized available research on the role of aesthetics in the realm of American law, proposed that:

> *Law is an aesthetic enterprise. Before the ethical dreams and political ambitions ... can even be articulated ... aesthetics have already shaped the medium within which those projects ... work.* (Schlagg, 2002, p1049)

And in analysing how modernity has come to reflect upon itself, and comparing his views to those of Beck and Giddens, Lasch (1994, p212) concluded that: 'Well before the post-traditional society of the past two decades, the first instantiation of reflexive modernity was through the aesthetic.'

In addition to how judges in the US interpret the law, how mathematicians work (see also Penrose, 1974) and how reflexive modernization operates, aesthetics over recent years has also been applied to:

- understand organizations (Ramírez, 1987, 1991, 1996, 2003; Strati, 1999; Lindquist, 2001; Ramírez and Young, 2003) and how people in them behave and understand them (Dean et al, 1997);
- how organizations present themselves (Schmitt and Simondson, 1997; Dickinson and Svensen, 2000), how they are experienced by others despite these efforts (Downs, 1995) and how some think they ought to be experienced (Guillet de Monthoux, 2004);
- how urban policy is enacted (Floyd, 1983);
- how exhibitions are organized (Lind, 2001);
- how the law is experienced (Elliott, 2002; Schlagg, 2002);
- how forests are managed (Gobster, 1999);
- how patterns of decision-making at NASA come to be ineffective (Feldman, 2000);

- how service firms select personnel in Glasgow (Warhurst et al, 2000);
- how digital technology is assessed (Beardon, 2002);
- how formulae are evaluated in theoretical physics (Farmelo, 2002);
- help understand which modes of business innovation managers prefer (Ramírez and Arvidsson, 2005).

Links between scenarios and aesthetics

Taylor and Hansen (2005) offer four categories of organizational aesthetics research. Their framework rests on two criteria: the content (instrumental versus aesthetic) and the method (artistic versus intellectual) employed. Thus, one can use an artistic method for instrumental or aesthetic purposes; or one can use an intellectual method for instrumental or aesthetic purposes.

This chapter fits the 'intellectual–aesthetic' agenda in the Taylor–Hansen framework. For them, the intellectual–aesthetic category includes work on:

- industries and products that are fundamentally aesthetic in nature (not the purpose here);
- aesthetic forms within organizations (partly the purpose here); and
- the direct sensory experience of day-to-day reality in organizations (more of the purpose here).[2]

In this first part of the chapter I have tried to show that scenarios are experienced by those who have not produced them as very real and imagined stories about possible futures. I have proposed that the measure of performance for scenario effectiveness rests on clarity. And I have argued clarity is an aesthetic category. So the central proposition that this chapter contributes is that scenarios have an aesthetic aspect – clarity – which is important for their effectiveness since this aesthetic element is apprehended or perceived through senses, in a feeling/limbic/pre-rational manner which I explore in the next part of the chapter.

In the second part of the chapter I describe a workshop I organized and ran to assess the above connections, which I here report in public for the first time. I did this as part of my assignment as a visiting professor of scenarios and corporate strategy in Shell's scenarios team during 2000 to 2003. At that time, the scenarios team in Shell was an open-ended, creative enquiring community, and it was well accepted for us to explore topics that contributed to keep Shell at the leading edge of scenarios thinking and practice.

Part Two: Workshop to explore the aesthetics of scenario work

On 26 November 2002, Kees van der Heijden, Louis van der Merwe and I met for two hours to design the three-day workshop to explore the 'art of' aspects of scenario practice and thinking. We agreed all participants would do preparatory reading on the work of Vickers's (1968) 'appreciative behaviour' and the work of Schlagg (2002), Strati (1999), and Ramírez (1996) on aesthetics so we could all start with a common understanding of how aesthetics informs social processes.

Day I of the workshop: Introductions and positions

The three-day workshop on aesthetics and scenario practice and thinking was held in London on 3 to 5 March 2003 (the attendees are listed in the appendix to this chapter). After introducing everyone and their take on the role of aesthetics in scenarios, Louis van der Merwe made a presentation, which I here summarize as follows.

> *I have been taken with the notion from Japan that if you get the process design right, content will look after itself. How does this apply to our work? Like Barbara Heinzen, I have also done quite a lot of work in Africa, with people [who] are not entirely in the Western culture sphere... Questions I have thought about include:*
>
> * *Are bushmen systems thinkers?*
> * *What is the role of conversation in these 'pre-industrial' communities?*
> * *What can we learn from them and how does this inform Western scenario practice?*
> * *What are some of the natural processes that we can even now examine in these cultures, and what can we learn about the role of aesthetics in their settings?*
>
> *... these cultures have had no direct influence from the Enlightenment and therefore, in my view, they offer a window into a more balanced use of the rational and the aesthetic as sense-making methods in language and conversation... In my work, I have used artists to develop scenario presentations and illustrations; artists capture the gestalt of time in ways that are communicable [where] words are not. In some work we did with corporations, we followed this method. We monitored whether the scenarios would diffuse more widely into the culture of the organization – results appeared mixed. In ongoing scenario-building in the South African President's office, one outcome was, in effect, anti-Mbeki. Artists could render it understandable and acceptable and discussible in ways words could not.*
> *... I would thus like to contrast evocative information gathering and feedback forms with the decision-making that scenarios entail. I would like to suggest that scenarios work much better as evocative systems – which manifest (the) aesthetic–*

limbic understanding – than as informational systems. They should be developed to evoke strategic conversation… I believe in aesthetics as a perspective to enhance and enlarge access and engagement in this mode. There is something serious in 'the art of' scenario planning, 'the art of' the long view. Aesthetics in my view informs this seriously, it informs scenario practice and it supports practitioners in enactable theory building (see Chermack and van der Merwe, 2003).

… How does aesthetics do this? I like the connectivity in the Batesonian view of aesthetics. Good scenario practices work when we help them to make connections… The largest conversation I encountered was a conversation among 65,000 people in Botswana, when Sir Seretse Khama consulted the nation to ask for their support to marry a woman who was British by birth, white and not from the Tswana royal lineage. Much of these conversations – as the material on aesthetics shows too – was centred on how it felt to have a member of the royal family marry a white person. The conversation was held in football stadiums in three cities across Botswana. Memories of these large conversations are still carried orally and their core is aesthetic. In my view, there is an unbalance in that the rational aspects were in this case a minor aspect of their value. It is the aesthetic dimensions that endure and have the greatest influence on the warm racial attitudes that still exist in Botswana.

… I like Wack's emphasis that scenarios must [effect] real change, and I believe that this notion of 'FIT', which is crucial to this impact and which is also in Christopher Alexander's design processes, is what Bateson's aesthetic connections are about … 'The pattern that connects.' It is about new recognition of things matching, or potentially matching. I found the material by Geoffrey Vickers on appreciative behaviour also resonated for me on this… Vickers reminds us that the schemata on which reality judgements are based are in constant development under three main pressures:

1   *pressure of event;*
2   *pressure of other men's schemata;*
3   *pressure of one's own internal requirements.*

… Adaptation in complex adaptive systems may, in effect, involve a triple loop that because it is inherently aesthetic is not captured by Argyris's (1992) discursive representation of learning. The third loop is a non-discursive, yet very real, choice of schemata for second- and first-loop learning.

… The value of systems diagrams as a natural way of providing an aesthetic dimension within this third loop lies in the observation that systems dynamics loops and links (see Senge, 1990) provide not only the 'pattern that connects', but also structure a pattern supporting learning. The systemic structure provokes 'strategic conversation', enabling a conversation about assumptions and causal relationships. Systems diagrams are thus a form of 'wrapping' (as Ramírez, 1996, put it) complex dynamics so that they can be held in memory. Inasmuch as this third-level choice of schemata is aesthetic, it involves aesthetics having a lot of power. If I am right, this says something about how aesthetic judgement provides fit – and, in this sense, closure – in scenario thinking.

> *... If I am right, we have a model for differential modes in the aesthetic judgements of scenarios. The Batesonian pattern that connects really means that the most relevant measure of performance for a scenario is: does one scenario 'feel' better for decision-makers than the other ones?*

A discussion followed that is not reported here.

This first day of the workshop confirmed for me that both concepts – clarity and aesthetic understanding – resonated with the group of experienced scenario practitioners participating in the workshop. The conceptual architecture that aesthetics offers – as described in the first part of this chapter – makes it possible to articulate aspects of scenario practices that had either been taken for granted, left in the background or had not been attended to as something that matters for scenario work to be effective.

As a result, day one of the workshop confirmed for me that bringing these aspects and/or appreciations into the foreground of scenarios that practitioners can attend to connects people engaging in scenario work to each other in ways they find significant. Highlighting the aesthetics in scenario work enables a useful conversation that allows good but diverse practice of scenarios in different settings to be compared. The clarity aspect of the scenarios' aesthetic in effect creates a common ground that experienced scenarios practitioners can use to understand their work more fully.

Day 2 of the workshop: Linking aesthetics and scenarios

In the second day of the workshop, three themes emerged that are relevant to this chapter: wrapping, rendering and reconnecting.

Wrapping

One suggestion was that perhaps it is not helpful to think of aesthetics in terms of a 'dimension'. This is just one metaphor and a rather limiting one at that. Instead, if (as Ramírez, 1996, suggested) aesthetics in organizations often consists of 'wrapping form', scenario practitioners have to explicitly attend to how we wrap a discussion in a syndicate room so that in the plenary the discussion enhances clarity of that which is being addressed.

Rendering

Hardin Tibbs suggested that aesthetics helps scenarios with *rendering*. 'Render' is a word full of meanings. Depending upon the context, it can mean 'convey', 'return', 'give', 'interpret or express or translate', 'provide', 'dispense or administer or do' (e.g. justice), 'make' (someone happy), 'produce effectively', 'provide' (recognition, homage). 'Render down' is used in cheese-making, and involves taking out the essentials by melting; thus, the fat is extracted by heating. 'Render up' involves surrendering a fortress or handing over a treasure. Hardin told the group that rendering is also an important part of architectural practice.

Thus, in scenario practice, one renders an original understanding to others for whom it evokes comparable feeling. As this feeling extends well beyond words, one must be attentive to the vehicle of this rendering that is the self. This prompted Kees van der Heijden to point out that some of the best presenters of scenarios, such as Pierre Wack, attend to rhythm and tone as they speak, as well as to silence and repetition, and to captivating metaphors and images that capture the pattern they want to render. It is this pattern in their stories that they hope will connect or resonate (Amado, 1993, 1994) with the audience. Such people, Kees suggested, use not only the story but also the storytelling and themselves as agents of connection.

Reconnecting

Another view in the discussion was that in dealing with intractable problems, people rarely have a complete appreciation of what the whole situation may entail. In situations that, as I said at the beginning of this chapter, Ackoff called a 'mess' and Rittel 'wicked problems', the situation is ill defined and not structured. To address such wicked messes one seeks patterns that connect, co-producing what Trist called 'common ground'. This is a shared meaning of a whole that provides what Maturana and Varela (1987) called an 'identity', a supple and adaptable continuity of the self in relation to the other that ensures viability. It is this auto-poietic co-produced viability that allows the system in question to live on, preventing it from fragmenting (as would be the case in moving from turbulence to hyper-turbulence – see, for example, Chapter 8 in this book) and disappearing. The 'patterns that connect' connect in two ways: they connect the enacting subjects to each other, and they connect the subjects to the object they are jointly enacting. Put simply, without the other, one no longer exists – which is why isolation punishment universally, from the 'go to your room' to a child, to isolation cells in prisons, is considered severe.

So, in this perspective, in constructing scenarios what we are actually doing is exploring and creating, forming and connecting (not finding) new worlds. In other words, we render anew a world by manifesting our connections to that world as 'new'.

We show and experience and interpret possible worlds intuitively – and we try to get people to experience how it would feel to be in them. It is no accident that as scenario designers we build in so many learning journeys for workshop participants. We may then ask them to return from these explorations of plausible futures with poems or images, not with words alone, to express what they connected with. We seek to inspire illuminating, clarifying experiences and to elucidate patterns that connect anew.[3]

The aesthetics of scenario purpose

The group brainstormed the purposes of scenario projects in which they had been involved or knew about. The list we came up with is:

- making sense of intractable problems;
- reducing complexity;
- reframing a situation or dissolving a problem;
- finishing a problem;
- surfacing assumptions to test them;
- testing strategic options;
- wind tunnelling a given strategy;
- team building;
- changing organizational culture;
- anticipating events (particularly when forecasts are not reliable);
- entertaining;
- sensitizing;
- engaging stakeholders;
- enhancing organizational learning;
- mapping/assessing uncertainty;
- creating a better world or future;
- challenging the official future groupthink;
- increasing future orientation;
- storytelling of the sources of the future;
- facilitating emotional change;
- understanding systemic behaviour;
- building confidence to act;
- developing language to articulate thinking;
- rendering disagreements assets;
- helping disagreements to become more constructive;
- enabling and eliciting innovations and options;
- preparing efforts to move beyond scenarios: simulations/war games (trainer cockpit – refining cases).

We decided to put the list of purposes on hexagons with magnets on them and to cluster these purposes into families that *felt* to us as if they had the same type of purpose. The result of the clustering – for which there was a remarkable level of consistency – is seen in Figure 11.1.

We then organized the clusters in a triangle that follows Vickers's (1968) idea of the elements needed to make judgments – instrumental (action oriented to direct, conclude and close), coupling (creating relations and their norms) and appreciative (sensing what the context might hold in the future).

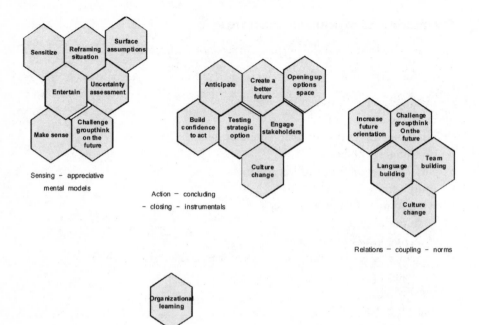

Figure 11.1 Aesthetics clusters of *purposes*

In Figure 11.2, the realm of what is possible to do is designated by the white space, and actual possible interventions by the grey or black forms within it.

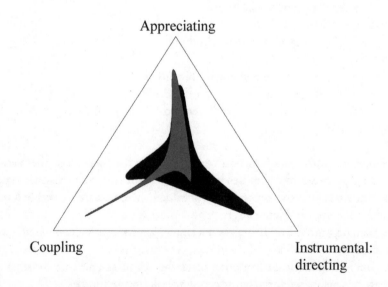

Figure 11.2 The aesthetic space of every scenario intervention

We then returned to the original clustering of scenario purposes and attempted to distil what the scenario addressing that type of purpose would *feel like* for a participant – if aesthetic quality were the single most important purpose of a scenario intervention. We also related these aesthetic appreciations to Vickers's appreciative judgement categories. The result is found in Figure 11.3: what is in bigger font text is the aesthetic aspect of each of the three elements of making decisions.

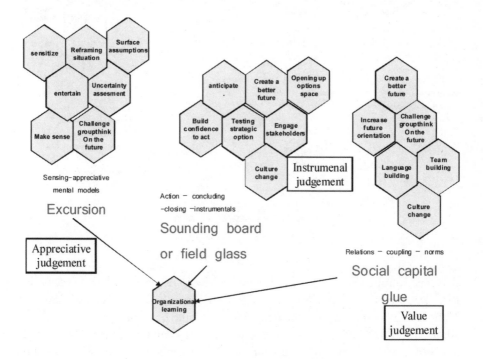

Figure 11.3 *Aesthetics* clusters of purposes

We then moved on to what criteria could be used in order to judge each cluster as 'appropriate'. The findings of this discussion were so powerful that one of the most experienced participants in the workshop called a major corporate customer during a coffee break and redesigned a process planned for the following week. The comment made was: 'I now really know why these people have been stuck. They are stuck in one of the clusters, and I must move them into another one if we are going to get their situation unblocked.' The results are manifested in italics in Figure 11.4.

Returning again to both the original clustering and Vickers's judgement typology, we considered the type of temperament that would be most at ease with each cluster, and how this would be manifested again in Vickers's types. We felt

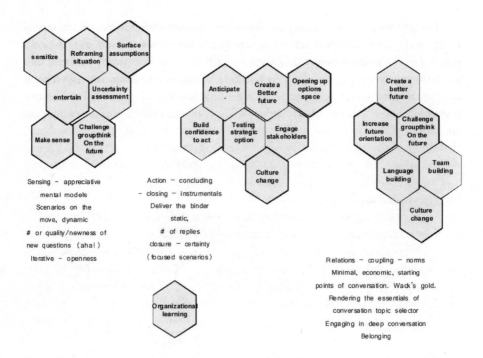

Sensing - appreciative
   mental models
Scenarios on the
   move, dynamic
or quality/newness of
new questions (aha!)
Iterative - openness

Action - concluding
- closing - instrumentals
Deliver the binder
   static,
# of replies
closure - certainty
(focused scenarios)

Relations - coupling - norms
Minimal, economic, starting
points of conversation. Wack's gold.
Rendering the essentials of
conversation topic selector
Engaging in deep conversation
Belonging

Figure 11.4 Aesthetics clusters

that this would be far more helpful than the Myers' Briggs or Belbin frameworks that some practitioners have used to research scenario work effectiveness (Islei et al, 1999). For a *sensing* purpose, the temperament would be exploratory, curious and appreciative; for the *norming–coupling* purpose, it would be collegial, emphatic and other centred; and for the *strategic–directive* purpose, the temperament would be pragmatic, courageous and centred on benefits and risks and actionable initiatives.

Conclusion

All workshop participants had extensive scenario-making, scenario-thinking and scenario-using experience. All were familiar with the major articles and books on the subject. No other similar group in the world could claim to be more knowledgeable than this group on scenarios, although several other equivalent groups could be convened. All participants had assiduously read extensive readings on aesthetics and on appreciative judgement circulated before the workshop. In other words, the conditions for relating aesthetics to scenario thinking and practice we had thus obtained could hardly be stronger.

The group gave face validity to the connection between aesthetics, the clarity it articulates and scenarios. Thus, from a Popperian point of view, if this group rejected the hypothesis that aesthetics is helpful to scenario thinking and practice, it would be safe to conclude that the rejection would apply to many more scenario cases and their relevant purposes than those represented in the workshop. But this was not the case. Instead, those in the workshop sustained the idea that aesthetics appears to matter in scenario effectiveness. In effect, the group unanimously felt that the workshop had shed new light on scenario thinking and practice. Through the workshop, we found that the old adage that scenarios are an 'art' and not only a 'science' now had a rationale grounded in aesthetics which had not previously been examined explicitly and systematically.

Making ourselves attentive to aesthetic knowing, and our willingness to consider the information that this form of knowing produces, helped us to clarify common purposes of scenario work by finding new 'patterns that connect' what we had experienced in our professional practice. We related these to the three elements needed to make judgements identified by Vickers. Our enquiry made us responsive to patterns connecting each of our deeply felt experiences to those of the others, and as such broadened and deepened our understanding of scenario work.

Attending to the aesthetic qualities of our own understanding, such as good scenario work, produced clarity. Bateson (1979, p7) famously stated that 'by aesthetic, I mean responsive to the pattern that connects'. In the first part of this chapter I used the analogy of the novel in literature to highlight the aesthetics of scenario work. As Williams (1996, pp232–233) put it:

> *For Fuentes ... the novel ... offers a variety of languages in opposition to the official languages and voices of governments, institutions, the mass media, and the like. In addition, Fuentes proposes that the novel is always the genre of the future, always associated with the world as it is being made and as it will come into being ... the novel (for him) is the genre of the future, in two senses:*
>
> *1 as an always evolving genre of new languages and new ideas;*
> *2 as the genre that invites its creator to imagine the future.*
>
> *Novels in the eyes of Fuentes are open and inconclusive, and so it is with conversations – and with scenarios.*

Having introduced the workshop in the second part of this chapter, I can now say that clarity helps not only with the imagining mind, but with the conversations among those minds to jointly produce imagined figures considered plausible. Thus, clarity also helps to co-produce common ground.

This insight about clarity's role in creating common ground is important for decision-makers coping with turbulent conditions. Turbulent environments are often experienced not only as very unclear, but also as disconcerting. So, in addressing turbulence, people seek methods that help them to find or produce clarity. As I have tried to show in this chapter, the scenario method offers this possibility of clarity. Attending to this search for clarity explicitly helps scenario practitioners to produce or find common ground with others.

Appendix: Workshop participants

- Gerard Drenth: Shell;
- Barbara Heinzen: independent scenarios consultant;
- Lennart Nordfors: scenarios consultant;
- Hardin Tibbs: independent scenarios consultant;
- Rafael Ramírez: Shell and HEC Paris;
- Angela Wilkinson: Shell;
- Louis van der Merwe: independent scenarios consultant;
- Kees van der Heijden: ex-Shell, University of Strathclyde;
- Marshall Young: Leadership Programme Director, Oxford University.

Notes

1   Professor Peter Homenuck, lecture in Management in Turbulent Environments, MES course, Faculty of Environmental Studies, York University, Toronto, Canada, 1979.
2   It is worth noting that while the purpose of this chapter might be seen as fitting their 'intellectual–instrumental' category, it does not. This is because it is not about any of the elements in their category:
   - It is *not* about 'artistic forms as metaphors for organizations'.
   - It is *not* about 'lessons for management from the arts'.
   - It is *mostly not* about 'using aesthetics to deepen our understanding of traditional organizational topics'.

   Instead, the chapter is about how aesthetics informs aspects of scenario practice that have otherwise been missed – not 'deepening' according to Taylor and Hansen, but about 'complementing' or 'broadening' these.
3   This, in turn, entails an ethical stance, which we discussed at some length. While it is an important element of our work, this was not the central concern of our workshop, centred on aesthetics. See Chapter 13 in this book, which analyses these aspects extensively.

References

Ackoff, R. (1970) *A Concept of Corporate Planning*, John Wiley and Sons, New York, NY

Amado, G. (1993) *La Résonance Psychosociale*, PhD thesis, Université Paris, France

Amado, G. (1994) 'La résonance psychosociale au coeur de la vie et de la mort', *Revue Internationale de Psychosociologie*, vol 1, October, pp87–94

Amado, G. and Ambrose, A. (2001) *The Transitional Approach to Change*, Karnak Books, London, UK

Argyris, C. (1992) *On Organizational Learning*, Blackwell, Oxford, UK

Atlan, H. (1991) 'L'intuition du complexe et ses théorisations', in Soulié, F. (ed) *Les Théories de la Complexité*, Editions du Seuil, Paris, France

Bateson, G. (1979) *Mind and Nature: A Necessary Unity*, Fontana, Isle of Man

Beardon, C. (2002) 'The digital Bauhaus: Aesthetics, politics and technology', *Digital Creativity*, vol 13, no 4, pp169–179

Beck, U., Giddens, A. and Lasch, S. (1994) 'Replies and critiques', in U. Beck, A. Giddens and S. Lasch (eds) *Reflexive Modernization: Politics, Tradition and Aesthetics in the Modern Social Order*, Polity Press, London, UK

Cassirer, E. (1964) *Philosophie des Symbolischen Formen*, Wissenschatliche Buchgesellschaft, Darmstad, Germany

Chermack, T. and van der Merwe, L. (2003) 'The role of constructivist learning in scenario planning', *Futures*, vol 35, pp445–460

Churchman, C. (1979) *The Systems Approach and its Enemies*, Basic Books, New York, NY

Damasio, A. (2000) *The Feeling of What Happens: Body, Emotion, and the Making of Consciousness*, Vintage Books, New York, NY

Dean, J., Ottensmeyer, E. and Ramírez, R. (1997) 'An aesthetic perspective on organisations', in C. Cooper and S. Jackson (eds) *Creating Tomorrow's Organisations*, John Wiley and Sons, Chichester, UK

Dickinson, P. and Svensen, N. (2000) *Beautiful Corporations: Corporate Style in Action*, Prentice Hall, New York, NY

Downs, A. (1995) *Corporate Executions: The Ugly Truth about Downsizing: How Corporate Greed is Shattering Lives, Companies and Communities*, Amacom, New York, NY

Elliott, E. (2002) 'Beautiful day, awakening to responsibility', *Law and Critique*, vol 13, no 2, pp173–195

Farmelo, G. (ed) (2002) *It Must Be Beautiful: Great Equations of Modern Science*, Granta Books, London, UK

Feldman, S. (2000) 'Micro matters: The aesthetics of power in NASA's flight readiness review', *Journal of Applied Behavioural Science*, vol 36, no 4, pp 474–490

Floyd, C. (1983) 'Billboards, aesthetics, and the police power', *American Journal of Economics and Sociology*, vol 42, no 3, pp369–382

Fuentes, C. (1993) *Geografía de la Novela*, Ediciones Santillana, Madrid, Spain

Gobster, P. (1999) 'An ecological aesthetic for forest landscape management', *Landscape Management*, vol 18, no 1, pp54–64

Guillet de Monthoux, P. (2004) *The Art Firm*, Stanford University Press, Stanford, CA

Islei, G., Lockett, A. and Naude, P. (1999) 'Judgemental modelling as an aid to scenario planning and analysis', *Omega*, vol 27, pp61–73

Langer, S. (1942) *Philosophy in a New Key*, Harvard University Press, Boston, MA

Lasch, S. (1994) 'Reflexivity and its doubles: Structure, aesthetics, community', in U. Beck, A. Giddens and S. Lasch (eds) *Reflexive Modernization: Politics, Tradition and Aesthetics in the Modern Social Order*, Polity Press, London, UK

Lind, K. (2001) 'Organising aesthetics: The case of exhibition in enterprising – managing vision, will, and realisation', Paper presented at the Academy of Management Conference, 6–8 August, Washington, DC

Lindqvist, K. (2001) 'Where's the aesthetic? From the aesthetics of organisation to the organising of aesthetics', Paper presented at the Academy of Management Conference, 6–8 August, Washington, DC

Maturana, H. and Varela, F. (1987) *The Tree of Knowledge*, Shambala, Boston, MA

Monnier, R. and Roche, A. (eds) (2006) *Territoires du Scénario*, Centre Gaston Bachelard, Dijon, France

Morgan, G. (1986) *Images of Organization*, Sage, Beverly Hills, CA

Ocasio, W. (1997) 'Towards an attention-based view of the firm', *Strategic Management Journal*, vol 18, pp187–206

Penrose, R. (1974) 'The role of aesthetics in pure and applied mathematical research', *The Institute of Mathematics and Its Applications*, July/August, pp266–271

Ramírez, R. (1987) *Towards an Aesthetic Theory of Social Organization*, PhD thesis, Social Systems Science Department, Wharton School, University of Pennsylvania, PA

Ramírez, R. (1991) *The Beauty of Social Organisation*, Accedo, Munich, Germany

Ramírez, R. (1996) 'Wrapping form and organisational beauty', *Organisation*, vol 3, no 2, pp233–242

Ramírez, R. (2003) 'The aesthetics in and of metaphor', *Revue Internationale de Psychosociologie*, vol IX, no 21, pp123–132

Ramírez, R. and Arvidsson, N. (2005) 'The aesthetics of business innovation: An exploratory distinction of two archetypes', *Innovation: Management, Policy and Practice*, vol 7, no 4, pp373–388

Ramírez, R. and Vasconcellos, F. (1999) 'The co-evolution of knowledge and ignorance', 19th Annual International Strategic Management Society Conference, 4–6 October, Berlin, Germany

Ramírez, R. and Young, M. (2003) 'Aesthetics and scenario thinking and practice', Aesthetics, Art And Management: Towards New Fields Of Flow Conference, Gattières, France

Rittel, H. and Webber, M. (1973) 'Dilemmas in a general theory of planning,' *Policy Sciences*, vol 4, pp155–169

Scarry, E. (2001) *Dreaming by the Book*, Princeton University Press, Princeton, NJ

Schlagg, P. (2002) 'The aesthetics of American law', *Harvard Law Review*, vol 115, February, pp1047–1118

Schmitt, B. and Simondson, A. (1997) *Marketing Aesthetics: The Strategic Management of Brands, Identity, and Image*, The Free Press, London, UK

Schwartz, P. (1996) *The Art of the Long View: Planning for the Future in an Uncertain World*, John Wiley and Sons, Chichester, UK

Senge, P. (1990) *The Fifth Discipline: The Art and Practice of the Learning Organization*, Century Press, London, UK

Sinclair, N. (2004) 'The roles of the aesthetic in mathematical inquiry', *Mathematical Thinking and Learning*, vol 6, no 3, pp261–284

Strati, A. (1999) *Organization and Aesthetics*, Sage, London, UK

Taylor, S. and Hansen, H. (2005) 'Finding form: Looking at the field of organizational aesthetics', *Journal of Management Studies*, vol 42, no 6, pp1211–1231

Trist, E., Emery, F. and Murray, H. (1997) 'Formulating the perspective', in E. Trist, F. Emery and H. Murray (eds) and B. Trist (assistant ed) *The Social Engagement of Social Science, Volume III: The Socio-Ecological Perspective*, University of Pennsylvania Press, Philadelphia, PA

van der Heijden, K. (2005) *Scenarios: The Art of Strategic Conversation*, 2nd edition, John Wiley and Sons, Chichester, UK

Vickers, G. (1968) *Value Systems and Social Processes*, Penguin, Middlesex, UK

Wack, P. (1984) *Scenarios: The Gentle Art of Re-perceiving*, Harvard Business School Working Paper 9-785-042

Warhurst, C., Nickson, D., Witz, A. and Cullen, A. (2000) 'Aesthetic labour in interactive service work: Some case study evidence from the "new" Glasgow', *The Services Industries Journal*, vol 20, no 3, pp1–18

Williams, R. (1996) 'Carlos Fuentes: The reader and the critic', *HISPANIA* 79, pp222–233

12

From Causal Textures to Predetermined Elements to New Realities in Scenario Thinking and Practice

George Burt

Un fait mal observé est plus pernicieux qu'un mauvais raisonnement. [A fact poorly observed is more treacherous than faulty reasoning.] (Paul Valery, 1960, p621)

Introduction

Reflecting on his experiences in Shell, Pierre Wack (1985a, 1985b) advocated that planning should be based on a better *understanding of predictability*, rather than best guesses made from established norms and assumptions. Wack argued that a better understanding of predictability could be achieved by identifying predetermined elements in the contextual environment. Wack defined predetermined elements as 'those events that have already occurred (or that almost certainly will occur) but whose consequences have not yet unfolded' (Wack, 1985a, p77).

Pierre Wack set out to understand why Shell's planning was ill adapted to address turbulence (Wack, 1985a, p74). In a way that is compatible with Emery and Trist (1965), Wack learned to view context as an interconnected system within which it was possible to identify predetermined elements. While Wack is recognized as one of the pioneers in scenario planning, Wack's inclusion of systems analysis within the process of scenario building to help reveal the conditions that drive predetermined elements in the contextual environment (van der Heijden et al, 2002) is less well known. It is this aspect of his work I explore in this chapter.

Wack realized that (until now) undetected systemic conditions, emerging from interacting systemic structures, were important driving forces that contribute to the creation of turbulence. Wack understood that it was possible to convey systemic understanding of predetermined elements through a story about the future. He suggested that once identified and understood, predetermined elements would enhance an organization's ability to plan strategically by providing the underpinning logic of the specific environmental conditions so that a business plan could address them.

Predetermined elements are not predictions or forecasts. A prediction is a more or less well-substantiated guess by someone on what he or she thinks will happen in the future. A forecast is estimation or calculation of what is likely to happen based on past experience recurring in the future. Instead, predetermined elements emerge from a systemic understanding of driving forces pushing for inevitable outcomes and these outcomes can be planned for. In this chapter I explore this important idea to help enhance our understanding of the contextual environment and how scenarios help to address the turbulent conditions in it.

Purpose and contribution of the chapter

There is a threefold purpose for this chapter. The first purpose is to provide a new synthesis of Wack's (1985a, 1985b) seminal thinking on scenario planning, which articulated three integrated fundamental principles for such work:

1   the 'macroscope';
2   predetermined elements; and
3   change in managerial thinking and acting, previously described sketchily in a working paper entitled *The Gentle Art of Reperceiving* (Wack, 1984).

I elaborate upon each principle below.

The second purpose is to explore and expand upon the second of the three fundamental principles – predetermined elements. This is the focus of the chapter. I explain how the recognition of predetermined elements in the contextual environment helps to create new understanding of an emerging reality. The chapter adds to our comprehension of predetermined elements by showing the conditions for potential discontinuity, captured and modelled by system analyses. In the example I use to ground my argument, the scenario planners themselves became conscious of the inevitable outcome that they had identified from their scenario-building and sense-making activities. They realized that past historical industry actions, whose outcomes would emerge as their future context, were consequential for their industry in ways that they had not previously perceived. In my experience of over 15 years of scenario work, such occurrences often occur during scenario-planning exercises.

The third purpose of this chapter is to illustrate the integration of system analysis with scenario planning to help structure managerial understanding of the key variables and their interrelationship within a scenario story. This helps to structure the unfolding logic of the predetermined elements.

While predetermined elements can be recognized as crucial for business planning, for Wack they were only a step towards being able to '*see*' a new reality (Wack, 1985a, 1985b; Burt and Wright, 2006). Wack suggested one can only 'see' a new reality by moving on from the conceptual constructs in which the old reality was expressed. In this respect, Wack was on the same wavelength as Irwin's well-known maxim: *seeing is forgetting the name of the thing one sees* (Weschler, 1982). Therefore, one outcome of a scenario-building process is the combination of knowing the limitation of one's perceptions and experiences, and reinterpreting and transforming such perceptions and experiences to produce a new and reframed understanding of the contextual environment.

Layout of the chapter

In the next section of the chapter I review the flaws in planning that Wack recognized from his experiences. Following on from that section, I develop the historical link between the work of Emery and Trist and that of Wack. The historical link concerns causal textures arising from outcomes of the interaction between interrelated actors and driving forces, and how Wack's work makes it possible to investigate and identify them, and the unfolding consequences for the organization – if nothing else changed. Such understanding can be represented in scenario stories. Following on from the discussion of the historical link between the work of Emery and Trist and Wack, I present a new synthesis of Wack's ideas about the purpose of scenario planning. The rest of the discussion in the chapter is based around a case study to help discuss and elaborate upon the idea of predetermined elements as a precursor to developing an understanding of a new contextual reality (that ultimately should lead to new organizational action).

Wack and flaws in planning

Wack was attempting to address what he saw as two major flaws in planning as it existed in his time:

1   plans based on business-as-usual thinking and predictions; and/or
2   the acceptance of recasting plans year on year based on a (seemingly) more confident set of new (but not always fully substantiated) assumptions, which he referred to as the 'phenomenon of moving sands'.

The use of the metaphor 'moving sands' was to highlight phenomena that looked similar in nature to the original phenomena but had, in fact, changed in its inherent state due to external forces, with the changes unrecognized.

In the first of these flaws, Wack was challenging the belief that the future would be the same as the past, but later. Wack had recognized that such beliefs (and consequent behaviour) would make an organization vulnerable to (unexpected) discontinuities. In the second of these flaws, Wack was concerned about the ease with which managers would accept limited bases for facts when developing plans. Wack saw these flaws as 'excuses' for an inability or unwillingness to embrace, explore and, ultimately, incorporate uncertainty within planning.

Historical link between Emery and Trist and Wack

This book makes it possible to begin to understand the historical link between causal textures, especially 'turbulence' (Emery and Trist, 1965) and the need for a more insightful approach to explore and understand context (Wack, 1985a, 1985b). During the 1960s, Emery and Trist were theorizing about 'context' as the emerging challenge to strategy (and planning) in organizations. They identified four types of causal textures (or environments), differentiated by the degree of interconnectedness between the organizations creating their shared context and the resulting extent of relevant uncertainty (Emery and Trist, 1965).

Wack was influenced by the idea of the organization as an organism, operating as part of an open system, as opposed to a closed system. The open system influences the organism, and the organism influences the open system. However, at that time many managers considered their organization to be a closed system. Like Emery and Trist, Wack advocated for proactive engagement in exploring the contextual environment to understand the driving forces for change, rather than a reactive response when change was imposed by the contextual environment on an organization.

During the 1970s, scenario planning was emerging as an approach to explore and understand change in the contextual environment. Wack experimented with it as an (alternative) approach to overcome difficulties that he experienced in planning at Shell since it had the potential to represent and explain the, until then, unexplored causal relationships between contextual variables.

Synthesizing Wack's ideas on scenario planning

The starting point in the Anglo-Saxon literature on scenario planning is widely recognized as Herman Kahn's innovative work with the RAND organization and the Hudson Institute. Kahn is recognized as the founding father of scenarios or alternative futures, and scenario planning, contributing to our understanding with his books *On Thermonuclear War* (Kahn, 1962), *Thinking about the Unthinkable* (Kahn, 1964) and *The Year 2000* (Kahn and Wiener, 1967). Wack was intrigued by Kahn's thinking and set out to explore and understand the scenario approach and how it may be relevant in a corporate setting.

After many years in practice, Wack set out his reflections on scenario planning in two papers (Wack, 1985a, 1985b). I argue here (I think for the first time) that Wack's three fundamental principles are intrinsically linked to each other as a process to challenge how managers perceive, interpret and understand change in the contextual environment. Below I explain the three fundamental principles briefly, and later in the chapter I develop the interlinkages between the principles. The three fundamental principles are:

1   The '*macroscope*', which is a metaphor for the process of engaging in exploring and understanding context beyond thinking of it as the bigger system in which an organization operates. It enables managers to see distant (in time and space) yet interconnected events. Such a process therefore stretches what they perceive, bringing issues into view that were previously not recognized or understood, which allows for the identification of the following.
2   Predetermined elements (events that have already happened, although possibly not yet unfolded) as the basis of planning. As a consequence, this leads to the next principle.
3   The entrenched belief systems of shift managers to make them act on these new insights, leading to re-perception. This, in turn, results in change (what Wack called the gentle art of re-perceiving).

In this chapter I show that the systemic structures that are discovered with scenarios were *not* previously visible to the (case study) managers and that they emerge from their joint construction, exploration and understanding of scenarios constructed to address relevant uncertainty – and, thus, the turbulent field. However, the neurobiology or cognitive psychology of this has not, to our knowledge, been elucidated to date.

Wack based his work on the premise that scenarios have the ability to help people explore their environment, harness multiple perspectives about it, and structure their thoughts and understanding in a way that is meaningful for the 'explorers'. Wack (1985b, p150) stated:

> ... *scenarios allow managers to break out of a one-eyed view. Scenarios give managers something very precious: the ability to re-perceive reality. In a turbulent environment, there is more to see than managers normally perceive. Highly relevant information goes unnoticed because, being locked into one way of looking, managers fail to see its significance.*

Let's now look at the second principle – predetermined elements – which is the focus of this chapter.

Predetermined elements

Wack suggested that within the environment, predetermined elements could be identified as:

- events that are already in the pipeline and will emerge in time;
- a series of interrelated actions that will together be co-producing a particular outcome; and/or
- inertial forces within the wider contextual environment, which are slow to change.

An example of 'events that are in the pipeline and will emerge in time' would be the number of children born in a particular year who will enter primary school five years after birth, with the implication that could be drawn about the demand for teachers in the future.

An example of 'a series of interrelated actions that will together be co-producing a particular outcome' would be how transportation, congestion and emissions in a country, taken with an inability of the rail network to attract freight from trucks and lorries; government policies and/or interventions; and car manufacturers' product development and consumer attitudes increasing the demand for cars, especially four-by-four sports utility vehicles (SUVs) will all increase the demand for petrol and diesel, with the consequent impact upon air pollution.

An example of 'inertial forces within the system, which are slow to change' would be universities and their role as broad educational institutions that facilitate knowledge transfer from generation to generation.

I now put some 'flesh on the bones' of how predetermined elements connect with Emery and Trist's (1965) ideas on turbulence by developing Wack's second principle in relation to a recent case study I was involved in as consultant.

Case study context and exploration

The case study presented here arose from an action-learning intervention (Revans, 1982; Morgan and Ramírez, 1984) with the managers of an engineering original equipment manufacturer (OEM) and power-industry service provider in the UK. These managers were attempting to understand the future basis of British power generation, given the experience of power shortages and industry deregulation, as well as proposed future deregulation in the UK and North America. I believe that the approach set out in this chapter can be adopted in other settings.

Case study outcomes

Scenarios provide a description of a future end state of the context of an organization in a horizon year, as well as an interpretation of past and current events of that context and their propagation into the future, in an internally consistent account of how a future world might unfold. The scenario story captures a representation of the dynamic interplay of events, showing how these interconnect and impact upon each other, revealing their logical consequences in the horizon year (Burt et al, 2006).

In the case I present here, the managers prioritized the range of uncertainties, from their perspective, concerning the future of UK power generation. They then identified the two critical uncertainties that would have the highest impact upon their context, in this case:

1   change in the global economy driving energy demand; and
2   change in the global nature and structure of the market.

These two critical uncertainties were then further discussed and explored to identify possible developments in the future in terms of plausible polar outcomes depicting the future possible contexts. These were articulated as follows:

1   Change in the global economy driving demand for energy:
    - harmony, growth and increasing demand for energy; or
    - conflict and fragmentation with little or no increase in energy demand.
2   Change in the global nature and structure of the market:
    - many and diffused customers; or
    - fewer customers with increasing buying power.

Combining these outcomes by using a two-by-two scenario-structuring matrix, the managers defined four different, but plausible, alternative futures (end states). These plausible alternative futures were entitled:

1   'retrenchment';
2   'fill your boots';
3   'survive or die'; and
4   'win or lose'.

For the managers, these scenario titles captured and represented the emerging nature and logic of each of these futures. The two-by-two matrix is presented as Figure 12.1.

The following sub-sections provide a snapshot of the scenarios based on these end states.

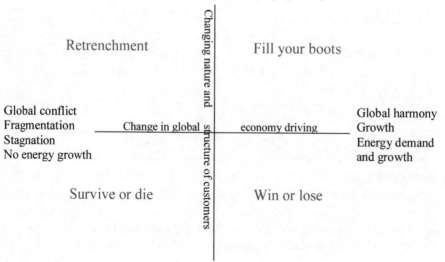

Source: From participants in scenario workshop

Figure 12.1 Scenario-structuring matrix

'Retrenchment'

In this scenario, the global economy will have stalled due to increased terrorism, which will have dampened business activity in many sectors. Business travel was hit hard, and over time the worries over terrorism led to increased regional, and less global, trade. Consequently, for the industry there was less energy technology transfer, fewer new plant builds, and a cutback in their expenditure in research and development. New build commissioning was deemed 'risky' in newly admitted European Union (EU) countries. Customers were bound by tight local regulatory controls that were governed by the EU, which made design specification complex and legalistic. All of this resulted in little opportunity for growth in the energy market and led to increased competition, resulting in a scaling back of business for power industry service providers.

'Fill your boots'

In this scenario, the global economy will have expanded on the back of market deregulation. The EU has expanded its boundary to capture the benefits of global growth and confidence. Demand for electricity has increased, with a bigger energy market, with many opportunities. As a consequence of growth, the labour market is tight, with labour becoming expensive. The threat of terrorism continues. A major French nuclear plant is attacked, which results in increasing public concern over nuclear technology. Fears over the threat of dirty bombs have increased debate and protests over nuclear power. This public backlash, in turn, leads to increasing political pressure to decommission nuclear energy in Europe and the UK. The political reaction is to change the energy supply mix away from nuclear power, resulting in power shortages and a step change in the search for alternative technology solutions. In a surprisingly short period of time, energy supply moves from traditional large plant provision to a distributed solution; at the same time, technological advances and declining costs result in many households becoming reliant on the self-provision of energy.

'Survive or die'

In this scenario, the global economy will have declined due to increased conflict, which, in turn, augmented economic rationalization. Stock markets across the world decline. Consequently, merger and acquisition behaviour has resulted in the emergence of a few large and powerful players in the global energy market. In some European countries, the additional barrier of national interests had become a factor. Those power industry service providers who survived were able to maintain strong working relationships with customers; others went bust.

'Win or lose'

In this scenario, the global economy has grown, with energy demand also expanding. The EU has expanded its boundaries, resulting in many opportunities in the extended EU. The EU, as part of its expansion plans, has provided financial support to new members for new job creation, and domestic power plants do not fall in this category. A trend emerged in Europe was for three or four large-scale generators to supply the majority of the extended EU power needs. The logic of the EU policy was based on European economic growth, supported by a stable energy supply from key countries in the original EU. Those power industry service providers who were successful did so from strong historical working relationships with customers; others pared back the scope of their activities.

I will now use this case study to explore Wack's principle of predetermined elements.

The scenario workshop process: From business as usual, to discontinuity, to predetermined elements

During the scenario-building exercise, the managers identified the conditions for two discontinuities – first, structural change in the power generation industry in the UK, and, second, what they came to see as *inevitable* growth in small-scale distributed power generation.

The first discontinuity concerned how two or three large European power generators might determine the nature and conditions of service provision. It surprised these managers since:

1 It could occur more quickly than they would have expected.
2 The EU system of anti-trust would support and reinforce the resulting situation over time rather than hinder it since the need to ensure stable and low-cost energy supply to underpin EU competitiveness was paramount.

This discontinuity occurred in the 'win or lose' scenario.

The second discontinuity is the focus of the rest of this chapter. It concerns changes in power generation and distribution which appeared in the 'fill your boots' scenario.

The combination of continued terrorist threats and the increasing fear of 'dirty bombs' led to a public backlash against nuclear energy. This led the government to delay investing in 'new build' nuclear power plants, enforcing planned closure of nuclear plants, which resulted in power shortages and speculative searches for alternative technologies that produced a technological breakthrough. As one manager put it, this was a 'sea change from the existing, traditional (power generation) approach'.

The breakthrough moved energy generation and supply from the position of a traditional large-scale and centralized system to a more distributed system. This made many households independent self-generators of energy. As one manager stated: 'If we think like this, then we are further into this scenario than we believe.'

The reason for this 'felt difficulty' (Emery and Trist, 1965, p29) was the ageing and unreliable UK power-generation plant fleet, and the worsening supply-and-demand tensions given legally mandated planned nuclear closures. For the first time, these managers recognized that a combination of events in the pipeline (nuclear decommissioning and fear of terror), together with a series of interrelated actions pushing for a particular outcome (ageing power generation with reducing generation output capacity and nuclear protests), would create the conditions for discontinuity.

So, how did these managers capture and represent their thinking to help them identify such a predetermined outcome?

Applying systems analysis within scenario building

Scenario stories are developed by linking the past to the present to the future (Burt et al, 2006) through internally consistent cause-and-effect reasoning, using influence diagrams and feedback loops (Meadows et al, 1972; de Rosnay, 1979).

These stories manifest themselves as models of the interaction of events over time, reflecting the logic of how such events and outcomes relate to each other and to their consequent implications.

Representing 'their' environment as a number of influence diagrams and feedback loops was novel for these managers. Previously, each manager held an individual and unique – implicit and untested – perspective of their contextual environment. These perspectives often contradicted those of other managers. Events were viewed only in the context of today, rather than as pertaining to systemic structures and driving forces.

For these managers, there had not been an overall collective sense of the relationships and structure of their contextual environment. They had not articulated such relationships, or the tensions created by these relationships, and therefore did not understand that the resolution of the tensions might produce their future environments.

Identifying feedback loops in scenarios

A systems dynamics feedback loop can either be generative (reinforcing) or negative (balancing) (Senge, 1990). Predetermined elements can therefore be understood as feedback loops in the form of generative and/or balancing loops. Feedback loops help in capturing and structuring managers' perceptions of contextual elements and the behaviour of such elements in their contextual environment. This helped them to understand the dynamic causal interrelationships and interactions among the elements, and the logic behind the growth or collapse of a given environmental situation, such growth or collapse being the basis of identifying predetermined elements. In developing the 'fill your boots' scenario, the managers identified three potential generative feedback loops driving the scenario-specific environment to a new situation: the movement from centralized to decentralized power generation.

The feedback loops revealed the underlying systemic drivers that could ultimately bring the contextual environment of these managers to a new state of equilibrium, which would arise after the turbulent contextual conditions had been addressed, centred on small, distributed power generation. Clearly, such a discontinuity would have a profound impact upon the industry.

The managers then proceeded to retell the scenario, but now making sure that events in the story line projected fully the behaviour and outcomes of the systems representations that they had developed. The need for the scenario to be 'internally consistent' now included the need to be fully compliant with the newly identified systems models.

Seeing the previously unseen

By articulating and sharing their individual perceptions and ideas about the contextual environment, the case study managers were able to conceptualize these elements into a meaningful interconnected understanding (i.e. the 'macroscope' view), moving well beyond their individual understanding with which they arrived into the scenarios process. Together, they were able to '*see*' the wider interconnected system, revealing the emerging basis of decentralized power generation which, if the scenario held, would continue unfolding.

Although they were surprised at the outcome, they recognized that they had developed scenarios about their future context from their existing knowledge. All of the models and insights that emerged during the process arose from their dialogue. Following the ideas of Emery and Trist (1965), scenarios act as a methodology to capture and structure perceptions of the causal texture surrounding and interacting with the organization, and to co-produce common ground.

The scenarios were developed without any (external) third-party input. Yet, the outcomes were counterintuitive to the managers' pre-workshop understanding. Prior to this intervention, managers had presumed that the business-as-usual portfolio mix of power generation (coal, gas and nuclear) would continue into the future. As a result of their scenario thinking, they recognized a shift in their consciousness and external structures that was moving towards self-organizing, decentralized systems.

By understanding how the tensions in the power-generation and distribution system were resolved, these managers were then able to identify and articulate the logic of conditions for the predetermined outcome of decentralized power generation during their strategic conversation. As a result of mapping the dynamics of the situation, visualization was expressed in terms of a system of feedback loops, and interactions were highlighted of what had, until then, appeared to be unconnected elements in their contextual environment. Within this scenario these interactions would bring about inevitable structural discontinuity.

At one point during the scenario-building process, one of the managers commented: 'It feels like we are already there. We seem to be accepting the conclusions of our thinking, no matter the consequences that it has for us.'

This is, in my experience of scenario work over the last 15 years, a frequent expression. The conditions that resulted in the predetermined outcome 'surrounded' the managers. They identified a number of events that had already occurred and others that they expected would occur, but whose consequences had not yet unfolded. The case study managers could now for the first time recognize the significance of a number of historical events about which they knew; however, they had considered them in isolation and had not developed a clear understanding of their relationship to each other. Their interaction and the inevitable outcome had now become evident. The managers were able to understand what they had seen but had not made sense of.

Towards a better understanding of predictability within plausible scenarios

The purpose of this chapter has been to reflect on the second of Pierre Wack's three key principles – predetermined elements. Wack's ideas are, in my view, influential because of the message of planning to be based on a better *understanding of predictability* (in my view more than uncertainty) within very uncertain contexts.

The case study managers recognized the logic and limitations of elements of their worldviews. Acceptance of continued business-as-usual technological, organizational and human thinking and acting had created their 'taken-for-granted' assumptions. These 'taken-for-granted' assumptions were based around large-scale centralized power generation. The assumptions were also their perceptual filters (and perceptual limiters). They could not 'see' what was now becoming inevitable without the aid of the scenarios.

If the identification of predetermined elements within a scenario results in the creation of knowledge based on their insights and it then becomes confirmed by facts as they unfold, the managers will gain some certainty that these outcomes will occur. The power generation and distribution system had remained largely unchanged during the previous 50 years. Until the early 1990s, ownership of the UK power generation and distribution systems had been in the hands of a few organizations and they were controlled by government. In this regime, plant registers of asset life and maintenance were well kept. Deregulation during the 1990s changed this situation, with ownership of the power plants and other assets changing frequently. The managers knew that the change in ownership had resulted in a decline in investment in plant and equipment due to a 'sweating-the-assets' economic model following privatization, which was a major contributory factor in the growth in contemporary power shortages. The continued deterioration of assets and the planned nuclear plant closures would inevitably result in even more power shortages in the future, though it remained uncertain where and how fast it would spread. Such conditions would create opportunities for alternative sources of energy to emerge and these would replace the incumbent system.

Conclusion

In this chapter I have examined Wack's (1985a, 1985b) idea of predetermined elements. Deploying systems dynamics and feedback loops as part of the scenario-building process has extended our understanding of predetermined elements and how they can clarify contextual conditions that would otherwise remain highly uncertain and complex.

These insights were developed from the four scenarios that challenged managers' dominant view of their context and industry, which was based on the historical logic of large-scale centralized power generation. This logic was the 'perceptual filter' through which they perceived events in the world. Until that juncture they had never considered that there would be an alternative future. While their *certainties* were grounded in the logic of large-scale centralized power generation in which they were embedded, re-conceptualizing these elements in systems models led them to see that the combination would change this fundamental aspect of their industry. The conditions for change surrounded them; yet they had failed to make the connections between the factors creating those conditions.

Using the macroscope approach in scenarios helped them to make connections between issues and events that surrounded them in a way that they had not previously done. By making such connections they were able to construct a shared understanding of 'their' environment that they had failed to see before. This is paradoxical as the organization itself was operating within these systemic structures.

For these managers, the scenario approach was a (self-)reflexive process providing time and space to enable them to articulate, share, question and collectively make sense of their tacit knowledge (Polanyi, 1958) about their context. Making sense of this tacit knowledge enabled them to 'see' patterns and trends about factors that would inevitably impact upon them.

While this chapter is focused on the power industry, I am convinced that the three fundamental principles generally apply. The principle of predetermined elements is central to the purpose of scenario work. By opening up and exploring contexts that are becoming salient (in this case, an industry-wide business model following on from privatization whose long-term future was becoming ever more uncertain), it is possible to narrow down to a limited number of issues that can be planned for.

It is now almost 25 years since Pierre Wack (1985a, 1985b) wrote his two seminal articles reflecting on his experience of scenario planning. He was arguing that planning should be based on an understanding of predetermined elements rather than best guesses. Wack's thinking was *not* based on futurism, but a sound understanding of the reality that we cannot always see. The challenge is to make the hidden visible, and the knowable known and understandable. His legacy is still relevant today, tomorrow and in the future.

References

Burt, G. and Wright, G. (2006) 'Seeing for organizational foresight', *Futures,* vol 38, no 8, pp887–893

Burt, G., Wright, G., Bradfield, R., Cairns, G. and van der Heijden, K. (2006) 'Limitations of PEST and its derivatives to understanding the environment: The role of scenario thinking in identifying environmental discontinuities and managing the future', *International Studies of Management and Organizations*, vol 36, no 3, pp52–77

de Rosnay, J. (1979) *The Macroscope*, Harper and Row, New York, NY

Emery, F. and Trist, E. (1965) 'The causal texture of organizational environments', *Human Relations*, vol 18, pp21–32

Kahn, H. (1962) *On Thermonuclear War*, University Press, Princeton, NJ

Kahn, H. (1964) *Thinking about the Unthinkable*, Avon Books, New York, NY

Kahn, H. and Wiener, A. (1967) *The Year 2000: A Framework for Speculation on the Next Thirty-Three Years*, Macmillan Company, New York, NY

Meadows, D., Meadows, D., Randers, J. and Behrens III, W. (1972) *The Limits to Growth*, Universe Books, New York, NY

Morgan, G. and Ramírez, R. (1984) 'Action learning: A holographic metaphor for guiding social change', *Human Relations*, vol 37, pp1–28

Polanyi, M. (1958) *Personal Knowledge: Towards a Post Critical Philosophy*, Routledge, London, UK

Revans, R. (1982) *The Origins and Growth of Action Learning*, Chartwell Bratt, Bromley, UK

Senge, P. (1990) *The Fifth Discipline: The Art and Practice of the Learning Organization*, Century Press, London, UK

Valery, P. (1960) *Tel Quel, Oeuvres II*, Bibliotheque de la Pleiade, nrf Gallimard

van der Heijden, K. (1996) *Scenarios: The Art of Strategic Conversation*, John Wiley and Sons, Chichester, UK

van der Heijden, K., Bradfield, R., Burt, G., Cairns, G. and Wright, G. (2002) *The Sixth Sense: Accelerating Organizational Learning with Scenarios*, John Wiley and Sons, Chichester, UK

Wack, P. (1984) *The Gentle Art of Reperceiving*, Harvard Business School Working Paper, Harvard

Wack, P. (1985a) 'Scenarios: Uncharted waters ahead', *Harvard Business Review*, September–October, pp73–89

Wack, P. (1985b) 'Scenarios: Shooting the rapids', *Harvard Business Review*, November–December, pp139–150

Weschler, L. (1982) *Seeing Is Forgetting the Name of the Thing One Sees: A Life of Contemporary Artist Robert Irwin*, University of California Press, Berkeley, CA

13

Conceptions of Fairness and Forming the Common Ground

Shirin Elahi

Introduction

I doubt any parent has survived the experience without regularly hearing those four words: 'It is not fair.' In this chapter I explore the nature of fairness, its innate importance to human beings, and – drawing on the work of Emery and Trist (1965) – I argue that in turbulent complex environments, it is critical to attend to conceptions of fairness. Indeed, the formation of the common ground creates a climate of cooperation and social adaptability and thereby enhances the possibility of a positive response to such challenging environments.

Scenarios offer a means to form this common ground. By their very nature, they incorporate elements of fair process – if for no other reason than that the process actively incorporates the perspectives and values of multiple stakeholders. If scenario practitioners consciously consider the various elements that underpin fairness, thereby making an implicit practice more explicit, I believe it would both enhance the impact and reach of their work and make the scenario process fairer. Fairness is one of the key dimensions of trust, so by extending an implicitly fair process to a wider field of actors and stakeholders, the scenario roll-out offers a means to achieve not only a fairer outcome, but also a more trusted one.

I have structured this chapter as follows. I first examine how the increasing complexity and relevant uncertainty in turbulence render the formation of the common ground important. I then briefly summarize the theoretical underpinnings of fairness and suggest how understanding them can improve scenario practice and its acceptance. After that I describe the issues that contribute to fair process, most of which are implicitly part of scenario practice. I then argue that scenarios, by bringing together multiple worldviews of the future into a shared framework, provide the potential to create the common ground so that attending to fairness in scenario practice can produce a fairer outcome.

Why common ground?

In a globalized interconnected world, issues become more transparent and divisions more apparent. The issues that receive widespread attention and generate concern tend to be tangled, complicated affairs. Such 'wicked' problems, as termed by Rittel and Webber (1973), reflect the coalescence of social, technical and political dilemmas that can cut across the boundaries of communities, organizations or nations. Although policy-makers and government departments are neatly divided into constituent parts, complex human, technological and environmental systems are not. So, more often than not, decisions impacting upon such multifaceted issues are made with a single-issue lens, giving rise to conflict between multiple stakeholder groups affected by cumulative impacts or unintended consequences. Such controversies then compound the systemic volatility of these already turbulent environments.

Wicked problems are characterized by uncertain facts and involve high stakes and disputed values. Although some appear to require urgent decision-making, this is difficult to achieve due to the complex interrelationships among diverse actors where power relations and roles are fluid and dynamic. Examples include the division of highly valued indivisible or finite resources, the partition of transboundary risks, or ethical life-or-death issues. Wicked problems defy solutions by analytical methods as they come together in non-linear combinations that are not only unexpected, but which can also fundamentally change the texture of the context – for example, the 11 September 2001 attacks by Bin Laden's men or the AIDS epidemic (see Chapters 5 and 7 in this volume for similar analyses of how single events can change causal textures). Wicked problems exhibit the type IV turbulent field conditions identified by Emery and Trist (1965), where the inherent nature of the field, combined with the dynamic interaction among disparate parties, has amplified levels of uncertainty and created emergent field forces.

It is almost half a century since Emery and Trist (1965) demonstrated that organizational survival and effectiveness in turbulent social fields required new forms of cooperation by former competitors under the rubric of shared values. They believed this required a new set of 'values that have overriding significance for all members in the field', and at that time they suggested that this would be a very slow process. Establishing such social values would require new forms of cooperative relationships where parties would have aligned their interests and created mutual goals in order to create a common future desired by all (i.e. the 'common ground').

Good scenario practice, drawing a diverse group of disparate stakeholders together to search for shared future interests, offers a potential framework for building the common ground – and to do so perhaps faster than Emery and Trist originally suggested (see Chapter 8 in this book). The scenario stories produced by this process in turn then offer the potential to move the collaborative scenario-building exercise conducted among a limited group of key stakeholders to a wider group able to share a common framework and language. My research shows that this cooperative process of discovering the common ground has the potential to transform the turbulent field into a less complex environment for those involved, underpinned by a shared set of values or a common ethical code.

Research suggests that fairness is particularly important for decision-making that involves long timescales, both for negotiation and decision maintenance (Albin, 1991; Young, 1994b) – and many of these are type IV environments. Considering fairness as an issue is useful not only from the ethical perspective in order to achieve acceptable decisions, but also from a pragmatic perspective to ensure compliance and to avoid constant confrontations and stalemate or the need for enforcement mechanisms to implement unpopular decisions. In contrast, fairness is of less significance in the decision-making process for the hierarchical type II environments, which are more likely to have centralized control and coordination structures, or type III environments, where power struggles between competing organizations, interest groups or even governments are likely to take place (Emery and Trist, 1965).

Conceptions of fairness

Fairness is embedded in our social vocabulary; yet, paradoxically, in many situations it appears to be neither well defined nor well researched. Fairness can be defined as 'free from bias, fraud or injustice, equitable, legitimate, impartial' (*Oxford English Dictionary*). This definition raises the fundamental intractable question: 'Fair to whom?' This question is one that many scenario exercises would be wise to consider explicitly. Indeed, the question of 'whom' depends entirely upon the size of the group identified as that sharing a common sense of identification – from organization or neighbourhood, to even a nationality or the human race as a whole (Rorty, 1997). An outcome that is fair to a group of parties at one level may not be fair at a different geographic or temporal scale (i.e. the wider international level) or to future generations.

Conceptions of fairness vary depending upon culture, age, gender and status. Yet, the concept of fairness is believed to be a universal notion (Rawls, 1972). Views on fairness are contained in the Bible, the Talmud and in Chinese writings. Recent research indicates that the frontal lobe of the human brain, the dorsolateral prefrontal cortex (DLPFC), is programmed to suppress basic human self-interest and enables humans to control fairness within society (Phillips, 2006), and that primates also sanction those who do not meet their concept of fairness (De Waal, 2006).

Fairness as we have come to understand it in the West falls into two basic categories. The first attends to method and the second to results. Procedural or process fairness is achieved when the method by which a decision is reached is fair, while outcome or substantive fairness is the result of a decision that is intrinsically a fair one. Undoubtedly, achieving outcome fairness is more desirable than achieving process fairness as the result is (generally) more important than the means. However, there are instances where no outcome will be fair to all parties (i.e. the allocation of a resource or burden for which there is no adequate compensation), such as the siting of a nuclear waste processing plant or the provision of life-saving drugs to only a proportion of a larger group. In such cases, parties may agree to a fair process and accept the resulting solution even if the outcome is an unfair one (Albin, 1993, Renn et al, 1995).

There are three major philosophical doctrines on which the concepts of fairness are based – equality, equity and priority – which I summarize below. Parties tend to view fairness from their own distinct vantage point, and research (Albin, 1993; Young, 1994a) indicates that the preference of doctrine will depend upon several factors, most notably the parties' perceptions of power and status. Strong parties favour equity, while weaker parties favour equality. Similarly, men generally favour equity and most women equality. Very small children will choose strict equity; but as they grow older they will favour equality before reversing to equity when they mature.

Equity (proportionality)

Fairness is a distinct principle in justice – in Greek times known as natural justice. Aristotle was the first to articulate this form of justice based on balance, arguing that social good and bad should be allocated in proportion to the contribution of each party to the asset. He distinguished between justice and equity and recognized that no system of justice could anticipate every circumstance that arose, and that in certain cases legal judgements required adaptation in order to achieve fairness. This distinction has continued – for example, in the UK, the Lord Chancellor had the power to redress harsh judgements, utilizing a system of equity courts, separate from the courts of law until the courts were merged in the early 20th century.

With equity, resources (rewards such as honours, public property or profits) or burdens are meant to be distributed proportionally to relevant contributions (inputs). Contributions can take many forms: wealth, skills, intelligence, effort – such as hours worked or tasks completed. However, these contributions are likely to be valued differently by the various parties negotiating, and although they are sometimes easy to measure, they can also be qualitative rather than quantitative by nature, making the allocations problematic. Similar problems occur when the resources are indivisible, such as a famous painting or children in a divorce.

Equity distribution can be used for several procedural mechanisms that I discuss in more detail below, such as rotation, sale and compensation. The partition of Pakistan and India is an example of division based on the principles of equity. All cash and government debt was divided in a ratio of 17.5: 82.5 per cent (based on the proportion of the population at that time); while other divisible goods were divided in a ratio of 20: 80 per cent (the rounding of the proportion). One of the most important indivisible items – the name, India – was kept by the larger half (Young, 1994b).

Equality (egalitarianism)

Equality is also called impartial justice or parity. It is based on the philosophy of Jean-Jacques Rousseau (1762) and the principle that all men are born equal. This implies all parties should receive an equal share of rewards and burdens, irrespective of their needs, differing resources and contributions. It provides clear-cut choices and can therefore be perceived to provide a fair outcome. While, in principle, this approach to equal shares or equal sacrifice appears to be unambiguous, economic costs and benefits are often unfairly distributed. This means that achieving an outcome of equality when parties are unequal is difficult to achieve and also often fails to provide an efficient distribution of resources.

Decisions based on equality rarely rectify current inequalities, perpetuating any existing perceptions of unfairness. For example, during the mid 1970s, Sweden initiated multilateral negotiations regarding transboundary air pollution, based on research proving that foreign sulphur dioxide (SO_2) emissions were responsible for acidification of their lakes. Equality had been established as the distributive principle in international negotiations, so the resultant 1985 Helsinki Protocol mandated a uniform 30 per cent reduction of SO_2 emissions, without taking into consideration that certain parties, such as Norway and Sweden, were benefiting more from the agreement. Other less developed countries, reliant on polluting technologies, were financially penalized by these obligations.

The perceived unfairness of this outcome and some other international agreements led to newer agreements taking a wider perspective to include economic, environmental and other factors, with the bias shifting towards equity. The subsequent 1994 Second Sulphur Protocol to the Convention on Long-Range Transboundary Air Pollution, aimed at achieving a 60 per cent reduction in acid rain in order to rid the European continent of its effects, was signed based on principles of equity and efficiency. The Regional Acidification Information System (RAINS) model developed at the International Institute of Applied Systems Analysis (IIASA) was used to determine a fair balance, as parties perceived it to be politically neutral, scientifically sound and an acceptable alternative to arbitrary fixed-percentage reductions.

Priority (compensatory or redistributive justice)

The third principle of fairness is based on fair distribution, priority or need, and has most famously been studied by Rawls (1972). It maintains that one cannot achieve fairness by using the system of equity between contributions and gains (which will usually reward those already well endowed) until resources have been divided so as to improve the well-being of the worst-off members of society, up to a basic minimum level of well-being to meet basic human necessities. However, an unresolved and problematic issue is how to define this base level, which can range from access to health, education, employment or a safe environment. The criteria specifying the most suitable or most needy parties also require definition, potentially an emotive process. Redistributive justice is attractive from the victims' point of view, but is likely to be resisted by those members of society benefiting from the status quo.

Other principles of fairness

Precedent has sometimes formed the basis for outcome fairness – and it is a particular feature of common law countries. A fair decision here will be based on a previous comparable decision, which serves as a rule for determining allocations. Precedent is commonly used in planning law, labour management negotiations and rent negotiations.

So-called super-fairness or envy-free distributions are based on the principle that no party should prefer the portion of another to his own (Baumol, 1987).

Fair process

'Fair process profoundly influences attitudes and behaviours that are critical to high performance. It builds trust and unlocks ideas' (Kim and Mauborgne, 1997, p66). Scenarios by their very nature incorporate elements of fair process, and most scenario practitioners implicitly incorporate some, if not all, of these aspects into their work. I believe that articulating the many issues underpinning fair process can enhance scenario work.

Procedural fairness or fair process refers to the ability of all parties to take part in the decision-making process, and it concerns the methods used for arriving at an acceptable decision. In law, this is termed *audi alteram partem* – hear the other side. How the selection of the 'other' side is structured, and how much involvement of third parties there is, will affect the formation of the common ground. There are a number of aspects to involvement in the process – namely, attendance, initiation, discussion and decision, and achieving. For more detailed information, refer to the Nominal Group Technique (NGT), the most common format for this in group work (van de Ven, 2007).

Having discussed the various conceptions of fairness, I now briefly set out the issues that determine procedural fairness. Many argue that even when a fair outcome cannot be achieved, a fair process will go a long way to ensure acceptance, linked to perceptions of respect and fair treatment (Lind and Tyler, 1988).

Attendance

A most critical aspect of fair process is whether all stakeholders affected by, or who affect, the situation are represented in the process and that they have a genuine opportunity to participate. The choice of representatives is very important since the identity of participants, their number and attributes will affect the fairness of the process. Unfortunately, all too often there are minority groups with little means of finding representation in decision-making processes affecting them. In some cases, parties cannot physically attend – for example, future generations or other species. In these cases, the question is how their interests can be measured and who can or should represent them fairly as the presence of outsiders can affect the balance and create asymmetry. The rise in civil society groups purporting to represent these constituents has been dramatic over the past years (Glasius et al, 2005). Whatever the choice of representation, it is essential that all participants commit to attending the whole process – partial attendance is unacceptable. In addition, participants have to have the freedom to move from the party line and explore alternative viewpoints. This 'representation' aspect in scenarios contrasts with the approach which search conferences take in this regard – where participants attend as individuals, not as representatives (see Chapter 3 in this book).

Initiation

The codes of initiation are an essential part of the issue of process fairness. In order to be fair, all parties require an equal chance to formulate and agree upon these structures and codes. Here issues hinge around the ability of all parties to be heard and to have their interests aired. The design of the process (i.e. the agenda, timescales for particular tasks, as well as the physical features of the location and the modes of communication – including the languages used for the process and the availability of communication channels) will also be important to establish process fairness, particularly when parties do not share the same language and customs.

Discussion and decision

Open and frank discussion without repercussion is a feature of procedural fairness. In practice, this means ensuring that all parties are heard and multiple issues are part of an integrated whole – incorporating the linkages between these issues and the relationships among various parties. The extent to which this is achievable will depend upon the ability of the facilitator to ensure that the agreed code of engagement is adhered to, and that the issues aired are equally represented and reproduced during the scenario-building process. Naturally, of key importance is that the forum in which the scenario process takes place protects those involved in candid engagement from unfair consequences due to this behaviour elsewhere.

One of the strengths of scenario practice is its broad Olympian view across stakeholders and issues as well as the inclusion of their interrelationships. This approach contrasts with many other forms of problem definition that utilize an analytically narrow focus of the subject. Although the latter course might make initial agreement simpler, it is likely to reduce the perception of fairness due to the lack of recognition of the complex linkages and the cumulative impacts between entities and issues. However, it is worth noting that the framing, that is, the interpretation used by individuals and the group to perceive, identify and label events and issues will affect understanding and guide actions, particularly when dealing with complexity (Goffman, 1974). Framing takes place in many ways that affect fairness: in terms of the division of a good or a bad, the timescale (long term, short term; intergenerational), and the size or dimensions of the units considered.

In some instances, there are sensitive issues that can be described as unmentioned or even unmentionable due to social or psychological taboos of the group, culture or society. For example, in the United Nations Joint Programme on HIV/AIDS (UNAIDS) scenario process I was involved in (UNAIDS, 2005), certain elements of sexual behaviour fell into this latter category. However, in order to find a shared solution it is important to try and raise such taboos, which, while unmentionable, are likely to have strong subconscious impact upon decisions and behaviours. In a similar vein, should there be any perception that there are undisclosed or hidden agendas, or that sensitive issues have been removed from the discussion, in this way influencing the framing, there will be a perceived lack of procedural fairness.

Achieving

Information and access to knowledge are currencies of power: if withheld or manipulated, no decision will be considered fair. The quality and extent of information available affects fairness. There are many examples of negotiations where information asymmetry has affected the outcome, and in such cases the distrust engendered makes future negotiations and consensus much harder to achieve. Good scenario practice ensures that all voices are heard, overcoming this.

A classic example where knowledge asymmetry led to an outcome perceived as unfair is the Trade Related Aspects of Intellectual Property Rights (TRIPS)

Agreement. Many argue that developing countries did not understand the impact that this agreement would have on their economies, but accepted the terms as a means of securing agreement on agricultural reforms which would provide revenue (Finger and Schuler, 2004; Correa, Huther, Visser interviews in EPO, 2007).

Fair outcomes (substantive fairness)

Substantive fairness means a fair outcome. In essence, fair outcomes will be those that enlarge the group with whom there is shared identity. Fair outcomes enable stakeholders or actors to find a means of co-existing without conflict by establishing a new shared set of beliefs and values, working out a *modus vivendi* or building a community of trust (i.e. creating the 'common ground').

Fair outcomes require that the principles underlying the distribution of resources or rewards, and burdens or risks, within the agreement itself are fair, using various mechanisms (Albin, 1991, 1993, 1995; Mellers and Baron, 1993; Young, 1994a, 1994b). Goods are not necessarily tangible or quantitative, making distribution complex. They can include clean air, social order, employment opportunities, security, power, physical land, or even political and social recognition. Liabilities can include both real or potential negative consequences and losses to human beings or the things they value.

There are a number of mechanisms used to distribute goods and liabilities, some of more relevance to scenarios practice than others. However, understanding these mechanisms is likely to provide practitioners with a theoretical framework to apply in the search for balance and fairness as necessary:

* *Division:* the value of environmental goods is seldom equal; but in some cases a fair division can be achieved based on reciprocity. This can take the form of equal sacrifice, tit-for-tat, split the difference or an exchange of equal concessions. This mechanism is only fair when the parties are equally far from the initial positions and when partisan biases (the tendency to overvalue one's own concessions and undervalue those of the other parties) can be avoided. Division is more difficult when one party has better information regarding the value of the resource. In such cases, the fairest method of division is for one party to divide and the other party to choose.

   This method was used in the international Law of the Sea negotiations, where a key issue was the division of the mining rights for the ocean floor. Developing countries were concerned that they would be left with the less valuable areas of what was a global commons resource as only some industrialized countries were in a position to exploit the seabed profitably. The resolution to this controversy was to ensure that any mining company applying to the International Seabed Authority (ISA), which licenses all mining activities, must develop two parallel deep-sea mining sites. An international mining company working for the developing countries is then given the choice of one of these sites. This ensures that the developing countries glean at least half the benefits of the process (Sebenius, in Young, 1994b).

* *Destruction or delegation to a third party:* when parties cannot agree on how to distribute a resource, it might be fairest to destroy it or give it to a third party. A classic case illustrating this mechanism is King Solomon's judgement made to two mothers claiming the same child (Kings I, 3: 16–28). Solomon's decision to divide the baby in two enabled the real mother to be identified. When the threat to the baby's life was about to materialize, the real mother was willing to lose her child to preserve its life. However, in today's world the concept of destruction of an asset could be unacceptable, and finding an arbiter who is perceived as sufficiently legitimate to all parties is often unlikely (Albin, 1991).

* *Random chance:* when an asset cannot be divided simply, random chance can be used to share an asset or liability. This could take the form of a lottery: flipping a coin or tossing the die and the winner takes all. Such a strategy could be perceived as fair when the outcome is either of very small or great importance, or when the disputed resource is indivisible. However, this practice is quite uncommon as most people are psychologically risk averse and will not accept risk-taking when the likelihood of loss is high (Tversky and Kahneman, 1981).

* *Rotation:* sometimes joint custody or rotation of the possession is a fair solution to the decision-making process. An example of rotation was adopted by Turkish fishermen in Alanya, where approximately 100 fishermen were competing for the best fishing spots at an inshore fishery. As the resource dwindled, fishing was no longer economically viable and the competition led to fierce conflict and increased production costs. A solution was found by identifying and listing all of the usable fishing locations. Every annual fishing season, fishing boats are put into a rota, which enables the fishermen to have access to fishing in every location sequentially. This is done by rotating their daily positions eastwards as the fish migrate westwards, ensuring that all fishermen have a fair opportunity to fish at the best locations at some point during the season. This system of rotation has also ensured that their common resource is maintained, removing the threat of over-fishing (Berkes, 1986b, in Ostrom, 1990).

* *Ownership in common:* when an area is indivisible, it can be possible to achieve a fair division by sharing ownership. In 1959, the Antarctic Treaty was signed by the 12 powers who had all made claims on the continent: Argentina, Australia, Belgium, Chile, France, Japan, New Zealand, Norway, South Africa, the Soviet Union, the UK and the US. The countries agreed to preserve the territory for peaceful purposes, particularly scientific research, and to ban colonization or development of its economic resources.

- *Sale:* there are cases when the value of an asset is realized and the proceeds shared among the parties. An auction is a fair means of determining which party values the resource most and their willingness to pay for it. However, should knowledge about the resource be asymmetric, it can lead to strategic bidding and perceptions of unfairness.
- *Compensation:* in some cases, a loser can be compensated with goods of equivalent value to achieve fairness; but there are some who perceive this as bribery. For example, in a bid to find locations for locally unwanted land uses (LULUs), such as hazardous waste disposal units that would be accepted by communities, some authorities attempted to compensate poor areas by offering improved education and health facilities in return. This caused moral concerns, with people questioning how financial payment could be balanced against the increased risks of a poor environment, ill health or even death (Field et al, 1996). It will be interesting to see whether these debates apply in the case of the United Nations Framework Convention on Climate Change (UNFCCC), which has introduced a Joint Implementation (JI) Programme where rich nations can be absolved from their requirements to reduce emissions under the Kyoto Protocol by paying developing countries to do it on their behalf through the means of emission reduction units (ERUs) (see http://unfccc.int/2860.php). At the moment, industrialized nations are required to reduce the majority of emissions themselves; but Yvo de Boer, executive secretary of the UNFCCC, argued that the challenge is so great that urgent action is required (BBC News, 22 August, 2007).

Using scenarios to form the common ground

> *If you listen to somebody else, whether you like it or not, what they say becomes part of you. So if the temperature is high, a conflict is generated inside and out. But in the dialogue, the temperature is lowered, and the common pool is created, where people begin suspending their own opinions and listening to other people's – so everybody's opinions will be held by everybody.* (Bohm, 1989, in Weisbord, 1992, p119)

Over the years I have had the good fortune to work on a number of scenario projects dealing with type IV turbulent fields. It is this experience that has made me so conscious of the value of fairness and the role it plays in the creation of trust, and, therefore, the 'common ground'. Fairness, alongside competence and consistency, is one of the three dimensions of trust (Renn and Levine, 1991; Cvetkovich and Löfstedt, 1999; Löfstedt, 2005). Without trust to lubricate the inherent frictions between disparate stakeholder groups there is little likelihood of forming the common ground – and navigating the systemic volatility of these environments.

Earlier in this chapter, I discussed the importance of forming the common ground, underpinned by a new set of values 'that have overriding significance for all members of the field', as Emery and Trist (1965) suggested, and I argued that scenarios could potentially speed up a process which would otherwise, according to Emery and Trist, require at least a generation to permeate a whole modern society.

In my work I have come to the conclusion that in almost every scenario-building exercise where issues of balance and trade-offs between different stakeholders and issues need to be explored, addressing fairness explicitly and systematically will improve effectiveness. This is so whether the issues under consideration are the ethics posed by a health risk such as AIDS in Africa; the economic, political or social impacts of an environmental catastrophe or a natural hazard; or the tensions between public and private ownership of intellectual property rights. In all such cases, finding a balance between the conflicting interests of diverse stakeholders that is perceived to be reasonably fair to all parties is of paramount concern in determining how successful the outcome will be.

I believe that the reason for this is that good scenarios integrate a jigsaw of collective mindsets, described by Bohm (1989), where the whole becomes greater than the sum of the parts. This process creates a set of scenario futures which form a robust framework from which a full range of perspectives can be viewed together as a whole. Many people will have preferences for one particular scenario; but the framework enables them to evaluate their ideas alongside those that might, under other circumstances, provide cognitive dissonance and thereby be rejected out of hand (Festinger, 1957).

To build scenarios that are fair, relevant and challenging, I have found that it is important to keep the following question firmly in mind: are there any major perspectives left out, and if so, why? An aim of scenarios is to widen thinking by setting out as many relevant facts of a larger whole, thereby helping people to think collectively, deal with complexity and engage in strategic conversation (van der Heijden, 1996). The resultant set of scenarios can then be used as a series of wind tunnels in which an organization or stakeholder can play out future strategies and test roles.

It is the focus on a shared future that enables scenarios to circumvent entrenched conflicts and form the common ground. By moving problems and ideas as far into the future as the scenario builders can tolerate, the process can break the current mindset of historical constraints that characterize type IV environments. The scenario stories produced in this way then offer the potential to move the collaborative scenario-building exercise conducted among a limited group of key stakeholders to a wider cooperative roll-out exercise. The set of scenarios form shared visions of the future, some of which will not be desirable for particular groups. By referencing a shared framework and language, people can collectively determine what decisions to take and what trade-offs these decisions might entail. In most cases, parties can find trade-offs that meet disparate interests which they consider fair because, generally, the same item is valued differently by the various parties and can therefore be traded by concessions on less-valued items for concessions of greater value. Because scenarios enable future trade-offs to be considered, people can experiment with possible valuations and evaluate options before exercising them – as they have considered not only the inherent fairness of the option they can adopt, but also the less fair alternatives which they can then modify or reject.

This process enables disparate stakeholders to explore the possibilities for cooperation, and potentially find shared values to achieve a future that can be shared by all or most parties. As they share the learning journey and its outcome, they co-produce the common ground and, hence, tap the potential means to deal with turbulence.

Building scenarios fairly

There are several phases in scenario building – namely, exploration, orientation, scenario building and affirmation. My work suggests strongly that when fairness is consciously integrated as a central element in each phase, the result is trusted more. This concerns procedural fairness at each stage, as well as frankness in addressing outcome fairness particularly in the roll-out phase – where a set of scenarios are shared with wider groups not involved in their production.

The exploration phase of scenario building usually entails a literature review and interviews to establish a landscape and set out a range of viewpoints. Interviewing both in person and by telephone provides a useful and low-cost means of incorporating multiple viewpoints within the process. The interviews are then synthesized in a search for patterns and structures that kick-starts the collaborative orientation process. However, it is important to be aware that there is a stage where the viewpoints are no longer original and the returns become progressively lower on the effort expended – which resembles what scientists call 'theoretical saturation'. Having first learned scenario practice in Shell, I believed that by the time one reaches approximately 20 interviews there would be usually sufficient repetition; yet this is not always the case. I found on my most recent project for the European Patent Office (EPO) that the range of viewpoints was so wide, and the issues were so contested, that we undertook well over 100 interviews with little duplication of ideas. The reasons were the complexity of the subject and lack of interdisciplinary research in the field, the sheer scale and diversity of stakeholders, as well as vested interests.

It is often good practice to ensure that interviews remain confidential and non-attributable, with the key points raised distilled and disseminated by the scenario team. However, I have found that putting the contents of each interview, edited and approved by the interviewee, into the public domain can maximize the value of the exercise by exposing diverse stakeholders (who are often reluctant to accept a change to the status quo) to the high probability or inevitability of change. Putting conflicting viewpoints coming from respected yet disparate parties into the public domain can set out clear markers and validate positions, thereby increasing trust and encouraging the formation of the common ground.

Since scenario processes deal with type IV environments, issues of trust between stakeholders are important. Ensuring that all dealings are transparent and that all outputs are clearly documented is an essential part of trust-building. Perhaps the most important outputs to document are workshop reports, which contain the contents of all flipcharts and exercises, while ensuring confidentiality by putting information in a non-attributable format. This ensures that every stage of the process is in the public or semi-public domain where the reasoning and proceedings are open to scrutiny.

Ensuring that all perspectives are considered equally is essential for fairness. This applies particularly to third parties who might be unable to participate in the process. Sometimes these viewpoints are those of minority groups who have been excluded due to logistical constraints of the process. For example, on the AIDS in Africa scenarios project I was involved with, it became clear that the downtrodden poverty-stricken sub-Saharan women, street children and AIDS orphans were not able to be represented in the room; yet they were some of the parties most affected by all of the future scenarios (UNAIDS, 2005). Once this problem was identified, the workshops used 'stick-holders' to ensure that these perspectives were not missed, and the director of the project explicitly invited these groups to meetings to ensure that the scenarios produced incorporated their perspectives. Similarly, the interests of unborn future generations facing massive socialization problems without the middle-aged income-generating and social norm-setting generations were going to be critical over the 20-year time horizon of the project. Therefore, exploring the social, political and economic issues and challenges they were likely to face was a major part of the exercise.

Building scenarios in multi-stakeholder settings takes more time and more substantial intellectual and financial resources than it does when working for individual focal organizations. In my experience, this complexity means that there are seldom sufficient resources available to explore every issue at the same level of detail, yet deciding which issues to concentrate on is inherently a subjective process, thereby creating a potential dilemma. It is therefore important to ensure that the issues considered are those that encompass the meta-level, and that the decision-making regarding the focus of research is transparent.

The process of using a 'parking bay' can enable those participants who do not want to let go of a given perspective to 'park' their ideas temporarily in order to examine alternatives. Acknowledgement of their views is a key aspect to achieving outcome fairness, and revisiting the 'parking bay' enables worthwhile ideas to be used later.

Ground rules are critical in order to ensure a fair process, and it is the role of the facilitators to ensure that they are maintained, and revisited and adapted, if appropriate. Some of ground rules I have worked with are:

- Confidentiality – what is discussed here stays in this room and the ideas remain non-attributable. The contents of the flip charts form the community record: they are easy to capture via digital photographs.
- Fairness – everyone has an equal right and responsibility to be heard. Different languages are welcome.
- Problem definition, not problem-solving – the focus is on shared learning, awareness, understanding and mutual support.
- Roles – participants generate and analyse information, derive meanings, propose action and take responsibility for output. Facilitators structure tasks and manage time.
- Status – speak as a person, not as a position; and listen to the person, not the position.
- Timeframes – activities are task oriented, so programme times matter.
- Validity – every idea or comment is valid and people need not agree.

Finally, the choice of location is critical to the physical access and comfort that the parties have, and it is important that one holds events in a neutral site. More often than not, I would try and persuade a client to hold a meeting offsite where everyone has the time to digest what is said and the opportunity to make new connections. When choosing venues, it is helpful if it is equally unfamiliar to everyone or, if this is not possible, a site where everyone is offered equal accommodation and related amenities.

Roll-out of the scenarios

Van der Heijden (2005) describes scenario practice beautifully as the art of strategic conversation. Scenarios provide a series of different perspectives that integrate mental models and open thinking, so enabling the strategic conversation to take place. This process creates learning loops linking thinking and action. However, when working with wicked problems beyond the scope or adaptive capacity of a single organization (see Chapter 10), achieving a strategic conversation is more difficult, even though it is more pressing to create the context where new ideas can be discussed without being rejected out of hand. Some scenario exercises never manage to move beyond interesting academic treatises; others create memorable metaphors and stories that enable the wider group to turn a theoretical exercise into reality. To the best of my knowledge, there is little research undertaken on how a given set of scenarios is shared with a wider audience, a practice termed 'roll-out'.

I have been arguing in this chapter that by their very nature scenarios incorporate elements of fair process within scenario building. A key question I now attempt to address is how an exercise among a relatively small group of scenario builders can best be utilized to extend the fair process and to touch a wider group of interested parties. Here the scenario builders become the obvious advocates – a group of people who have jointly shared a process of shared learning and created the framework that forms the basis for the common ground. These are the people who can form the nodes of an expanding network of people with cooperative attitudes and a shared understanding of the many facets around a particular issue, so galvanizing others and gradually creating momentum for cooperation, in this way increasing the area of common ground.

Scenarios – without denying conflicts – enable fewer, better arguments to be presented. For me, this roll-out process can be likened to a black-and-white image of a situation versus the different-coloured lenses of a prism through which to view it as a more complex and holistic set of issues, interests and viewpoints. An example of the successful use of scenarios for creating new forms of cooperation is the Mont Fleur scenarios, often cited as having contributed to the peaceful transition of government in South Africa (Kahane, 2004; see also Chapter 9 in this volume). In this instance, a multi-racial group of diverse decision-makers from across the political spectrum created four memorable possible futures, which varied from Lame Duck, Ostrich and Icarus to Flight of the Flamingos. These metaphors created the context for widespread strategic conversation and galvanized action.

This example illustrates how scenarios can be utilized as a means of establishing common ground beyond the scenario building itself, creating the context for cooperation and, possibly, the achievement of outcome fairness. In my experience, the roll-out process fails in such type IV environments unless the scenario-building exercise is trusted and the product perceived to be a resultant set of fair scenarios worth harnessing by others.

Conclusion

As I stated earlier, negotiations are more often than not adversarial by nature, presenting two opposing views of the future. This is in contrast to the integrative process that scenarios adopt and one that is particularly effective in easing friction between different stakeholder groups, forming a community of trust and establishing the common ground. An effective and fair roll-out process enables people who have not been involved in scenario production to modify their worldviews and redefine their social values. But why would they choose to do so? It could be recognition of the inevitability of change or the deep-rooted psychological need to understand and control the future (Gilbert, 2006).

Alternatively, the scenarios and their message could be unsuccessful, and the response to this new information could be to ignore, misinterpret or deny it. The first reaction to information that does not fit cognitive beliefs is denial, then anger, bargaining and depression before achieving acceptance (Kubler-Ross, 2005). In such cases, the responses to type IV turbulent environments will be business as usual until this can no longer be sustained. Should a crisis then occur, responses will probably be reactive, potentially creating chaos and a type V hyper-turbulent or vortical environment (McCann and Selsky, 1984; Selsky et al, 2007). In vortical environments, fairness across groups will be largely irrelevant as each group will be fighting for survival and ignoring the others.

It is in the turbulent complex type IV environments that common ground has a chance and makes strategic sense. The formation of the common ground creates the climate for cooperation and social adaptability and thus enhances the possibility of a positive response to such challenging environments. Scenarios are a tool that offers the potential to form this common ground – and by their very nature, scenarios incorporate elements of fair process. I believe that considering the various elements which underpin fairness and taking them into account in the building and roll-out of scenario work will make an implicit practice more explicit. Doing so, I have argued, should contribute to not only a fairer process, but potentially also a fairer and more trusted outcome, enhancing the impact and value of scenario work.

Acknowledgements

I am indebted to Roshana Kelbrick, William Cotter, Konstantinos Karachalios and John Selsky for their helpful comments on earlier drafts, and a special thank you to Rafael Ramírez for his insightful challenges and sympathetic editing.

References

Albin, C. (1991) 'Negotiating indivisible goods: The case of Jerusalem', *The Jerusalem Journal of International Relations*, vol 13 (March), pp45–76

Albin, C. (1993) 'The role of fairness in negotiation', *Negotiation Journal*, vol 9, no 3, pp223–244

Albin, C. (1995) 'Rethinking justice and fairness: The case of acid rain reductions' *Review of International Studies*, vol 21, pp119–143

Aristotle (translated by D. Ross) [1925] (1972) *The Nichomachean Ethics of Aristotle*, Oxford University Press, London, UK

Baumol, W. (1987) *Superfairness: Applications and Theory*, MIT Press, Cambridge MA

Bohm, D. (1989) 'Can lessons learned from subatomic particles help solve social problems?', Interview with John Briggs, *New Age Journal*, reprinted in M. Weisbord (ed) (1992) *Discovering Common Ground: How Future Search Conferences Bring People Together to Achieve Breakthrough Innovation, Empowerment, Shared Vision and Collaborative Action,* Berrett-Koehler, San Francisco, CA

Cvetkovich, G. and Löfstedt, R. (eds) (1999) *Social Trust and the Management of Risk,* Earthscan Books, London, UK

De Waal, F. (2006) 'The animal roots of human morality', *New Scientist,* 14 October 2006, issue 2573, pp60–61

Emery, F. and Trist, E. (1965) 'The causal texture of organizational environments', *Human Relations,* vol 18, pp 21–32

EPO (European Patent Office) (2007) *Scenarios for the Future: How Might IP Regimes Evolve by 2025? What Global Legitimacy Might Such Regimes Have?,* EPO, Munich, Germany

Festinger, L. (1957) *A Theory of Cognitive Dissonance,* Stanford University Press, Stanford, CA

Field, P., Raiffa, H. and Susskind, L. (1996) 'Risk and justice: Rethinking the concept of compensation', *Annals of the American Academy of Political and Social Science,* vol 545, pp156–164

Finger, J. M. and Schuler, P. (eds) (2004) *Poor People's Knowledge: Promoting Intellectual Property in Developing Countries,* World Bank and Oxford University Press, Washington, DC

Gilbert, D (2006) *Stumbling upon Happiness,* Harper Collins, London, UK

Glasius, M., Kaldor, M. and Anheier, H. (eds) (2005) *Global Civil Society 2005/6,* Sage, London, UK

Goffman, E. (1974) *Frame Analysis: An Essay on the Organization of Experience,* Harper and Row, London

Kahane, A. (2004) *Solving Tough Problems: An Open Way of Talking, Listening and Creating New Realities,* Berrett-Koehler Publishers, San Francisco, CA

Kim, W. and Mauborgne, R. (1997) 'Fair process: Managing the knowledge economy', *Harvard Business Review,* July–August, pp65–75

Kubler-Ross, E. (2005) *On Grief and Grieving: Finding the Meaning of Grief through the Five Stages of Loss,* Simon and Schuster Ltd, New York, NY

Lind, E. and Tyler, T. (1988) *The Social Psychology of Procedural Justice,* Plenum Press, New York, NY

Löfstedt, R. (2005) *Risk Management in Post-Trust Societies,* Palgrave Macmillan, Hampshire, UK

McCann, J. and Selsky, J. (1984) 'Hyperturbulence and the emergence of type 5 environments', *Academy of Management Review,* vol 9, no 3, pp 460–470

Mellers, B. and Baron, J. (eds) (1993) *Psychological Perspectives on Justice,* Cambridge University Press, Cambridge

Ostrom, E (1990) *Governing the Commons: The Evolution of Institutions for Collective Action,* Cambridge University Press, Cambridge

Phillips, H. (2006) 'Sense of justice discovered in the brain', *New Scientist,* Breaking News, 5 October, www.newscientist.com/channel/health/dn10239-sense-of-justice-discovered-in-the-brain.html

Rawls, J. (1972) *A Theory of Justice,* Clarendon Press, Oxford University Press, Oxford

Renn, O. and Levine, D. (1991) 'Credibility and trust in risk communication', in R. Kasperson, and P. Stallen (eds) *Communicating Risks to the Public: International Perspectives*, Kluwer, Amsterdam, The Netherlands

Renn, O., Webler, T. and Wiedemann, P. (eds) (1995) *Fairness and Competence in Citizen Participation: Evaluating Models for Environmental Discourse*, Kluwer, Dordrecht, The Netherlands

Rittel, H. and Webber, M. (1973) 'Dilemmas in a general theory of planning', *Policy Sciences*, vol 4, pp155–169

Rorty, R. (1997) 'Justice as a larger loyalty', *Ethical Perspectives*, vol 4, no 2, pp 139–151

Rousseau, J. (translated by G. D. H. Cole) [1762] (1913) *The Social Contract: A Discourse on the Origin of Inequality, and a Discourse on Political Economy*, J. M. Dent, London

Selsky, J., Goes, J. and Babüroğlu, O. (2007) 'Contrasting perspectives of strategy making: Applications in "hyper" environments', *Organization Studies*, vol 28, no 1, pp71–94

Tversky, A. and Kahneman, D. (1981) 'The framing of decisions and the psychology of choice', *Science*, vol 211, p453–458

UNAIDS (2005) *AIDS in Africa: Three Scenarios to 2025*, UNAIDS, Geneva

van der Heijden, K. (1996) *Scenarios: The Art of Strategic Conversation*, John Wiley and Sons, Chichester

van der Heijden, K. (2005) *Scenarios: The Art of Strategic Conversation*, 2nd edition, John Wiley and Sons, Chichester

van de Ven, A. (2007) *Engaged Scholarship*, Oxford University Press, Oxford

Weisbord, M. (ed) (1992) *Discovering Common Ground: How Future Search Conferences Bring People Together To Achieve Breakthrough Innovation, Empowerment, Shared Vision and Collaborative Action*, Berrett-Koehler, San Francisco, CA

Young, H. (1994a) *Equity in Theory and Practice*, Princeton University Press, Princeton, NJ

Young, H. (1994b) *Dividing the Indivisible*, IIASA Working Paper, WP-94-10, March

14

Turbulence and Corporate Social Responsibility: Is There a Role for Scenarios?[1]

Andromache Athanasopoulou

Introduction

Environmental complexity and uncertainty have bedevilled organizations and organizational actors alike because decision-making is often conducted under muddled conditions. In their seminal work on the 'causal texture' of the environment, Emery and Trist (1965) presented a typology of environments through which the notion of turbulence was introduced and the complexity of organizational environment highlighted. As was explained in Chapter 2, 'turbulent fields' are produced as a result of causal interconnections among the different parts of the environment within which organizations operate. In this chapter I seek to contribute to the causal texture framework by highlighting the role that corporate social responsibility (CSR) can play as a control, or regulatory, mechanism between a system and its environment in situations of environmental turbulence, as well as by indicating how CSR-based scenarios can help in addressing this environmental complexity and uncertainty. I illustrate this argument by using qualitative data from two case studies – a recently privatized public-service utility and a multinational tobacco company – in which the respective top management teams espoused explicit CSR strategies grounded in stakeholder responsiveness. I will use evidence from the fieldwork to argue that CSR can serve as a stabilizing mechanism for mitigating environmental turbulence by producing a 'common ground' among a firm and its various stakeholders. Evidence where the opposite occurs – that is, where CSR practices become a *destabilizing* mechanism further contributing to environmental turbulence – will also be discussed with regard to a company's environment and internal processes. Considering these observations, I argue that CSR-based scenarios can be an immense help for decision-makers in organizations in better addressing environmental uncertainty.

It is important to note at the outset that neither of the two companies studied actually used scenarios. I argue that the effectiveness of both companies' CSR strategies would have been strengthened if scenarios had been deployed. More generally, I illustrate how CSR may be strengthened in the future by using scenarios and, conversely, how scenario practice may be strengthened by considering CSR.

Causal texture and CSR

Emery and Trist's (1965) work falls under the broad area of open systems thinking which views systems as open to their environments and boundaries as permeable (Barton et al, 2004). In this approach, a system is conceptualized as 'people and organizations-in-environment, acting purposefully both to influence the environment and to learn from it' (Barton and Selsky, 2000, p706).

Emery and Trist (1965) identified the four 'ideal' types of causal texture of the environment discussed in Chapter 2. With regard to the turbulent-field texture, they suggested that in such a highly volatile environment, stability becomes tenuous and 'values' that have an 'overriding significance for all members of the field' can serve as a possible stabilizing or 'control mechanism' for actors as they cope with areas of uncertainty. Indeed, as Emery and Trist (1965) suggest, shared values provide the foundation for collective action that might change the texture of the field back to a less turbulent state. In that sense values serve as a common ground, which facilitates stability. Chapter 8 in this volume explores how this was made possible in Swedish healthcare.

One of the key challenges associated with CSR is an ongoing lack of agreement on its fundamental scope and content. Basu and Palazzo (2008, p122) identified three main lines of CSR enquiry prevalent in the academic literature: the stakeholder driven (where CSR is viewed as 'a response to the specific demands of largely external stakeholders'); the performance driven (which 'emphasizes the link between external expectations and a firm's concrete CSR actions', focusing on CSR performance measurement and selection of the activities that can best deliver the requisite performance); and the motivation driven (which examines either 'the extrinsic reasons for a firm's CSR engagement' or the 'intrinsic rationales' of the associated obligations and responsibilities).

CSR has been defined in numerous (and often contradictory) ways over the past 50 years that the concept has been discussed in the management literature. Andrews (1973, p58) sorted these views into two categories: the 'social interventionists' (i.e. CSR supporters) and the 'economic isolationists' – i.e. supporters of economic imperatives expressed by Friedman (1962), Arrow (1997) and others. This dichotomy exists even today.

The *social interventionists* view CSR as extending beyond the minimum legal requirements and give emphasis to companies' voluntary engagement in activities that would advance societal well-being. On the other hand, the *economic isolationists'* view is best represented by the well-known CSR definition provided by Milton Friedman in 1962: 'there is one and only one social responsibility of business – to use its resources and engage in activities designed to increase its profits so long as it ... engages in open and free competition, without deception or fraud' (Friedman, 1962, p133). Unlike earlier definitions, Friedman (1962) implied that corporations and managers have responsibility only to shareholders.

For the purposes of this chapter, CSR is defined as 'the notion that corporations have an obligation to constituent groups in society other than stockholders and beyond that prescribed by law or union contract' (Jones, 1980, pp59–60; Jones et al, 2002, p21). CSR is strongly linked (in the academic literature and in everyday business practice) with the notion of business ethics; but the relation between them remains contested. Some argue that CSR is a subset of business ethics and others that business ethics is a subset of CSR. For instance, Carroll (1991, p42) proposed that CSR consists of four responsibilities which form a 'pyramid'; ethical responsibility is one of them. Chapter 13 in this volume on fairness in and of scenarios shows that ethical considerations in CSR are also important in scenario work.

Zenisek (1979, pp363–364) reflected on Emery and Trist's (1965) work and noted that business ethics in the form of social responsibility can transform the environment so that a new, 'no longer turbulent and relatively static' environment is created. In other words, CSR represents the degree of 'fit' between the ethics of business and society's expectations of the business community. Several scholars studying social issues in management have also embraced the idea that CSR or other similar concepts can serve as 'common ground'. For instance, Savage et al (1991) argued that stakeholder management can serve as a means of coping with environmental uncertainty. Based on this overview, the question arises as to whether scenarios can play a role in better preparing organizations to survive in a turbulent environment. This will be discussed particularly with regard to the growing concern and demand from society and corporate stakeholders for companies to be more actively (and proactively) involved in CSR practices.

Scenario planning and CSR

Scenario planning can find application in different types of decision-making associated with high levels of turbulence. Ellis and Feinstein (2000), for instance, underlined the robustness of scenario learning as a tool for better decision-making, particularly with regard to financial planning. Similarly, within the context of risk management, Miller and Waller (2003) suggested that the combination of scenarios (from the strategic management field) and real options (from the finance field) can more effectively help a company to improve its flexibility and the quality of its investment decisions. As these examples indicate, decision-makers can (and do) use scenario planning in a variety of contexts and situations either as a stand-alone technique or in combination with other approaches in order to better prepare their organizations in times of increased uncertainty.

One development is the effort to use scenario planning to address CSR issues, particularly those related to sustainability. Early advocates of the value of CSR-related scenarios were Elkington and Trisoglio (1996), who focused their attention on 'sustainability scenarios'. They observed that with sustainable development becoming a strategic issue for organizations, managers were increasingly realizing the need to develop win–win solutions for them and their stakeholders. This requires having a better understanding of sustainability and its implications. They claim that the development of sustainability scenarios can help companies to better cope with the complexity of doing business in international environments because this planning technique can effectively prepare business executives and their companies for strategic 'surprises'. One such surprise the authors analyse is Royal Dutch Shell's messy involvement with the *Brent Spar* events of 1995.[2] Elkington and Trisoglio (1996) evaluated the well-known *Shell Scenarios* published up to 1995 and identified what they call a 'blind spot' – namely, the absence of an egalitarian perspective. More broadly, they also underline that the egalitarian perspective has been missed by much of the international business community. The authors argue that 'had Shell included an egalitarian perspective among its scenarios, it would have been much less likely to have been surprised by the Greenpeace response to the *Brent Spar* issue' (Elkington and Trisoglio, 1996, p766). However, this in my view involves the erroneous use of scenarios as forecasts – one cannot consider that a scenario set 'should have had' a viewpoint after the fact: that is what forecasts, not scenarios, are meant to do. It may well be the case that Shell's 1995 scenario set had a built-in bipolar scenario structure. In its most recent scenario set, the company proposed three, not two, scenarios that allowed for an egalitarian perspective that was meant to open the possibility of a dialogue space that the bipolar structure disallowed.

Recently, Stormer (2003) suggested that the economic paradigm, which sees profit maximization as the primary obligation of corporations, does not allow CSR to shift beyond the notion of an enlightened self-interest (in the sense of acting socially responsibly in order to further one's own ends). The author noted that such a neoclassical economic justification of the stakeholder model of the corporation is no longer pertinent within an increasingly complex environment. Linking the concept of environmental complexity with the use of CSR scenarios, Stormer (2003) called for CSR to be conceptualized within an 'inter-systems' model where business is seen as one of several interrelated systems. She argues that the shift from one model to another may be facilitated by the use of a modified version of the scenario-planning process. To be effective this requires the participation of an outsider (an 'authentic critic') in the scenario-planning process since the scenarios that are developed solely by managers within the organization (the insiders) would probably recapitulate the enlightened self-interest model. It is the participation of the critic (who may or may not be a stakeholder) with a completely different mental model of business-and-society relations that can make CSR scenario planning effective. Medjad and Ramírez (2007) explored how legal professionals would be affected if they used scenario planning in CSR; but they also suggest that this possibility does not exist in practice or, if it does, is not well documented.

The growing societal pressure pushing organizations to act in a socially responsible manner makes CSR scenario planning an important method for organizations that want to better prepare themselves for future challenges. It is not just of academic interest.

Two case studies

The above discussion opens up a set of questions with regard to the role of CSR amidst environmental turbulence and the role that scenarios can play: can CSR serve as a control mechanism for organizations operating in turbulent environments by providing a platform for common ground between organizations and their stakeholders? Can CSR-related scenarios help in mitigating the turbulence faced by organizations?

I examined these questions in two case studies that were conducted as part of a large-scale research project, the aim of which was to understand why organizations engage in CSR practices (Athanasopoulou, 2007). The study involved qualitative, mainly face-to-face, interviews with managers of two organizations during July to November 2004, based on an interview schedule of 38 open-ended questions. The interviews were coded and analysed using the NVIVO 2.0 software.

Both companies studied are multinationals: one is a public-service utility and the other is a tobacco company. For reasons of confidentiality, pseudonyms are used. At the time that the fieldwork was conducted, both companies were among the leading organizations worldwide in their respective industries in terms of market share. The study entailed interviews with managers from each of the two organizations. At the public-service utility (UTIL) 22 managers from various departments (CSR and non-CSR) were interviewed. At the tobacco company (TOB) the interviewees were 15 internal TOB managers (from CSR and non-CSR departments) and 3 external managers of consulting organizations, who were working with the TOB on its CSR implementation efforts.

UTIL: The utility company

UTIL used to be a state-owned organization that was subsequently privatized and some years later was acquired by a large conglomerate. UTIL belongs to a heavily regulated industry. The company recently set up a CSR department but has done considerable work on the area of environmental management and has produced environmental reports for many years before that. At the time the fieldwork was conducted, UTIL's CSR efforts were project-specific rather than CSR being an integral part of the way in which the company operated. Recently, UTIL faced an important challenge: it was pressured by its parent company to make a major shift in its expansion strategy, which directly contradicted UTIL's prior decision to help in pressing developing world issues. To find a balance between these somewhat contradictory pressures, UTIL's CSR department worked together with a member of the top leadership to develop a large-scale CSR project which was arranged in such a way that both objectives would be satisfied.

TOB: The tobacco company

TOB is a leading tobacco company, holding a significant percentage of the world's global tobacco market with hundreds of brands in its portfolio. As a tobacco company, TOB faces stringent regulation and numerous litigation cases due to the potential risk its products pose to public health.

TOB started its CSR implementation efforts a few years ago as a result of an internal recognition that the company was gradually becoming isolated from its stakeholders. This was primarily due to the defensive posture it had adopted over the criticism it had been receiving as part of changing societal perceptions regarding tobacco use. The company developed a new corporate vision with CSR set as an integral part of TOB's corporate strategy. This meant that from then onwards, every strategic decision would be filtered from a CSR perspective to ensure that it was socially responsible. The company also engages in a variety of CSR practices, including charitable donations, sponsorships of biodiversity programmes, employee volunteering and stakeholder dialogue sessions.

In the TOB, CSR is perceived as the way in which the company operates, rather than a project-based stand-alone process. The company has developed elaborate social reporting and governance mechanisms, which are gradually being adopted by its local operations across the world. One of the key elements of the company's CSR efforts is a stakeholder engagement process, which includes regular stakeholder dialogue sessions, where TOB employees (including its top leadership) participate.

Findings

Considering that UTIL's public service offering is vital for everyday life, whereas tobacco poses health risks, one might assume that the tobacco company would face greater turbulence than the public service company. However, a closer look at the case backgrounds revealed that both companies are in highly turbulent environments, each of a different nature. At the time of the research, UTIL faced heightened turbulence in its environment. The type and nationality of UTIL's ownership had changed, and the company had also to balance between the parent company's objectives and its previous commitment to help in addressing pressing developing world issues – two seemingly opposite objectives. Furthermore, the public-service industries remain highly regulated with regard not only to the operational aspects of the services that these companies provide, but also the prices they set for those services. Due to the importance of their service, public service companies are under very strict monitoring from public regulators and non-governmental organizations (NGOs).

I found that the TOB also faced high turbulence in terms of its external environment. It was (and still is) made up of potentially hostile stakeholders such as governments, public regulators or non-governmental advocacy organizations, the latter being particularly hostile towards the company due to the potential risk tobacco causes to health. The analysis of the data led to the following findings with regard to the role of CSR as a vehicle for developing common ground between companies and their external environment.

CSR: Stabilizing through common ground?

Interviewees were asked to comment on what their company seeks to achieve though CSR practices. Through this, the aim was to understand whether CSR serves as a link between the company and the environment in which it operates and, if so, how.

Interviewees' responses confirmed that CSR can serve as the common ground between the organization and its turbulent environment and as a means of improving its internal processes. Specifically, interviewees in both companies described CSR in the following terms: a safety mechanism in cases of failure of reputation; a source of differentiation and leadership; a boost to employee morale and good-quality employee recruitment; an opportunity for the company to 'give back' to society; to contribute to sustainable development; to improve the way/quality/effectiveness of doing business; an internal and external validation of being a responsible company (i.e. a legitimization tool); the right thing to do; preferred by shareholders since the lack of CSR may entail financial implications for the company; a source of organizational learning and improvement; and, finally, a means of enhancing corporate reputation. Some of these elements were highlighted as more important in UTIL than in TOB and vice versa. For instance, the view that CSR constitutes a means of differentiation and leadership was noted by 6 out of 22 UTIL managers interviewed, but by only 1 out of 15 TOB managers. On the other hand, the view that CSR is a legitimization tool was espoused by 3 TOB managers, while no UTIL manager expressed such a view.

The above clearly addresses different aspects of environmental turbulence and confirmed that managers tended not to agree with Milton Friedman's (1962) 'isolationist' view, but instead saw CSR as a way of bridging what were often perceived as irreconcilable differences between what a company seeks to achieve and what the society expects from the company. For instance, by stating that CSR is 'an opportunity to give back to society', or that 'it is the right thing to do', or that CSR efforts 'contribute to sustainable development', these managers, in essence, saw CSR as a tool for addressing the gap between the company's performance and society's expectations, and softening the frictions that they faced (or may face in the future).

This was particularly pertinent to the TOB, which had been enduring acute stakeholder hostility. Among the many different types of CSR practices in which the TOB was active, my sense from the fieldwork was that the ones which tended to be most valuable and helpful in creating common ground were the stakeholder dialogue sessions (compare with Martin Thomas's experience in Venezuela, documented in Chapter 9, where he found it impossible to organize such sessions). This is because each of these sessions entailed active participation of managers (from CSR and non-CSR relevant departments and from very different levels in the organizational hierarchy) in dialogue with the TOB's stakeholders. As some of the interviewees noted, this sometimes made for a difficult experience because they were exposed to often hostile attitudes or ironic comments by some of the participating stakeholders. However, even the fact that stakeholders agreed to attend such a session and engage in dialogue with the company was considered a great step forward. This helped in the company's effort to identify a common ground where both the company and the stakeholders could communicate, with the ultimate objective being the stabilization (as much as this is feasible) of the volatile environment. This was the conclusion I reached based on the examples that several interviewees offered to indicate how from the first stakeholder session to the second or third they clearly felt less hostility from the stakeholders who were invited in each session. The following quotes are indicative of this:

> ... *the first year that we did stakeholder dialogue in the UK, a lot of it was spent in talking about how we run our business ... about our product because many people clearly had misconceptions of what the product was, what we did, how we did it; and so it very much was closing a knowledge gap to reset the baseline on which we and stakeholders actually engage.* (Head of corporate social and regulatory affairs, TOB)

This suggests that like scenarios, CSR may have a role in producing clarity (see Chapter 11):

> *When we first invited anti-smoking activists to participate in dialogue, many of them would either not even respond or simply say: 'You can't be serious; why on*

earth would I come and talk to you'; and as the second and third round has gone on, we find that we are beginning to get a wider group and, if you like, a more critical group of our industry coming to our dialogue session. (Global head in research and development strategy, TOB)

There were numerous accounts by interviewees which illustrated that CSR served as a stabilizing mechanism. These were best identified when interviewees were asked to comment on measures of CSR success. The following quote is indicative of this:

... [success is] when you invite people for a company party and you have [many] more people attending, so people feel good to be together and when you invite external people to engage and you have [many] more people than you were expecting. (International regulatory and consumer affairs manager, TOB)

Along similar lines, another manager said:

I actually think that probably two-thirds of the employees want some form of CSR programme because it actually makes them feel better about [whom] they work for. And I think you need that if you work for the tobacco industry. I mean: what we are often sort of saying, when you go to a dinner party and people say: 'Who [do] you work for?'; sometimes it is quite uncomfortable giving the answer... So I think CSR will always continue to have support from the workers because (a) they think it is essential and (b) it makes them feel better about their work. (International regulatory and trade affairs manager, TOB)

The above quotes indicate that CSR became a point of contact not only internally among TOB's employees, but also externally between the company and its external stakeholders. With regard to the company's internal environment, as these interview excerpts illustrate, CSR gave TOB employees a sense of pride in their company and in what they do. The interviewees reported that this improved employees' morale and had a positive impact upon their work environment.

With regard to the company's external environment, clearly CSR became the common ground to which the company and its stakeholders can come together. The way in which a CSR project was communicated across different contexts and different audiences indicated how CSR could help in creating 'areas' of common ground, hence serving as a stabilizing mechanism. Specifically, I observed that CSR managers may use the same CSR project across different contexts, interpreting it in different ways according to the audiences whom they wanted to buy into the idea of CSR. For instance, UTIL developed a small CSR project which was then used by the CSR team as an example of the company's CSR efforts; depending upon the target audience, specific elements of the project would be highlighted. When this CSR project was presented to UTIL's parent company, the CSR team highlighted the way in which this project had brought positive publicity to the company. Therefore, the CSR team used this example to justify the resources put into CSR projects. In this way, the CSR project became a potential platform for common ground between the CSR team and the parent company. On the other hand, the same project was used in UTIL's external publications to signal to external stakeholders that UTIL is a responsible company. In that case, the project served as a potential platform for common ground between the company and its external stakeholders, some of whom may have been sceptical about the company's operations. This CSR project helped to mitigate some of this scepticism and, hence, became a platform for stabilization. The customization of the project to different audiences allowed the CSR team to derive the maximum stabilization impact in each case, depending upon the target audience.

CSR as a destabilizing mechanism?

Delving into more detail within each of the organizations, there is clear evidence that CSR serves as a stabilizing mechanism, both internally and externally. However, I also found that, surprisingly, CSR may become a destabilizing mechanism. The evidence suggests that this is because:

- CSR implementation serves as an idiosyncratic change agent that can alter the balances of power within an organization.
- When CSR is not effectively communicated, the CSR implementation may end up destabilizing (rather than stabilizing) the environment in which a company operates.

These points are explained below.

In one of the two cases, which for confidentiality reasons cannot be identified, there were clear instances that CSR served as a destabilizing function internally. I found that CSR practices and the company's active engagement in CSR projects had triggered political controversies among departments that were opposed to CSR. For instance, a manager of one such department suggested that the introduction of CSR had unsettled the internal dynamics of the company:

> ... we have been cutting back on the staff, giving bigger and bigger job sizes to people. I work both evenings, weekends, and somebody says: 'This company should be doing CSR!'... They are all good to have, but if you are stressed ... and you are looking at your directors and they are all getting big bonuses and they are talking about CSR, [while] people are being made redundant, do you believe that they truly understand what they are talking about? Because I don't!

This example illustrates that the introduction of CSR had unsettled the political balances within this organization. Managers of this interviewee's department argued that, since its establishment, the CSR department had been taking much of the credit for the work that they, in the first department, had been doing. The following quote from one of that department's managers illustrates this:

> *We have the biggest resource because we are the biggest part of the company ... in America my equivalents are all ... scientists. The CSR people in America: they are communications staff or they are PR staff.*

This situation led to controversies between the departments which have a stake in the resources dedicated to the company's CSR efforts. However, it is particularly interesting to note that the controversy was not over whether CSR was something good to have, but over the way in which CSR was being implemented. In other words, the destabilizing effects of CSR were attributed to its role as a change agent, challenging the way in which the company had been operating, not to the idea of CSR *per se*. It can be argued that this constitutes a positive change since it signifies that CSR had 'unfrozen' the organizational system. However, delving further in the data, I concluded that the destabilization had much deeper roots than a simple departmental rivalry. These frictions appeared between several departments and the CSR department because the CSR department and the top leadership did not provide effective justifications for their choice of CSR projects (see Chapter 13 in this book for a critical assessment of fairness in such processes). In other words, a significant part of the organization had not bought into the manner in which the company decided to implement CSR – hence, tensions arose. The following quote from a manager of a 'neutral' department (i.e. one who was neither for or against the CSR department) illustrates this point and indicates that the destabilization effects of introducing CSR cannot simply be attributed to organizational politics:

> *So, the confusion, or perhaps that's too shallow a word, but there is certainly a tension at the moment ... between the CSR principles which we have all culturally accepted for a long time and believed in... There is a lack of clarity ... it doesn't link to business strategy ... and if you are not careful it will begin to look like tokenism ... a number of people ... have feelings like mine ... you could argue that we are being negative. We are not being negative. Culturally we believe that CSR work was right ... and a good thing to do.*

This observation indicates that the extent to which CSR serves as a stabilizing or a destabilizing mechanism may depend upon:

- the type of CSR strategies adopted by the company; and
- the extent to which the value of CSR and the reasons behind the selection of specific CSR activities over others are adequately communicated across the company and externally in order to secure CSR buy-in and minimize frictions.

Discussion and conclusion: CSR, turbulence and the value of scenario planning

These findings suggest that turbulence may be mitigated with the help of CSR. However, the opposite may happen if CSR is not implemented effectively. Within such a context, the managing of the relationships of the company with its various stakeholders emerges as key.

Indeed, Post et al (2002, p1) define the corporation as a collaboration of multiple and diverse stakeholders and argue that '*organizational wealth* can be created (or destroyed) through relationships with stakeholders of all kind'. The authors argue that effective *stakeholder management* in the sense of 'managing relationships with stakeholders for mutual benefit' is a critical requirement for corporate success (Post et al, 2002, p1; italics in original). Current research indicates that effective stakeholder management also requires high-quality organizational communication and CSR education to ensure that CSR plays a positive, stabilizing role. CSR and, particularly, stakeholder engagement practices can serve as a platform for common ground where organizations and their stakeholders meet and seek to identify win–win solutions so that both corporate objectives and societal expectations are met. However, the inability or unwillingness by one or both parties to engage in such a discussion, or a problematic CSR communication, can widen the gap between those involved. Consequently, organizations can become misaligned from their external environment. This disjuncture makes the environment in which organizations operate more uncertain. This situation is not uncommon and was observed, to some extent, in both organizations under study.

Can CSR-related scenario planning help? Can this common misalignment between a company and its stakeholder environment be prevented? Can the development of CSR-related scenarios serve as a means of shaping a shared context between the company and its stakeholders and thereby help in identifying a common ground in conditions of turbulent environments?

Watkins and Bazerman (2003) examined disastrous events that happened despite the fact that corporations could and should have seen them coming (i.e. 'predictable surprises', or what Schwartz (2003) called 'inevitable surprises'). The authors found that these take place due to one or a combination of three causes: psychological (i.e. cognitive defects of the decision-makers), organizational (i.e. barriers internal to the organization that impede communication) and political (i.e. decision-making flaws). They conclude that scenario planning (in combination with risk assessment) can help companies to avoid these predictable surprises. If Watkins and Bazerman's (2003) observations are juxtaposed with the case I have presented, where the CSR implementation became a destabilizing mechanism, at least two of the three causes leading to predictable surprises can be identified – namely, organizational (i.e. poor justification of CSR choices and ineffective buy-in to the CSR efforts) and political (i.e. departmental conflicts leading to intra-organizational frictions) causes are clearly evident within this organization.

This implies that this company, because it is operating in a turbulent environment, may soon face predictable or inevitable surprises in its CSR arena. The company is finding itself in a situation where CSR engagement destabilizes rather than stabilizes its environment. I argue that this could have been avoided if CSR-related scenario planning had been undertaken before the company embarked on its implementation of CSR. If it had, then the company would have been better prepared for, or even arrested, the contentious situation that arose during this implementation. In other words, scenarios would attend to the psychological cause (Wack's 'microcosm', discussed in Chapter 12 of this volume). Going forward, scenario planning – and especially the 'egalitarian' scenarios proposed by Elkington and Trisoglio (1996) – could help the company to open up its perception of possible futures and, hence, be better prepared in the event that surprises arise again. This supports the advocates of scenario planning, who claim that every organization can better understand its past and present and sense the signs of future change that would later emerge in its environment. Moreover, Medjad and Ramírez (2007) have suggested explicitly that using scenarios might benefit the legalistic thinking that is often present in CSR.

CSR-related scenario planning can be valuable not only to organizations that have adopted CSR practices for some time, but also to companies (such as UTIL and TOB) which are new to this field. For instance, as discussed, the TOB ended up becoming isolated from its external environment by adopting a defensive attitude towards the criticism it had been receiving from hostile stakeholders. However, the TOB might have identified the possible future of 'isolation' earlier if it had actively used scenario planning and explored ways in which to avoid reaching a state of isolation. A scenario exercise could have surfaced the latent hostility earlier, enabling top management and the public relations department to prepare for it or deflect it better (see Chapter 6 in this volume on how scenarios can initiate and sustain a difficult strategic conversation among diverse stakeholders).

A similar conclusion could be drawn about the value of CSR scenario planning in the public-service utility. CSR-related scenario planning could clearly have helped UTIL to perceive its possible futures and better prepare itself for the challenges it now faces. The company's privatization and acquisition by a conglomerate is a scenario that a scenario-planning exercise might have foreseen when UTIL was still a state-owned enterprise. Scenario planning would have been equally useful with regard to what role UTIL could or should have played (and can play in the future) within the sensitive context of public service-related issues (Chapters 8 and 12 in this volume touch on these issues). I suggest that the lack of scenario planning on those issues contributed to increased complexity and, hence, more environmental turbulence, which could have been mitigated through CSR-related scenario planning.

Phelps et al's (2001) exploratory study is also pertinent to this discussion since it examined the value of scenario planning in one of the UK's public-service industries – water, in particular. Specifically, the authors observed that scenario planning contributed to improved financial performance (as measured both by service level and by financial return), but, interestingly, worsened customer service levels. The authors attributed the latter to the water industry's quasi-monopolistic structure.

The several examples and the discussion in this chapter have shown how CSR practice can be enhanced with the help of scenarios. Looking at this perspective within the CSR context, it also becomes clear that the opposite may apply – that is, scenario practice may be enhanced by explicitly including CSR principles and considerations (see Chapters 3, 8 and 13). Stakeholder engagement can be a key aspect of more effective CSR practice as the case of the TOB indicated. The ability to communicate with stakeholders, gauge their expectations and discuss how and whether the company can address some or all of these expectations is a valuable tool in the hands of decision-makers, not only with regard to the short-term day-to-day issues of the company, but also for its long-term strategic planning. This is aligned with Stormer's (2003) suggestion for the role that stakeholders can potentially play as 'authentic critics' in the scenario-planning process. CSR in the form of stakeholder engagement practices can become the basis for developing more effective scenarios and also for regular testing of these scenarios to ensure that they can best prepare the organization for its uncertain future(s). The engagement of stakeholders might enable this to happen more easily – as long as the stakeholders are not co-opted into the company's perspective (or they would lose their capacity to be authentic critics).

Overall, scenario planning can be as useful to CSR practices as CSR practices are to scenario planning. CSR and the development of CSR scenarios can contribute to the development of control mechanisms within turbulent fields and, where applicable, prevent the acceleration of turbulence. However, all of this effort will be ineffective if the organization is not fully committed and ready to take stock of the lessons that the scenario-planning process offers. Mercer (1995) notes that a key prerequisite for scenario planning to be successful is an organizational culture that encourages making the most of the scenario-planning process so that this process thrives and positively impacts upon the company's strategy in the long run. This might entail the promotion of the role of 'authentic critics' in the scenario-planning process, as discussed above, as an integral part of the organizational culture. As Wack (1985, p74) has eloquently explained: 'a willingness to face uncertainty and to understand the forces driving it requires an almost revolutionary transformation in a large organization. This transformation is as important as the development of the scenarios themselves.'

Considering this discussion, I believe that UTIL and the TOB would be well served in adding CSR-based scenario planning to their repertoire of CSR initiatives.

Notes

1   I am very grateful to the editors of this book for their very meticulous and most helpful feedback and editing of this chapter. I also owe a special thanks to Dr Angela Wilkinson for her elaborate advice on a section of this chapter.

2   Since there are quite contradictory views regarding what really happened in the *Brent Spar* events, I can only present here my understanding of the situation after consulting relevant material. In 1995, with UK government's regulatory support, Shell UK decided to sink its *Brent Spar* oil storage and tanker loading platform in the Atlantic Ocean. Greenpeace campaigned against this decision and under public pressure Shell eventually decided not to sink the platform, but to tow it to land for disposal. However, the company never abandoned its initial view that sinking the *Brent Spar* was the right approach according to health and safety and environmental criteria. In the end, the facts were with Shell, not Greenpeace – but Greenpeace won the publicity and political battle, not Shell.

References

Andrews, K. (1973) 'Can the best corporations be made moral?', *Harvard Business Review*, vol 51, no 3, pp57–64

Arrow, K. (1997) 'Social responsibility and economic efficiency', in T. Donaldson and T. W. Dunfee (eds) *Ethics in Business and Economics, Volume I*, pp137–151, Ashgate, Dartmouth, Aldershot, UK

Athanasopoulou, A. (2007) *Making Sense of Corporate Social Responsibility: A Study of the Implementation Process*, PhD thesis, Saïd Business School, University of Oxford, Oxford, UK

Barton, J., Emery, M., Flood, R., Selsky, J. and Wolstenholme, E. (2004) 'A maturing of systems thinking? Evidence from three perspectives', *Systemic Practice and Action Research*, vol 17, no 1, pp3–36

Barton, J. and Selsky, J. W. (2000) 'Afterword: Toward an Emery model of management: Implications and prospects of Emery open systems theory', *Systemic Practice and Action Research*, vol 13, no 5, pp705–720

Basu, K. and Palazzo, G. (2008) 'Corporate social responsibility: A process model of sensemaking', *Academy of Management Review*, vol 33, no 1, pp122–136

Carroll, A. B. (1991) 'The pyramid of corporate social responsibility: Toward the moral management of organizational stakeholders', *Business Horizons*, vol 34, no 4, pp39–48

Elkington, J. and Trisoglio, A. (1996) 'Developing realistic scenarios for the environment: Lessons from Brent Spar', *Long Range Planning*, vol 29, no 6, pp762–769

Ellis, J. and Feinstein, S. (2000) 'Scenario learning: A powerful tool for the 21st century planner', *Journal of Financial Planning*, vol 13, no 4, pp82–90

Emery, F. and Trist, E. (1965) 'The causal texture of organizational environments', *Human Relations*, vol 18, no 1, pp21–32

Friedman, M. (1962) *Capitalism and Freedom*, University of Chicago Press, Chicago, IL

Jones, T. M. (1980) 'Corporate social responsibility revisited, redefined', *California Management Review*, vol 22, no 3, pp59–67

Jones, T., Wicks, A. and Freeman, R. (2002) 'Stakeholder theory: The state of the art', in N. E. Bowie (ed) *The Blackwell Guide to Business Ethics*, Blackwell, Oxford, UK, pp19–37

Medjad, K. and Ramírez, R. (2007) 'When strangers meet: Scenarios and the legal profession', in B. Sharpe, and K. van der Heijden (eds) *Scenarios for Success: Turning Insights into Action*, John Wiley and Sons, Chichester, UK

Mercer, D. (1995) 'Scenarios made easy', *Long Range Planning*, vol 28, no 4, pp81–86

Miller, K. and Waller, H. (2003) 'Scenarios, real options and integrated risk management', *Long Range Planning*, vol 36, no 1, pp93–107

Phelps, R., Chan, C. and Kapsalis, S. (2001) 'Does scenario planning affect performance? Two exploratory studies', *Journal of Business Research*, vol 51, no 3, pp223–232

Post, J., Preston, L. and Sachs, S. (2002) *Redefining the Corporation: Stakeholder Management and Organizational Wealth*, Stanford University Press, Stanford, CA

Savage, G., Nix, T., Whitehead, C. and Blair J. (1991) 'Strategies for assessing and managing organizational stakeholders', *Academy of Management Executive*, vol 5, no 2, pp61–75

Schwartz, P. (2003) *Inevitable Surprises: Thinking Ahead in a Time of Turbulence*, Gotham Books, New York, NY

Stormer, F. (2003) 'Making the shift: Moving from "ethics pays" to an inter-systems model of business', *Journal of Business Ethics*, vol 44, no 4, pp279–289

Wack, P. (1985) 'Scenarios: Uncharted waters ahead', *Harvard Business Review*, vol 63, no 5, pp73–89

Watkins, M. and Bazerman, M. (2003) 'Predictable surprises: The disasters you should have seen coming', *Harvard Business Review*, vol 81, no 3, pp72–80

Zenisek, T. (1979) 'Corporate social responsibility: A conceptualization based on organizational literature', *Academy of Management Review*, vol 4, no 3, pp359–368

Part IV

15

Conclusion: The Conjuncture of Scenarios and Causal Textures – Contributions and Progress

John W. Selsky, Kees van der Heijden and Rafael Ramírez

In Chapter 2 we overviewed the history of scenario work and of causal texture theory as a way of framing the material in this book. The 12 chapters that followed made important contributions to moving forward the conjuncture of those two fields. In this chapter we review the new understandings enabled by the 2005 Oxford Futures Forum conversations and the works of this volume. We then raise and discuss several methodological and conceptual issues that have surfaced in the various chapters.

Author contributions

In Chapter 5, Mary Bernard explores how causal texture theory is developed further with Ilya Prigogine's views on order and chaos. In Chapter 7, Rob Roggema provides practical illustrations of this with his work in the world of urban and regional planning. John Selsky and Joseph McCann, in Chapter 10, explore how the causal textures view of the nature of disruption informs scenario work. In Chapter 13, Shirin Elahi focuses on the role and importance of fairness in the scenario method and in collaborations, in general. She then offers ways of extending that value of fairness out into the environment beyond any group of scenario participants. Chapter 11 by Rafael Ramírez forges the connection between clarity and the effectiveness of scenarios in addressing turbulent causal textures. George Burt, in exploring a case in the power generation sector (Chapter 12), draws attention to how scenarios help to identify predetermined elements in the contextual environment. Those elements are critical factors in developing the collaborations that are needed to address turbulence. In Chapter 8, Niklas Arvidsson raises the issue of governance in the institutionalization of such collaborations.

Two chapters in this volume draw linkages between the scenario method and other methods – to our knowledge, for the first time. Chapter 3 by Jaime Jiménez finds hitherto hidden similarities and differences between the method of scenarios in relation to the search conference method. Trudi Lang and Lynn Allen (Chapter 4) explore how scenarios are situated in relation to soft systems methodology. Both chapters seek to enrich scenario work by applying insights from the other methods.

The application of the scenarios method is explored directly in very diverse case contexts in the chapters on the Indian agricultural sector by Kees van der Heijden (Chapter 6), on Swedish regional healthcare by Niklas Arvidsson (Chapter 8), on Scottish energy by George Burt (Chapter 12), on Venezuela by Martin Thomas (Chapter 9), and on corporate social responsibility in the tobacco and public utilities industries by Andromache Athanasopoulou (Chapter 14).

Thus, as a set, the chapters in this volume explore how causal texture theory helps practitioners using scenario methods to understand how they might (and should) engage with turbulent fields. In an important sense, then, the book constitutes a theoretically grounded reflection on practice (Schön, 1983) since it seeks to render explicit assumptions used by practitioners in the choices they make and to relate these choices to an explicit intellectual framework.

While our focus in this book has been to use causal textures theory to better understand the method of scenario work, the authors' and our own confrontation with that theory in the context of scenario applications raise some important conceptual issues that we explore below.

Scenarios as method

Scenarios can be considered a method with which to engage some aspect of reality. However, they are not a method in the classic scientific sense.

Scientific method as it is typically construed is positivistic, deductive and prospective – that is, hypotheses derived from variances on accepted 'truths' are tested empirically against 'reality' under carefully controlled conditions. New truths are discovered with tightly bounded possibilities for generalization that are offered for future research. However, Paul Feyerabend, a philosopher of science, suggested in his book *Against Method* (1975) that in natural science, 'method' has always been a *retrospective* account of what the scientist has done. This account is made in order to enable another scientist to replicate the procedure or process – that is, to reproduce it under similar or at least comparable conditions in order to determine if the same or similar results are produced. Scientific truths that survive the disproving of falsehoods in methodical practice can thus be established through independent replication.

In social science, an important difference is that control over the conditions necessary for hypothesis testing is much more challenging. This is because the research method often involves intervention in the system, provoking a reaction that is often not desired. Another reason is that the researcher may become an important variable in the situation – for example, simply by choosing a set of techniques with which to investigate the phenomenon (Normann, 1975) or by interpreting findings in an idiosyncratic way. Gareth Morgan in his book *Beyond Method* (1983) suggests that the method that a social scientist employs in a research project strongly affects the type of result that the investigation will produce. This is because the method is not 'neutral'. Instead, the method itself helps to construct or make sense of the phenomenon the scientist is intervening in or enquiring about (see also Churchman, 1971). Thus, choosing a method in social science research is not trivial. As a result, this raises the question: how is a method chosen?

Where does scenario work fit in this categorization? It appears to us that the choice to utilize scenario methods, like other practitioners' crafts, lies largely outside the canons of natural or social science. One influential reflective practitioner has suggested that scenario work is an art (Schwartz, 1991). The production of knowledge from the arts proceeds inductively from specific cases to general regularities – the opposite of deductive scientific method. In the arts, each situation is idiosyncratic, with end points difficult to predict, and with a unique configuration of actors interacting in novel, creative and unexpected ways. Nonetheless, in scenario method some procedural and process-related regularities are able to be discerned. Over the years the community of scenario practitioners has gained some understanding of things that do and don't work in facilitating scenario projects.

Scenarios in this methodological respect are similar to search conferences and soft systems methods (see Chapters 3 and 4, respectively) in that they can be deployed as an intervention method and/or as a research method. Scenarios were developed as a method to engage with current realities and explore how the context of those realities might develop into the future. In that sense they also bear some similarities to action research – see Reason and Bradbury (2006) for a recent compilation. A scenario project is not *inherently* action research, which entails a deep engagement between a social scientist and a client, the outcomes of which explicitly seek to contribute both to the world of practice and to the world of social science. But scenarios can be deployed as part of an action research project (see Chapter 6). It appears to us that, thus far, engagements using scenarios which have documented histories in the public domain are policy, strategy or consulting engagements much more than they are scholarly contributions. Various efforts have been made to systematize the procedures involved for replication (e.g. Schwartz, 1991) and, in some cases, verifiability (Schoemaker, 1993; van der Heijden, 2005). The fact that many practitioners have taken up scenarios as an 'artful' consulting tool has accounted for its growth, as mentioned in Chapter 1. We have assembled this volume based on the belief that it is now time to reflect on what makes scenarios intellectually rigorous and 'scientific' in the sense above.

In Chapters 1 and 2 we noted that the theoretical grounding of scenario work has been weak until now and we have sought to redress this in this book. As an 'artful method', scenarios have a dual character: they are both prospective (scenario projects help participants to 'discover' or re-perceive 'new' futures) and retrospective (accounts of their success are written up for other practitioners to benefit from, as in van der Heijden, 2005).

Schwartz's (1991) work and Chapter 6 in this volume meet Feyerabend's description – their work consists of after-the-fact accounts of practices that worked well in a set of contexts. In Chapter 6 on Indian agriculture in this volume, van der Heijden revisits work he did in that sector during 2005 and makes sense of what was accomplished with the help of causal textures theory. Here, causal textures theory renders explicit why the scenario method worked well by relating the method to the kind of situation in which it was applied. But could that project be replicated? Arguably not because of the idiosyncratic factors in that unique situation, as well as the particular skills embodied in van der Heijden himself, accumulated over decades of experience. A novice practitioner reading this chapter could not expect to replicate the process or the success of that project, but could come to an appreciation of the process – and perhaps the skills 'behind the curtain' that were needed to orchestrate it. The engagement van der Heijden recounts in Chapter 6 produced *situated*, not *general* (replicable), knowledge.

Several people have attempted to theorize on the scenario method before – for example, by linking it to Belbin's role models in teams (Islei et al, 1999) and attending to how they relate to decision-making (Schoemaker, 1993) or to theories about iterative learning (van der Heijden, 2005). The methodological innovation that we have explored in this book concerns not only *how* scenarios are to be produced but also *whether* and *when* to deploy scenario methods – that is, the chapters in this volume have explored which type of situations are amenable to scenario work, and why and how scenarios might serve an explicitly defined and useful purpose in a process of guided enquiry and engagement.

In this respect, a theme in this book is the idea that knowing the role of the method in a particular engagement or enquiry is a requirement to its being effective. Accounts of failure – e.g. the Whittington (2006a, 2006b)–Hodgkinson and Wright (2002, 2006) debate mentioned in Chapter 1 – imply that not paying enough attention to purpose and the related methodological aspects in a project appears to contribute to failure. What we are suggesting is that attending to causal textures theory clarifies the type of situations in which scenarios are an appropriate and effective method. Chapter 9 pushes this envelope by suggesting that scenarios may be used for purposes other than the 'received wisdom' – namely, for purposes other than anticipating and appreciating turbulence collaboratively.

The nature of the turbulent causal texture of a field

Why is turbulence considered bad, uncomfortable or threatening? Why does it require 'coping behaviour'?

Various disciplines have explored why intense uncertainty in one's environment is problematic. Psychologists highlight the detrimental effects of stress and distress (e.g. in times of war), and how uncertainty challenges an individual's sense of identity (Sennett, 1998). Economists argue that lack of predictability destroys rent opportunities associated with long-term investments, and that creating external effects which cannot be traded is unsustainable. Anthropologists and sociologists consider how the dissociation and anomie created by maladaptive responses to uncertainty lead to passivity or conflict. Political scientists focus on how inter-group conflict often results from uncertainty regarding resource bases.

What does the causal textures theory suggest? On the one hand, it says that head-to-head competition in type III causal textures and the increasing salience of the forces driving the contextual environment in type IV causal textures are lived as 'increasing relevant uncertainty'. This creates anxiety among the actors in a field. This anxiety, as well as the failure to recognize the potential for the causal texture of the field to shift from type III to type IV, can lead actors into maladaptive behaviours that produce further turbulence. Chapters 8 and 9 make useful contributions to an understanding of this issue.

On the other hand, we have Prigogine arguing that increasing the complexity of a field increases the occurrence of 'dissipative structures' – new sources of order and predictability – in and around that field (see Chapter 5). So, 'objectively', more complexity (but according to Prigogine, only in a sufficiently large field) might be beneficial in that the probability of new sources of unexpected order increases. But, of course, the new sources of order and predictability would not be welcome if the field were not so complex and uncertain in the first place.

'Coping' with turbulence, therefore, means:

- recognizing that the causal texture of a field can become turbulent; and
- acting to prevent this by engaging in 'active–adaptive' behaviour and avoiding maladaptive behaviour (F. Emery, 1976; M. Emery, 1999).

Everything starts with recognizing turbulence, even if it is temporarily held in check by dissipative structures. Scenarios are an important and heuristic way to reach an understanding of how the contextual (L22) relationships may evolve in the future, and to understand what aspects of the contextual environment are preordained and inevitable, as Chapter 12 suggests.

But these perspectives on why turbulent causal textures are best avoided raise the question: how can we reconcile contextual forces in a field that risks becoming turbulent with the choices made by individuals and organizations in such a field? We explore this question next.

Macro-evolution or strategic choice:
Can the two be reconciled?

As we noted in Chapter 2, Emery and Trist produced their seminal 1965 paper before they had made the distinction between the transactional and the contextual environment. Based on their later writings, we have assumed in this book that for any given system, L12 (planning) and L21 (learning) relations connect that system with its transactional environment and L22 relations constitute its contextual environment, which 'bounds' the transactional one. The implication is that the contextual environment happens outside the sphere of influence of the system – affecting its transactional environment, but unable to be influenced by it. In contrast, the system *is* able to influence its transactional environment (L12, L21) since it transacts with it and co-determines it along with those with whom it transacts.

Emery and Trist (1965) suggested that the criteria for turbulence were related to the degree of 'salience' of the L22 relations, even if they did not indicate how 'salient' the L22 relationships had to be in order to shift the causal texture of the field from a type III to a type IV environment. They went so far as to suggest as criteria that in the type IV causal texture, the contextual environment becomes so important that it threatens to overwhelm and disable the L12 and L21 relations; but they did not work this out in any detail. However, the important point here is that the contextual environment (by definition) cannot be influenced directly by the individual system. That means that the increasing salience of L22, as the causal texture becomes turbulent, cannot be reduced by the strategy of any individual system in that field. The turbulence in the field follows its own evolutionary logic and individual systems can do nothing about it – alone. This then begs the question: what does coping behaviour mean if it cannot be grounded in the individual system's acting to reduce the turbulence of its contextual environment?

If an individual system in a field that is taking on a turbulent causal texture can do nothing about that on its own, the least it can do is to try to escape from it. This strategy of 'escape' is only effective if there is some place to escape to – that is, if turbulence is not a homogeneous condition in the field. Physical examples of such escape may be found in the Berlin Wall, the Israel–Palestine wall and the Great Wall of China; 'gated' residential communities; and military barracks and monasteries, with border patrols, moats, drawbridges and defensive fortifications protecting the certainty of the 'order inside' from the disordered uncertainty perceived to lie outside. For the excluded outsiders, these bounded spaces represent *another* (perhaps perverse) 'order', with which L12 and L21 relations are highly restricted, if not impossible. These barriers, from the outsider's point of view, reinforce enclave status and establish identity by clearly distinguishing 'Other' from 'Self'. McCann and Selsky (1984) believe such boundaries increase adaptive capacity within by restricting resource allocation from the 'Other'. But in and of themselves they do not reduce turbulence.

For the insiders in the bounded spaces, the strategy in the turbulent field consists of securing a niche of relative predictability, allowing growth and development. This involves setting up real or virtual barriers to the turbulent outside world that may have to be defended against incursions triggered in this turbulent context. Because of the outside's threat to the viability of the inside, it is crucial for the latter to understand the L22 forces in order to appreciate how such a niche might be designed, and where and when such new niches might be needed.

This is what active adaptation means in a turbulent causal texture. Emery and Trist (1965) believed that in turbulent conditions, systems could no longer act alone and expect to be successful. Instead, those sharing a field would need to act together. In pursuing this line of thinking, McCann and Selsky (1984) explored how it might be possible to create a low-uncertainty niche, which they called a 'social enclave'. Their idea was that while the violent L22 forces reign all around, the collaborating systems shut these forces out from the enclave by sharing sufficient basic values and resources to enable them to build and sustain institutional arrangements that keep turbulence on the other side of the enclave's boundary. Since no individual system could be resourceful enough to create a niche by itself, this strategy would require the collaboration of multiple actors. This seems to us the underlying explanation and justification for Emery and Trist's (1965) promotion of collaboration as the only effective response to turbulence.

It may be helpful to think of multilateral institutions, such as Bretton Woods, the International Monetary Fund and the United Nations in terms of this kind of collaborative niche-building. These collaborative arrangements allowed systems in that field to keep unpredictable fluctuations outside the door and encouraged long-term investments to be made. The relative stability and investments, in turn, generated a level of economic development that would otherwise have been impossible in the midst of post-World War II upheavals.

What this logic suggests is that a strategy to escape turbulence by collaborative action needs to be based not only on common values and ideals alone, but also on institutional arrangements that protect the collaborative enclave against incursions from outside and from opportunistic behaviour inside (see Emery and Trist's, 1965, discussion of 'organizational matrixes'; and Wilkinson and Young, 2005, for a more recent assessment of collaboration in turbulent conditions). With institutions come issues such as governance, compliance, enforcement and power. Once a viable niche has been created, it needs to be adapted actively over time through a continuous process of updating, renovating and improvising (see Chapter 10) in the ever-changing turbulent conditions with which it has to deal. When adaptation slows down, crisis is not far away. If a governance or regulatory system realizes that it is in 'crisis' due to some turbulent force in the causal texture, this is an invitation to renew the niche. Chapter 8 in this volume discusses governance issues and offers an example.

While collaboration is enacted at the micro-level – that is, individual systems exercise strategic choice to collaborate in forging and maintaining institutional arrangements – at the contextual macro-level the field evolves in ways beyond the control of any one system. In an important contemporary development, complexity theory has thrown new light on this link between individual system (or 'actor') strategies and macro-evolutionary processes. Prigogine showed how at certain sensitive moments in the history of a sufficiently large and complex field, which he called 'bifurcation' points, the direction of development of the whole field depends upon minor fluctuations of a few variables. In terms of causal texture theory, this means that under the right conditions, even a single individual, through an incisive decision or serendipitous intervention, can entrain a series of actions that may alter the trajectory of a field as it emerges in time. For example, in Chapter 7, Roggema shows how at such a sensitive fork in the road the ideas of one person may make the difference for a whole province or country trying to cope with climate change, arguably a turbulent field in a country such as The Netherlands today. It may well be that in the future, complexity theory will provide further insights that link micro-actions and decisions *in* a field with macro-evolutionary trajectories *of* that field. Perhaps this illuminates why remarkable individuals such as Ghandi and Mandela have been able to make such a big difference in their societies.

Meanwhile, we deal with turbulent causal textures through collaborative escape strategies. One day, complexity theory may teach us that the story of systems or fields at an actual bifurcation point can only be told in retrospect, that strategizing around such a point prospectively is impossible. Consider a scenario exercise pointing such a situation: the participants might be able to take plausible bifurcations into account in advance, but not be able to predict which road in the bifurcation the system will actually take since this is irreducible uncertainty and therefore unknowable. If that were to be the case, collaborative strategy would still be the best available recourse. This may explain why 'open innovation', 'open source' and 'corporate social responsibility' (see Chapter 14) have become big issues for large and small organizations as turbulence has become a more prevalent causal texture in their fields. However, it is too early to determine if the collaborative options now being developed will suffice to deal with the very big issues associated with contemporary turbulence, including climate change, disease pandemics, terrorism and other contextual disruptions discussed in Chapter 10, that are generated in the turbulent causal texture of the fields we now inhabit.

Silent voices

We acknowledge that a weakness in this book is that the excluded, the poor and the exploited are under-represented. This includes those 'Others' outside the institutionalized enclaves discussed above. The normative stance of causal textures theory provides an opening for discussing issues of power in collaborations and other engagements that can involve scenario methods. While we feel that such issues are real and important, we acknowledge that this area remains under-explored in this volume.

Conclusion

The conjuncture of causal texture theory and the scenario approach has led to new developmental ideas in both areas.

We now see the historically coincidental development of the two fields not as an accident, but as two areas of human activity, both addressing some of the prominent human needs of the times – perhaps with a lacuna in relation to power inequalities that future work in both areas might explicitly attend to.

The analysis in this volume on the nature of turbulence and how scenarios can help in turbulent causal textures contributes to contemporary efforts to address more effectively the questions of organizational resilience and sustainable societies.

We believe that this book has made four important contributions:

1 It advances our understanding of the nature of turbulent causal textures. And it does so in a way that should help reflective practitioners who are deploying scenario methods to become more effective.
2 Causal textures theory has been shown to have many interdisciplinary handles that can be deployed in its further development. A few of the new strands emerging from this book are the links with complexity theory, institutionalization, and inequality and power. The book has also provided grounds for further explorations – using causal textures theory – of the key success factors of fairness and responsibility, the importance of leadership in strategic choice, micro–macro connections across levels, and aspects of fields such as contextual disturbances, bifurcation points and (co-)evolution.
3 The book has highlighted certain issues of methodology: the nature and role of interventions in systematic enquiry, the importance of the choice of method, the features distinguishing 'scientific' versus 'artful' enquiry, and the role of clarity.
4 The book explains why scenario practices have been growing, and why they are relevant in searching for and developing collaborative innovations that will enable managers, consultants and scholars to address turbulence effectively. The scenario field has benefited as we now see more clearly the contribution that the field makes in developing resilience and sustainability in turbulent contexts.

References

Churchman, C. (1971) *The Design of Inquiring Systems: Basic Concepts of Systems and Organization,* Basic Books Inc, New York, NY

Emery, F. (1976) *Futures We Are In,* Martinus-Nijhoff, Leiden

Emery, F. and Trist, E. (1965) 'The causal texture of organizational environments', *Human Relations,* vol 18, pp21–32

Emery, F. and Trist, E. (1972) *Towards a Social Ecology,* Plenum Publishing, New York, NY

Emery, M. (1999) *Searching: The Theory and Practice of Making Cultural Change,* John Benjamins, Amsterdam, The Netherlands

Feyerabend, P. (1975) *Against Method,* New Left Books, New York, NY

Hodgkinson, G. and Wright, G. (2002) 'Confronting strategic inertia in a top management team: Learning from failure', *Organization Studies,* vol 23, no 6, pp949–977

Hodgkinson, G. and Wright, G. (2006) 'Neither completing the practice turn, nor enriching the process tradition: Secondary misinterpretations of a case analysis reconsidered', *Organization Studies,* vol 27, no 12, pp1895–1901

Islei, G., Lockett, G. and Naudé, P. (1999) 'Judgemental modelling as an aid to scenario planning and analysis', *Omega,* vol 27, no 1, pp 61–73

McCann, J. and Selsky, J. (1984) 'Hyperturbulence and the emergence of type 5 environ-ments', *Academy of Management Review,* vol 9, no 4, pp460–470

Morgan, G. (1983) *Beyond Method,* Sage, Thousand Oaks, Beverly Hills, CA

Normann, R. (1975), *A Personal Quest for Methodology,* Scandinavian Institute for Administrative Research, Stockholm, Sweden

Reason, P. and Bradbury, H. (2006) *The Handbook of Action Research,* Sage, Thousand Oaks, CA

Schoemaker, P. (1993) 'Multiple scenario development: Its conceptual and behavioral foundation', *Strategic Management Journal,* vol 14, pp193–213

Schön, D. (1983) *The Reflective Practitioner,* Basic Books, New York, NY

Schwartz, P. (1991) *The Art of the Long View: Planning for the Future in an Uncertain World,* Doubleday, New York, NY

Sennett, R. (1998) *The Corrosion of Character: The Personal Consequences of Work in the New Capitalism,* W. W. Norton and Company, New York , NY

van der Heijden, K. (2005) *Scenarios: The Art of Strategic Conversation,* 2nd edition, John Wiley and Sons, Chichester, UK

Whittington, R. (2006a) 'Completing the practice turn in strategy research', *Organization Studies,* vol 27, no 5, pp613–634

Whittington, R. (2006b) 'Learning more from failure: Practice and process', *Organization Studies,* vol 27, no 12, pp1903–1906

Wilkinson, I. and Young L. (2005) 'Towards a normative theory of normative marketing theory', *Marketing Theory,* vol 5, no 4, pp363–396

Postscript

Building Effective Future-Mindedness

Angela Wilkinson

I offer this reflection based on my personal interests and professional experiences – as a scenario practitioner, a business executive, a scientist and educator, and a mother of two young children. While reading this engaging book with these identities in tow, some rather large questions kept coming to mind.

When facing uncertain and puzzling situations and possibly catastrophic changes is there anything leaders, groups and organizations can do? Can they avoid looking to their past experiences and recasting tomorrow's challenges in terms of yesterday's solutions? Can they avoid or at least reduce their 'addiction to prediction'? And can they avoid defaulting to head-to-head competition as the winning strategy in an emerging world of intense interdependencies?

I believe the answer to all these questions is a resounding yes! But only if leaders, groups and organizations start to attend to how they think about the future and the role the future plays in the present. This is where this book makes an important contribution.

Lord Rees, UK Astronomer Royal, has estimated that humanity has a 50/50 chance of surviving the next century. Reading this book encourages me to think that we may beat these odds for two reasons.

First, the key insights provided by the authors and editors of this book concern how leaders, groups and organizations can develop a capability for matching increasing attention to the future to realizing more effective outcomes in their present-day actions. As such, this book holds insights about what I will call '*effective future-mindedness*', that is, learning 'with' rather than 'about' the future.

As such, it is relevant to leaders, groups and organizations from all walks of life, in all parts of the world.

Second, if the insights contained in this book are applied widely, we may see the dawn of a new era of human development, whereby effective future-mindedness is deployed to better appreciate and navigate the messy realities of today. This might be done in a way that enables institutional innovation and renewal, and a process of global civilization that is more inclusive and sustainable.

Permit me to paint a picture of the challenges we face and my reasons for hope as we navigate a turbulent future.

Current challenges

Balancing the co-evolution of knowledge and ignorance

The first challenge concerns whether we can know the future in advance. We cannot. Knowledge, uncertainty and ignorance are co-evolving and we need to attend to all three. Ignorance is overlooked or treated as a lack of knowledge. Despite the increasingly widespread rhetoric of embracing uncertainty, the reaction of individuals, groups and organizations tends still to be characterized by denial, complacency and even corruption. Is it more effective to think in terms of what is knowable about the future or how the future is open to influence? Should we act on what might conceivably happen or focus instead on what has already happened but has yet to play out in full? At present we seem to be obsessed with trying to know what the future will be rather than creating or constructing it, we focus too much on knowledge and too little on the coevolution of knowledge and ignorance.

Enabling a shift from risk management to shaping the future

The second challenge is about how we will influence the current course of civilization. The examples offered in this book demonstrate that the future is open to shaping; indeed, it *must* be shaped. It is not an uncharted territory obscured by clouds, but an unformed landmass. However, there is a tendency to invoke futures thinking in the service of risk management and contingency planning, in order to 'proof' ourselves, our organizations, our societies, against the vagaries (and possibilities) of the future.

As a result, key institutions act to maintain the situation for which they were designed rather than innovating and renewing themselves as the future unfolds. As highlighted in this book, organizations and institutions should instead seek to co-evolve with their environments. This, in turn, requires attention to the processes and practices of strategy and policy and the impact of dominant decision cultures on the 'evidence' of the future.

Futures thinking can become corrupted by vested interests in sustaining the status quo (more about this below).

Promoting collaboration as the winning strategy of the 21st century

The third challenge concerns the strategies that will be adopted. As the concluding chapter of this book highlights, competition is a strategy for failure in turbulent contexts; instead institutionalized collaborative efforts are needed to calm turbulence. This book also raises questions about approaches to corporate strategy and public policy in 21st-century contexts replete with dispersion of causes and effects (in both space and time), fragmentation of agency and institutional inadequacy. What is the purpose of strategy and policy, who does it, when and how should it be done?

Strategic planning is often thought of as a centralized leadership process to direct the actions of a firm to manage more effectively the risks associated with its growth, that is, the agility to do things faster, more efficiently, etc. In the latter decades of the 20th century, the winning strategy for business was simple, beat the (increasingly global) competition!

However, in the early 21st century we are faced with daunting interdependency, complexity, uncertainty, and discontinuous and surprising changes. Policies and strategies that are rooted in positivism, objectivism, optimization and continuity appear ill suited to the volatile conditions that characterize our world today. The key to success is ambidextrosity to manage both for agility (i.e. speed of change) and adaptability (i.e. discontinuity).

Building practical wisdom in future-mindedness on a global scale

The fourth challenge concerns whether we have the will to create and nurture the capacity for more effective (and therefore reflexive) future-mindedness, and whether we are capable of doing so rapidly enough and on a sufficiently global scale.

A strategic futures capability – that is, future-mindedness at the level of a group, organization or country – implies to me an ability to navigate and deploy multiple methods, with awareness that the effectiveness of the intervention is determined by the purpose and situation at hand.

If, as this book suggests, scenarios are an art, or perhaps a peculiar form of science that is different from mainstream notions, this raises questions about learning and education. How will we enable today's and tomorrow's leaders to equip themselves in the skills of effective future-mindedness? Training in a particular technique will only get you so far; apprenticeship, mentorship and action-learning will, I believe, take you much further.

I believe a certain paradox in future-mindedness and a certain addiction to prediction underpin this set of current challenges.

A paradox in future-mindedness

We live in an era when leaders, groups and organizations across the world are paying more attention to the future. There has been a proliferation of futures studies and foresight initiatives, some focused on particular challenges, such as climate change, nanotechnology and intellectual property, others focused on exploring or realizing a (better/more sustainable) future for a particular company, sector, city, country or world region.

Moreover, we are heirs to a rich history of over half a century of professional futures practices. This wealth of experiences is associated with an increasing diversity of methods, such as scenario planning, computer simulation modelling, forecasting, back-casting and others.

Nevertheless, we seem to have only a sketchy understanding of how (and in some instances whether) futures thinking translates into effective action, either in terms of securing the future survival or continued success of a specific organization, or in terms of realizing a better future for a greater proportion of humanity.

The result is a paradox: as the list of concerns about the future has increased, confidence that we have the 'right' methods, skills and tools for navigating the future has waned. Few ever bother to face up to the dizzying array of choices about futures methods.

This combination of more attention to the future, a diversity of futures methods and (at least, a rhetoric of) willingness to embrace the future as uncertain, often leads to three outcomes that are regrettably ineffective. As leaders, groups or organizations we tend to:

1   *Non-reflexive practices. Default to promoting methods of certainty in a context of confusion or ignorance regarding other methods and tools.* For example, we are drawn to a mode of futures thinking that best fits with the dominant decision culture. Since both evidence-based policy-making and adversarial legalism are on the rise, this tends to lock groups and organizations into methods that promote simple causality and quantification, and can demonstrate a consistent and systematic approach.

2   *Attending to knowledge but not uncertainty. Treat uncertainty as a lack of precise or accurate knowledge about the future, rather than addressing the need to continuously navigate knowledge, uncertainty and ignorance.* For example, consider proactive responses involving futures practices that imply we can 'know' the future by collecting and extrapolating the evidence gathered about the past and/or present. Or those studies and reports that promise we can

'determine' the future, that is, we can find solutions to the problems of the future by (better) harnessing and steering the development of science and technology.

3 *Defaulting to contingency planning. React to the uncertainty of the future by promoting the past as the future and/or emphasizing continuity of the present, rather than creating new possibilities in the future.* For example, the response of some groups and organizations, whether in the public, private or civic sector, is to cling to the certainties of the past and even attempt to reassert a historical idyll – a romanticized version of the past as the preferred and only future.

As a result, certain futures practices, for example, forecasting and quantitative modelling have become widespread. This leads to my second theme underlying our current challenges.

Our 20th-century addiction to prediction

Even with the increasing rhetoric of embracing uncertainty the ancient arts of prophecy and prediction are flourishing.

Visioning involves imagining the 'big' picture – where you would like to be in the future, then back-casting to determine what will enable (or disable) progress to this destination. It can encompass utopian and dystopian ideals, and can comprise realistic dreaming or the wildest flights of fantasy. Visioning can also unintentionally lock us into projecting today's challenges as tomorrow's problems.

Forecasting, on the other hand, tends to focus on one factor or trend at a time and assumes your future will be a continuation of the past, maybe a bit higher, or a bit lower – but basically somewhere along a single line of projection. Pierre Wack was fond of saying that the challenge with forecasting is that it 'will let you down most when you need it most'.[2]

Computer-based models and simulations, which enable more systemic (i.e. multi-factor) explorations of the future than forecasting, might be thought to address this problem. They have progressed greatly from their first applications (calculating nuclear bomb design and predicting the weather) over the past 60 years. Many can now provide reliable information. But a model is only accurate within the range of what it has historically described, whereas the unfolding future might be out of that range.

The inherent uncertainty of the future is its greatest promise, but tends to invoke the darkest fears of key decision-makers. Despite embracing the rhetoric of an uncertain world, key decision-makers still want certainty. In response, there has been a tendency to confuse certainty-seeking with accuracy-seeking and, in turn, accuracy with precision.

The result is an *addiction to prediction*. This addiction is in turn fed by the combination of factors I discussed above: the global spread of adversarial legalism, the increasing emphasis on evidence-based policy, the hubris of experts who drastically overestimate their own knowledge, and overconfidence in the benefits of quantitative approaches to risk management, often enabled through sophisticated computer modelling and a belief that quantitative analysis generates better truths about the future than more qualitative enquiry.

What if we were to think instead of interventions that help dispel the illusion of current reality and the constraints it imposes? Interventions that help us think about how we think about the future, as well as why and what we think about the future, and enable us to reflect on our assumptions about the future in the present?

This seems to be the appeal of scenarios – they can encourage and enable a reflection on deeply embedded worldviews. Some scenario practices attend to ignorance, uncertainty and knowledge; others focus on searching for predetermined elements; still others focus on clarifying critical uncertainties and delivering an array of possible futures. Coupled with other strategic methods such as Horizon Scanning, Early Warning Systems and Weak Signals, scenarios can avoid creating a new 'lock-in' in futures thinking. Without such additions, however, scenarios can so easily become the new frame of 'in the box(es)' thinking!

Furthermore, and different to forecasting or modelling approaches, scenarios appear to encourage reflection on the cognitive framings (schema, worldviews) through which novel signals and cues of environmental change get filtered.

Effective future-mindedness as a leadership skill

The insights offered in this book suggest that effective future-mindedness involves iterative and inductive processes of enquiry in an inseparable process of learning, unlearning and doing. In this process:

- *learning and unlearning* are better enabled through creative, imaginative thinking about the future. This should be taken as seriously as scientific knowledge about the past and present derived from empirical data;
- *doing* involves directly engaging in the world to change it and requires collaboration in order to see through the messiness of the present, calm the turbulence and enable future possibilities to be more effectively realized.

There is an important role for leadership here. The skill of 21st-century leadership is not in knowing more about the future, but in being able to enact different realities today. It also involves nurturing a strategic futures capability that involves being able to deploy different futures methods, rather than focusing on any one and being reflexive about how choice of method might impact outcomes. I believe that without such leadership skills and capabilities, groups and organizations will fail to embrace the possibilities to create and shape – but not control – the course for civilization in the 21st century.

How can we cultivate these crucial skills? Can we focus more attention to *how* we think about the future and its role in the present rather than what we can know about the future? I believe the answer is yes, if we promote changes to education, research and strategy. The kinds of changes I have in mind are described below.

Instilling future-mindedness in education

We need to pay more attention as parents to how our children are educated to think about the future, and as leaders to how we enable the role of the future in today's actions and decisions.

Humans are endowed with a capability to think about the future that matures as we grow older: infants and children are very present orientated (which parent hasn't experienced the demanding 'now' phase in a toddler's life!); on the other hand their imagination is strong.

Our children enter the world unfettered by a notion that the past binds us to the future. They are not burdened by the illusion of current reality – we can have many pasts and many futures but there is only one true interpretation of the present. Our children are ready to see, willing to learn and open to the possibilities of the future. They are able to absorb and observe the world through the many varieties, shades and colours of different pasts, presents and futures.

This inherent capability for future-mindedness is, however, fragile and can be easily derailed, depending on whether it is encouraged and how it is nurtured in the individual child, how it is influenced in later years by organizational culture, and how the maturing person cultivates it throughout life by reflexive practice – or does not.

How sad then, that through our modern processes of learning and socialization our open-to-the-future-minded children learn how to close their minds. They are conditioned by experience that the future is constrained and remote – it is for others (adults) to think about and determine. Technical training, in the Western scientific tradition, equips them to think in terms of 'straight line' futures, that is, projections of the past determine future possibilities. It encourages them to think that the path to fuller understanding is via the calculation of 'parts' rather than the visualization of 'wholes'. It teaches that so long as they can accurately define a problem, the answer will follow.

The conditioning of open-minded children into 'rear-view mirror' decision-makers continues as they progress through their education. For those who pursue graduate education, the courses offered by most business schools essentially teach students that every problem has a right answer! Why then are we surprised, when decades after such education and conditioning, so many individuals and organizations treat the future as though it is something to 'future-proof' themselves and their organizations against; that it can be understood simply as a continuation of the past; that our knowledge of it will improve so long as we bring together the right components of the past and present, for example, analysing so-called 'key trends' rather than telling a story about the whole?

I speak from experience: by the time I had reached a junior management position, with a doctorate in atmospheric physics, I realized how poorly my world class scientific training had prepared me for dealing with the messy realities of managing teams of people and resolving challenges involving different worldviews and contradictory certitudes. Leadership involved enabling better, collective judgement rather than the accumulation of expert and technical knowledge.

My response was to find a new position that also enabled my practical re-education. My own expertise in scenarios has been honed through a process of action-learning and reflexive practice. I was fortunate to have received encouragement from and the opportunity to work with some very experienced practitioners. Their mastery helped me reflect on and improve my performance. Since coming to Oxford, I have been inundated by requests from executives and graduates, some that possess Masters in Futures degrees from other universities, asking if there is some way I can help them secure practical experience.

All this suggests to me that we need a pedagogy of action-learning, apprenticeship and mastery in futures thinking. Currently the opportunities for practical education in future-mindedness are too limited compared with the availability of technical training in a particular technique.

I agree with the assertion in the concluding chapter of this book, that scenarios are more of an art than a conventional science. I believe it is important to recognize that in the education and research structures that support it.

Shifting from research using futures to research into futures

At the moment, there may be a lot of money and effort being devoted to futures studies and scenario-building initiatives, but funding for futures research tends also to be biased towards new knowledge generation rather than application, that is, towards Mode 1 rather than Mode 2 research. Mode 1 research can be summarized as 'the pursuit of "scientific truth" by "scientists"'.[3] This is the form of knowledge production supported through the hierarchical infrastructures of traditional higher education and concepts such as 'sound science'. It involves experts working in particular disciplines to produce scholarly output that is validated by their peers. By contrast in Mode 2 research, content is produced by heterarchical and cross-disciplinary groups, who are responding together to a perceived and transitory need. Consequently, efforts to clarify and extend the effectiveness of futures practices, including scenario-based interventions, are few and far between.

This book contains valuable lessons about the 'how' of scenarios – forged from learning honed through the trials-and-errors of futures practices and, as such, is a distillation of that most precious form of knowledge – practical wisdom. One of my few criticisms of this book is that it didn't provide enough practical guidance for me about how to translate these insights into more effective practice in different contexts.

In promoting research into how futures thinking works in practice, as well as using futures methods as a mode of research, there is an urgent need to cultivate in futures practices the equivalent of the tradition of clinical research in medicine.

In researching what 'works' some of the questions I would like to see addressed, include:

- What is the relationship between plausibility, accuracy and precision, and how desirable is each compared to the others?
- Which futures methods can help ensure more humane futures?
- What are the implications if scenarios are also social and political processes: who should be involved and when/how?

Conclusion: Cultivating responsibility for the future

The world is a dangerous place. Irresistible forces are emerging at an ever-increasing pace – urbanization, climate change, demographic ageing, to mention but a few. Existing institutional arrangements are found wanting: forged in a bygone era, traditional institutions are struggling to actively adapt to the changing world. Crisis can force a brutal re-perception but often promotes knee-jerk responses.

Alternative efforts to tackle the complex, socially messy, seemingly intractable and significant challenges of the 21st century are in evidence. For example, there are the increasing numbers of multi-stakeholder, public–private and international partnership arrangements catalysed after the second Earth Summit (Johannesburg, 2000), including the Global A Vaccine Initiative (GAVI), UN Global Compact, etc.

However, many of these valiant efforts will prove ineffective, for some of the reasons discussed above:

- lack of attention to the 'who' needs to be involved and the emphasis on more rather than more effective participation, i.e. ensuring requisite variety of worldviews throughout the process/intervention;
- the lack of reflexivity in future-mindedness;
- the emphasis on navigating change and risk management rather than catalysing transformative actions and sustaining collaboration over long timeframes, i.e. balancing agility with adaptability;
- the continued emphasis on global economic competition as winning 'national' and 'corporate' strategies in an interdependent world;
- comfort with the illusion of centralized command-and-control rather than a shift to adaptability enabled by inductive strategizing at the periphery.[4]

It is not enough to proliferate our studies of the future, instead, we must find a way to take responsibility for the future in our present decisions and actions, or else future generations will regard our era as one of short-term and narrow-minded selfishness.

As such, scenarios offer a means for collaborating in the creation of more sustainable and humane futures, rather than a means by which individual entities can react (i.e. future-proof) or compete for the future. Scenarios offer a means to act and learn in parallel, rather than postponing action in the absence of accurate knowledge.

Today's challenges do not lend themselves to the linear, problem-solving techniques of yesteryear. Indeed they call for the renewal of many of the institutions on which modern civilization is founded.

In the context of today's messy challenges and complex changes that seem to paralyse leaders and threaten to negate the very concept of leadership in all sectors of society, this book illustrates that groups and organizations can deploy scenarios to ensure shared progress, rather than defaulting to competitive tactics.

But in highlighting the possibility of 'individual exit' and 'collaborative escape' strategies for coping with turbulence (see Chapter 15) I am still troubled by questions of power and interests: who do these enclaves really benefit and does the calmness enabled within these enclaves result in new burdens on others beyond the enclave?

While such considerations are perhaps less necessary in the context of the hurly-burly of the so-called 'free' marketplace, they are fundamental to notions of societal progress, humanity and civilization. The freeness of the market produces negative externalities on society/humanity: deregulation provides openings for pollution and worker rights abuses.

In conclusion, we need to revisit key institutions to determine whether and how they 'fit' today's context. This in turn implies we need to focus attention to how to ensure 'more effective' rather than 'more' participation interventions aimed at creating and shaping more humane and sustainable development paths.

In this respect, scenarios appear to offer a means to enable gentle, rather than brutal, means to shared re-perception and effective action – but only if they reflect sufficient requisite variety of the worldviews.

Notes

1   Pierre Wack referred to these as 'predetermined elements' – future developments that had in fact already happened and would play out in a predictable way.

2   Pierre Wack.

3   Huff (2000), p288.

4   Wright, A. (2005) 'The role of scenarios as prospective sensemaking devices', *Management Decision*, vol 43, no 1, pp86–101.

Index